Linguistic Dimensions of Crisis Talk

Pragmatics & Beyond New Series

Volume 136

Linguistic Dimensions of Crisis Talk:
Formalising structures in a controlled language
by Claudia Sassen

Linguistic Dimensions of Crisis Talk

Formalising structures in a controlled language

Claudia Sassen

Universität Dortmund

John Benjamins Publishing Company

Amsterdam / Philadelphia

™ The paper used in this publication meets the minimum requirements
of American National Standard for Information Sciences – Permanence
of Paper for Printed Library Materials, ANSI z39.48-1984.

Library of Congress Cataloging-in-Publication Data

Claudia Sassen
    Linguistic Dimensions of Crisis Talk : Formalising structures in a
        controlled language / Claudia Sassen.
        p.   cm. (Pragmatics & Beyond, New Series, ISSN 0922-842X ; v. 136)
    Includes bibliographical references and indexes.
        1. Dialogue analysis. 2. Speech acts (Linguistics) 3. Head-driven
    phrase structure grammar. 4. Air traffic control--Language. I. Title. II.
    Pragmatics & beyond ; new ser., 136.

    P95.455.S277 2005
    401'.41--dc22   2005048398
    ISBN 90 272 5379 X (Eur.) / 1 58811 642 5 (US) (Hb; alk. paper)

John Benjamins Publishing Co. · P.O. Box 36224 · 1020 ME Amsterdam · The Netherlands
John Benjamins North America · P.O. Box 27519 · Philadelphia PA 19118-0519 · USA

For Inge and Thea

Table of contents

Acknowledgements

This book is based on my doctoral thesis that was partially funded by the Deutsche Forschungsgemeinschaft (DFG) through a scholarship of the Graduate Program *Task Oriented Communication* (GK 256) Universität Bielefeld. My thanks go to my colleagues at the Graduate Program and especially our speaker Dieter Metzing. For their invaluable advice and encouraging remarks I would like to thank my supervisors Dafydd Gibbon and John Brian Walmsley and the participants of their colloquia as well as two anonymous reviewers at Benjamins for their helpful comments. I also want to thank Andreas H. Jucker and Isja Conen for their friendly and professional communication during preparation of my manuscript and Sylvia Nasaroff and Donna Devine for final proofreading. I am grateful to Kim Cardosi, Kellye Je'anne Tanner and Bryan Rife for background information, Harro Ranter for his kind permission to use and transform the ATC/CVR transcripts he hosts on aviation-safety.net, Harald Lüngen for discussion and Benjamin Hell, Jens Pönninghaus and Marcus Grieger for support with the perl-scripts. I am indebted to my parents and my aunts Inge and Thea and last not least to my husband Peter Kühnlein for his patience and untiring willingness to discuss matters.

## CHAPTER 1

Towards an analysis of crisis talk

Aviation ranks as the most secure means of transportation when it comes to long-distance travelling. Despite a momentary stagnation in bookings, owing to the attacks of September 11, 2001, in the long run flight frequency is expected to rise steadily. Despite this anticipated increase, however, choosing an airline to fly with gives reason enough for fear. As is stated in the Weissbuch of the Commission of the European Community, one serious accident per week can be expected in the coming years (EU Kommission 2001:46).

Economy and efficiency of flights require optimisation; however, high standards in both profitability and security seem to contradict each other. For example, a shortened schedule maintenance and briefer training phases doubtlessly reduce costs, but add to the risk of flying. Truncated readback behaviour accelerates communicative exchanges and reduces the radio workload, but may have adverse effects on the understanding between participants, and so result in a disaster. In the present analysis, we will opt for the second reading of the effects. This is in accordance with the analysis of Devlin (2001:11), who blames many aircraft accidents on too little communication.

Status behaviour, in the form of a solid role definition that supresses any initiatives towards contradicting authorities, can be another serious challenge to flight security. This was probably at least a partial cause for the aviation disaster of the *Birgen Air B757 Accident*. Behaviour of this kind, however, will not figure in the focus of this work.

The current investigation concentrates on aviation communication as a domain. It seeks to identify conspicuous features and aims at pointing out how important a proper development of communication is, either in routine situations or in emergency cases. The latter, called *crisis talk*, plays an important role in this investigation. It aims at a juxtaposition of speech act sequences during crisis talk and speech act sequences before the crisis.

Crisis talk is defined as a dialogue genre that occurs in threatening situations of unpredictable outcome, with no obvious way out, and requiring spontaneous decision, unconventional strategies and unrehearsed actions (Sassen 2003). Classical spoken language scenarios are typically service encounters and construction dialogues. They are genres in the sense of Grice's conversational maxims (Grice 1975): cooperative, well-formed and often rehearsed. Unlike these scenarios, *crisis talk* is more disfluent; it violates Gricean maxims, is usually emotional, and shows high taboo word frequency, unterminated *uptake loops* (Gibbon 1981) and iterated utterances as well as greater speech output quantity. Crisis talk typically occurs in negotiations with criminals, political summits, interpersonal conflicts and disaster scenarios. In the context of this book, crisis talk relates to aviation disasters, namely, to cockpit voice recordings, which acoustically document the actions undertaken by the crew in order to avoid a disaster during the last few minutes before their airplane crashes. In aviation communication, crisis talk usually occurs during a plane's take-off or landing because during these phases safety and thus people's lives are most at risk.

This outline of the term *crisis talk* will undergo further specification in the course of the analysis. *Crisis talk* will be introduced as a technical term, which, according to an internet search and to bibliographical research of printed texts, is not widely used. Every type of conversation that does not bear the features of crisis talk will be called *non-crisis talk*.

Crises are acutely dangerous situations. They are less likely to have happy endings although they need not end in fatal results. They are situations with a turning point of unpredictable outcome, resulting from an unbearable *problem* or conflict and are connoted with personal traumas or political emergencies. Often unexpected, difficult and dangerous, a crisis may put the face or even the lives of the persons affected at risk, and to be resolved it requires quick decision and action (Kienle 1982; Sinclair 1987). Specific decisions and actions help solve or at least mitigate the situation. Crises develop from particular kinds of behaviour that deviate from everyday routines, partly because a person's confidence in someone or something is undermined to such a large extent that it is doubtful whether it can ever be fully regained. As a result, crises cannot be mastered by conventional problem-solving techniques, but instead require unorthodox strategies (Fuchs et al. 1978).

A *problem* is a state of affairs that causes difficulties for people and awaits resolution. A crisis is a possible result of a problem; i.e. if a problem cannot be conventionally solved because there is no convention for resolution, a crisis will unfold. A crisis presupposes a problem, whereas the occurrence of a problem in a situation does not necessarily mark a concomitant crisis. There are no clear-cut criteria that help decide at what point a problem turns into a crisis.

Starting with these intuitive definitions, a method will be elaborated that allows for determining formal criteria for the definition of crisis talk and non-crisis talk.

1.1 Objectives and requirements

The data for the present investigation are constituted by ATC/CVR (air traffic control/cockpit voice recordings) transcripts that document the recordings of airplane crashes. It is grounded in a corpus-linguistic and speech act-based approach, and relies upon the constraint-based grammar HPSG that is extended to speech acts. Modelling HPSG is achieved by employing XML as a denotational semantics. The analysis is an attempt at formalising discourse theoretical structures that especially occur in crisis situations involving aviation disasters. Of particular importance in this context are topic-oriented discourse sequences that help secure uptake among the crew and between crew and tower in order to coordinate actions that might result in avoiding a potential disaster.

The analysis is aimed at proposing a methodology for a speech act-based documentation and analysis of data that is extendable to other sets of crisis talk data. A central goal is to develop a model for the description and disambiguation of speech acts which does not only serve to (semi-)automatically identify illocutions in highly stereotyped communication, but also enables researchers to spot *leaky points*, i.e. non-professional communication within a professional setting (Gibbon 1981), in the efficiency of communication. Ideally, the analysis could assist in achieving more successful exchanges in crisis situations, which might allow a de-escalation of communicative crises, its long-term objective in this very special case being to make flights safer.

For an effective access to discourse sequences such as uptake securing, the data are subjected to empirical and formal processing. To generate a corpus of crisis talk data, the empirical process passes through corpus design, its collection and representation: The individual transcript files, which were prepared by various institutionalised transcribers, show differences and inconsistencies in their notational framework. Therefore, the format of the corpus has to be standardised (see Section 4.2) so that it can be used for retrieval software such as concordance programs (KWIC-concordance)[1] and, more importantly, to simplify semi-automatic annotation. Annotation will be accomplished by using the attribute value archiving and retrieval formalism XML. In doing so, the categories already provided by the transcribers can be documented. Further requirements, specifically of the crisis talk scenario, will be fulfilled by an en-

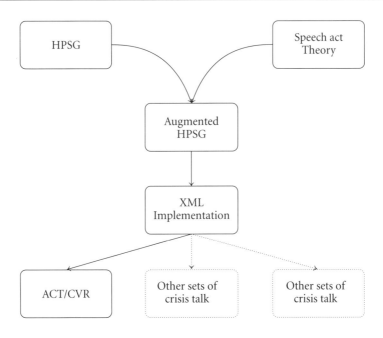

Figure 1.1 Diagram for the extension of HPSG and its later implementation in XML.

hancement strategy (see Figure 1.1). The XML format was chosen because it supports a flexible and platform-independent application enabling access and application of the data by internal and external users. The steps that are necessary for the annotation have been documented. The corpus is required to be available without XML-markup and in its marked-up form that meets the standard formulated by Bird & Liberman (1999b). The corpus can be looked up at http://pbns.claudia-sassen.net/.

On the formal level, the discourse sequences selected will be described by means of an attribute value formalism that is based on HPSG (Section 3). In order to ensure an extensive semantic-pragmatic modelling, the sentence-based HPSG-formalism will be expanded to the illocutionary logic of Searle & Vanderveken (1985). Bearing this requirement in mind, it should be noted that speech act theory is oriented towards strongly idealised examples and not towards modelling discourse. For the expansion of the HPSG-based formalism this means that the representation of utterance sequences must be accomplished as well (the relation of complex signs which may be produced by more than one speaker, see e.g. Heydrich, Kühnlein, & Rieser (1998); Kindt & Rieser (1999); Rieser & Skuplik (2000); Kindt (2001), in one HPSG-sign. In contrast to Kindt & Rieser (1999) and Rieser & Skuplik (2000), the focus of the analysis is not primarily on the cooperative production of single utterances, but on the interactive production of sequences thereof.[2] Thus, regularities of speech act sequences will be established while a modified HPSG-formalism for the integration of illocutionary logic and the disambiguation of speech acts is postulated. The investigation does not offer an analysis of individual words, but concentrates on functions that are independent of the lexicon. Lexical analyses and their results are presupposed.

The augmented HPSG formalism will be employed further in developing a new annotation category set by implementing HPSG-based attribute value matrices into the XML semantics (Section 5.4), see Figure 1.1. A strategy like this is necessary because the crisis talk scenario requirements are more demanding than the descriptive sets of existing annotation systems (e.g. the TEI): Crisis talk annotation requires detailed syntactic, semantic and pragmatic features for which a principled approach is preferred. XML is potentially flexible enough to be suitable for fulfilling crisis talk annotation requirements. XML annotation has been criticised for lacking a valid semantics. This problem will be circumvented by using XML simply as an algebra for domain structuring in a semantic document model: Together with the appropriate processing mechanisms, XML provides a denotational semantics for the attribute-value description. Starting from a basic XML data annotation, and based on the attribute-value description, an extended DTD (Document Type Definition) will be developed and the basic dialogue annotations enhanced semi-automatically. In a sense, the procedure extends, formalises and operationalises older proposals to formulate markup in terms of feature structures. Based on the theoretical background and its extensions proposed above, the following predictions are made:

- Crisis talk is different from non-crisis talk with respect to interactional patterns;
- In order to disambiguate speech acts, the model of Searle's and Vanderveken's illocutionary logic requires more precision with regard to the propositional content that is presupposed. This extension can be achieved by an HPSG-based formalism;
- An extended HPSG-formalism is an adequate model for the representation, description and explanation of the disambiguation of illocutionary acts;
- It is possible to extend HPSG-based structures and principles from the interactive sentence level to the utterance level. An extension of the HPSG-based inventory from the utterance level to the discourse level is also possible: speech act sequences may be modelled by one HPSG-based sign.

– XML uses an attribute value archiving and retrieval formalism, and is potentially flexible enough to fulfill the requirements of crisis talk annotation.

1.2 The scenario: Air traffic control

The term ATC has at least two different meanings. The first is "part of aviation parlance" and applies to the tasks which include the controller. The second meaning is metaphorical and explicitly pertains to the two-way communication between controllers and the cockpit and could be phrased more exactly by ATC-*system* or ATC-*communication*. Consequently, for reasons of clarity from now on the term ATC-*communication* will be employed to refer to the verbal exchange between tower and crew as a procedure. The term ATC may even have a third reading in that the regulated routine communication between the pilots in the cockpit is also a component of controlling air traffic. In order to distinguish cockpit-tower communication from communication within the cockpit, the former is called *extra-cockpit communication* and the latter *intra-cockpit communication*. This terminology deliberately stresses the cockpit side because more data are available from cockpit voice recordings than from ATC-recordings. The terms ATC and also CVR will be used in connection with the terms *corpus* and *transcript* if the documents that contain these data are referred to. *Aviation communication* is a general term that subsumes the two sorts of communication.

Constraints and consequences

Communication is a critical component in aviation. It is shaped by accuracy and efficiency constraints. Controllers and pilots use a "combination of English and special conventions that have developed in response to these constraints" (Morrow et al. 1994: 235). The *accurate* understanding of every unit of information is vital for air safety and has resulted in the explicit acknowledgement procedures, such as readbacks, that enable addressees (e.g. pilots) to repeat the sender's (e.g. the controller's) message so that the sender can check its interpretation. As important as accuracy is the efficiency-related factor of rapidity. Aviation communication must be *rapid* because all participants are involved in dynamically changing situations. A central type of transaction that requires quick behaviour is exchange via radio transmission, as many different pilots use the same radio frequency to talk to the same controller.

Consequently, aviation language is highly compressed, as becomes obvious from its abbreviated terminology and phrasal syntax. According to Morrow et al. (1994), both *routine* and *non-routine operations* are influenced by accuracy and efficiency constraints. *Routine operations* relate to transactions free from communication problems. *Non-routine operations*, in the present study called *crisis talk*, refer to sender and addressee interrupting their routine transaction in order to resolve a communication problem or a technical problem. The latter involves deviation from some standard collaborative scheme as perceived by Morrow et al. (1994), which people follow in order to ensure mutual understanding. Their standard collaborative scheme consists of the components "initiation of a transaction, presentation of new information about a topic" and "collaboration of sender and addressee(s) in order to accept the information as mutually understood and appropriate to the context" (Morrow et al. 1994: 236, see also Ringle & Bruce 1982 and Clark & Schaefer 1987).

For basic routine ATC-communication this means that controllers open a transaction with the intended call sign of the aircraft. Then they present a message by means of particular speech acts, e.g. statements about airspace conditions or instructions on the flight level. If pilots understand the message they update a mental model[3] of the flight conditions. Finally, pilots and controllers terminate the transaction by accepting the message as mutually understood and appropriate: Pilots acknowledge it using their call sign and a readback of it, while the controller validates the readback for accuracy (*hearback*) (Morrow & Rodvold 1993: 324).

Standard collaboration, of which the scheme is a convention, implies that communication takes place against a background of shared knowledge about language, here English, aviation communication conventions and the operational environment (the task to fulfill). As Morrow puts it,

> Controllers and pilots must agree that they share the same mental model before continuing to the next turn or transaction. (...) With understanding problems, addressees do not correctly update their mental model from the presented information (or speakers do not receive evidence that addressees did so).   (Morrow et al. 1994: 237)

The main function of extra-cockpit communication is to prevent a collision between aircraft that operate in the system and to coordinate and expedite the orderly flow of traffic (Federal Aviation Administration (2001a: Chapter: 2.1.1)). This service is provided by air traffic controllers. They stay on the ground, organise the routes that aircraft are allowed to take through the sky and stay in contact with the pilots by radio and radar. If indicated, the service includes safety alerts such as reporting abnormalities in weather conditions (Federal Aviation Administration 2001a: Chapter: 3.1.10, 4.), bird activity information (Federal Aviation Administration 2001a: Chapter: 2.1.22) or unknown aircraft in the area of the aircraft currently under jurisdiction.

ATC-communication involves entering into a highly rule-governed process. The *Airman's Information Manual (AIM)*, which forms part of the *Aeronautical Information Manual*, as well as the *Pilot/Controller Glossary* (Federal Aviation Administration 2000a)[4] along with the *Federal Aviation Administration Order* (FAAO)[5] equip aviation professionals in the United States by means of phraseologies with strict rules to achieve a standard of linguistic exchange that is (acoustically and semantically) unequivocal.[6]

The pilots' and controllers' duty is to use the words and phrases of these regulations to secure a complete and effective ATC-communication. Some examples of FAAO-regulations are given below. The following phraseology consists of an utterance without variables. Its context of use is cited first:

> In situations where the controller does not want the pilot to change frequency but the pilot is expecting or may want a frequency change, use the following phraseology:
> PHRASEOLOGY – REMAIN THIS FREQUENCY
> (Federal Aviation Administration 2001a: 2.1.17)

Example (1) displays a phraseology that consists of an utterance including a variable that is printed in round brackets. The template is used as a response to a request from another controller, a pilot or vehicle operator:

(1)   Restate the request in complete or abbreviated terms followed by the word "APPROVED." The phraseology "APPROVED AS REQUESTED" may be substituted in lieu of a lengthy readback.
      PHRASEOLOGY – (requested operation) APPROVED or APPROVED AS
      REQUESTED.   (Federal Aviation Administration 2001a: 2.1.18a)

Restating a request or instructions verbatim or by a completely synonymous equivalent is called *full readback* in aviation register (Cushing 1994; Rife 2000). The readback pattern represents an important part of the grammar of ATC-communication. Full readback is mandatory to attain clarity with regard to commands and responses. There are instances when readback is especially requested by the controller (see Example (2) and also Federal Aviation Administration 2001a: 4.2.3c).

(2)   Request a readback of runway hold short instructions when it is not received from the pilot [...]. NOTE- Readback hold instructions phraseology

may be initiated for any point on a movement area when the controller be-
lieves the readback is necessary.

(Federal Aviation Administration 2001a: 3.7.2d)

Unless otherwise indicated, readback may be abbreviated to backchannelling
behaviour, called *acknowledgements* here (Rife 2000) and, according to other
sources, *one-word acknowledgement* (Morrow et al. 1994; see Example (3) on
backchanneling).

(3)   When issuing clearances or instructions ensure acknowledgement by the
      pilot. [...] Pilots may acknowledge clearances, instructions, or other in-
      formation by using "Wilco," "Roger," "Affirmative," or other words or
      remarks. (Federal Aviation Administration 2001a: 2.4.3a; see also 2.1.18)[7]

To prevent the fatal consequences of misunderstandings the controller is
obliged to execute a linguistic repair mechanism (see Section 4.5):

If altitude, heading, or other items are read back by the pilot, ensure the readback is correct. If incorrect or incomplete, make corrections as appropriate.

(Federal Aviation Administration 2001a: 2.4.3b)

Example (4) displays an extract from an exchange between a pilot (caller) who
contacts the controller (receiver) and illustrates the principle of a full readback:

(4)   The caller states his or her operating initials. EXAMPLE- Caller- "Den-
      ver High, R Twenty-five." Receiver- "Denver high." Caller- "Request direct
      Denver for Northwest Three Twenty-eight." Receiver- "Northwest Three
      twenty-eight direct Denver approved. H.F." Caller- "G.M."

(Federal Aviation Administration 2001a: 2.4.12)

An *AIR (Aviation Interface Research) System Controller Grammar* can be found
in Cushing 1994: 137.

Apart from extra-cockpit communication, phraseologies are also indis-
pensable for intra cockpit communication to secure an accurate and effective
exchange between the pilot and his copilot.

Unlike extra-cockpit communication, there are no federal regulations governing communication between pilots. However, at all U.S. airlines a *Flight Operations Manual* (FOM) is prepared by the company and details the procedures
that are used by flight crews. The FOM is reviewed by a Federal Aviation Administration (FAA) *Principal Operations Inspector* who approves and certifies
the original FOM and revisions to the FOM.

The FOM is very detailed and lists the required procedures for completing
any task. For instance, it contains detailed instructions on how a takeoff is per-

formed and the required *callouts by the non-flying pilot*. The *callouts* are quite specific and intended to be followed to the letter. Any deviation from these procedures could result in a FAA violation for the flight crew for failing to follow required procedures.[8]

The *Pacific Northwest National Laboratory Manual 530* (PNNL-MA-530)[9] has been selected as one representative of the FOM. Like all the other FOMs that were found on the internet and acquired through contacts with aviation companies it does not contain the exact phrasing that should be used, but simply states the required procedure in a descriptive manner. This is exemplified for an *altitude callout* (Example (5)) and a *flight level callout* (Example (6)):

(5)   Altitude Callout
      Both pilots call out and acknowledge each altitude callout of 1000ft, prior
      to the assigned altitude (Federal Aviation Administration 1998:4.3.1.2).

(6)   Flight Level 180 Callout
      Both pilots call out the climb and descent altimeter settings for flight level
      (FL) 180 (18,000ft) (Federal Aviation Administration 1998:4.3.1.2).

The *Approach Briefing* is executed as follows:

> Upon receiving the appropriate approach information and verifying that both altimeters are correctly set, the Pilot Not Flying (PNF) will pull the approach plate for review by the Pilot Flying.
> (Federal Aviation Administration 1998:4.3.1.14)

Since the phraseologies assembled in the airline-specific FOMs are proprietary,[10] exemplifying phrases were taken from *MD-80 sample oral questions* (Hoesch 2000), a source that was found on the *World Wide Web*. It was designed to help pilots train for their exams. The chronological list of PF (pilot flying) and PNF (pilot not flying) callouts during a missed approach is embedded in the prescribed actions that the pilots have to execute (see Table 1.1).

Intra- and extra-cockpit communication represent a critical link in the aviation system. Radio communication, for instance, can be a strong bond between pilot and controller. The interruption of radio communication can have disastrous results, as the following quotation implies:

> The single, most important thought in pilot-controller communication is understanding.   (Federal Aviation Administration 2000c:4.2.1)

Factors influencing the quality of controller/pilot communication are volume of traffic, frequency congestion, quality of radar, or controller workload (Federal Aviation Administration 1995:2.1.1). Some aspects of the situational,

Table 1.1 List of PF/PNF-callouts during a missed approach, see Hoesch (2000). The callouts are marked in bold face. For further explanation see the glossary of aviation terms in Appendix A.

GO-AROUND		
Go-Around	PF	PNF
	"GO-AROUND" Press either TO/GA button	Verify EPR G/A, ALT, GO RND, GO RND annunciate on the FMA A/T, arm, roll, and pitch windows respectively
	"GO-AROUND POWER"	Select flaps 15 or 11 Make final thrust adjustments
	Verify throttles to GA thrust Rotate to F/D commanded attitude **"FLAPS 15"** ("**FLAPS 11**," if landing flaps were at 28) Maintain at least V_{ref}+5 knots	**"POWER SET"**
Positive Rate of Climb	Verify positive rate of climb **"GEAR UP, ADVISE ATC, ARM MISSED APPROACH"**	**"POSITIVE RATE"** Position gear lever UP Advise ATC
	Select/Request as level of automation dictates Verify missed approach altitude is armed Pull HDG select knob (if appropriate) Set airspeed command bug to appropriate maneuver speed Set missed approach course and Nav radios	
	Execute published missed approach or proceed as instructed by ATC	Disarm spoilers Monitor Missed approach procedure
Climbing through 1,000' AFE	Select/Request HALF RATE Reduce pitch and accelerate	Select one-half through vertical rate (not less than 1,000 FPM), if requested
At flap retraction speed	**"FLAPS UP, CLIMB POWER"**	Retract flaps and select CL on the TRI
At slat retraction speed	**"SLATS RETRACT, AFTER TAKEOFF CHECKLIST"** Accomplish checklist	Retract slats
At appropriate maneuver speed	Select/Request SPD/SEL, desired VERT SPD and BANK ANGLE 25° or 30°	Select SPD SEL, vertical speed, and bank angle 25° or 30°, if requested. -or- Select IAS HOLD and bank angle 25° or 30°, if requested

linguistic and technical behaviour that may cause serious problems as mentioned in this section will be discussed in more detail in Section 1.2. Some trouble sources are catered for by the aforementioned federal regulations; however, they do not cover many other problems. Project groups have been formed by organisations such as NASA in order to analyse the leaky points, i.e. non-professional communication in aviation transactions and to formulate recommendations that help avoid the occurrence of problems. Extracts from the regulations as well as recommendations designed to prevent potential problems will be included wherever possible.

Sources of error in extra- and intra-cockpit communication

According to Cardosi, Falzarano, & Han (1999: viii), pilot-controller communications (see e.g. Morrow, Lee, & Rodvold 1993; Cardosi 1994; Buerki-Cohen 1995) display an astonishingly low error rate. Corresponding studies reveal that less than one percent of the aviation communication analysed led to a communication error that would vitiate the accuracy of the exchange. Although the error rate is low, it does not reduce the potential seriousness of even a single error. Cardosi, Falzarano, & Han (1999: viii) particularly point out that the number of these errors per hour are close to one. In order to decrease the number of communication errors, several research projects have been inaugurated, because the first measure taken against communication errors must be to identify why they happen in the first place. Some of their results will be reviewed here. They can be categorised as factors that apply to personal and contextual aspects, to linguistic issues and to technical problems. As will be seen in the course of this section, however, the distinction is not selective, because the factors form a continuum.

Personal and situational factors

Personal and situational factors pertain to the personality of participants in aviation communication and to the situations they are in. *Readback behaviour* (or the lack of it) is considered a most critical and controversial factor of ATC-communication (Rife 2000). Despite an explicit appeal in the federal regulations to make use of full readback (Federal Aviation Administration 2001a: 2.4.3), this type of response tends to fall victim to routine behaviour on the one hand and to misunderstood efficiency on the other. Pilots acknowledging a controller's command with a partial readback leave the controller insufficiently informed on whether his instructions were interpreted as intended. The following instance comes from a three-hour listening session at a major airport: Although the controller issued the instruction *Squawk 1735* the pilot reduced it in his readback to *Squawkin'*. A similar instruction was read back by another pilot simply with *Awrightee* (see Cushing 1994: 40). Rife concludes:

> Pilots should acknowledge each radio communication with ATC using the appropriate aircraft identification, and read back critical information such as runway and altitude assignment. When critical information is not read back, the opportunity for the controller to correct the error is lost.
>
> (Rife 2000, see also Bürki-Cohen 1995; Cardosi, Falzarano, & Han 1999)

Rife cites an instance in which a lack of readback resulted in one aircraft entering another controllers airspace without coordination or approval.

Lax behaviour is frequently observed when it comes to the completeness of responses. *Completeness* does not only imply that the addressee is required to repeat the message of the sender verbatim but also that he prefix it with the call sign in question. According to a study conducted by the Volpe Center,[11] on average, 38 percent of pilots do not use their complete call sign (also known as aircraft identifier) in response to controllers. A lack of either component might result in misunderstandings and confusions. For this reason, Cardosi, Falzarano, & Han (1999: 10) issue the warning that it is not an excuse to omit the aircraft identification claiming that it *[tends] to clutter the frequency*). They cite an incident in which a pilot, who *did not believe in complete readbacks of clearances* because of possible radio overload, acknowledged the clearance *position and hold* that was addressed at another aircraft with a mere *roger*. In the end, this runway transgression made a go-around for an incoming aircraft necessary.

Cushing makes the critical point that the requirement of full readback along with other official constraints on language use can only be expected to be a valuable means in uptake securing when both interlocutors are

> fully cognizant of the subtle nuances of the language they are using and fully engaged in their role as interlocutors.   (Cushing 1994: 45)

As a central source of error with regard to the subtlety of a language he names speakers of languages in which explicit prepositions are not as essential for meaning as in English. They were more likely to omit words like these unless the potential danger of omittance was not clearly brought to their attention in training.

Routine behaviour ranks as a severe factor adding to the eventual inefficiency of full readbacks. Aviation communication is a matter of routine to a large extent, and particularly characterised by a massive amount of repetition. Therefore, it induces ritualisation whereby utterances and situations "lose their cognitive impact and participants [fall] into a pattern of simply going through the motions for their own sake" as Cushing (1994: 46) observes. To this problem add the closely related *hearback* errors, as an experienced pilot notes:

> After 27 years of flying I now find it becoming easier to "hear" things in a clearance that are not really there. More diligence is required.
> (cited from Cardosi, Falzarano, & Han 1999: 9)

With regard to the mnemonic qualities of a message, brevity is an essential issue for the success of readback behaviour and is integrated as an explicit recommendation in most of the analyses on pilot-controller communications:

> Controllers should be encouraged to keep their instructions short with no more than four instructions per transmission. The complexity of the controller's transmission has a direct effect on the pilot's ability to remember it – there are fewer pilot errors with the less complex transmissions.
> (Cardosi, Falzarano, & Han 1999: viii, see also Cushing 1994; Bürki-Cohen 1995)

In the context of message length, Morrow & Rodvold (1993) examined the timing of messages in cockpit-tower communication testing the effect of two short messages instead of one long message. For brief and portioned messages they state a dialectic nature:

> While long messages reduce comprehension or immediate memory for information by overloading working memory, short messages presented in quick succession are more likely to cause forgetting, with the later message intruding into memory for the earlier message.   (Morrow & Rodvold 1993: 326)

If controllers split long messages they will improve communication accuracy only if they also leave enough time between messages to avoid memory interference problems (Morrow et al. 1994). The strategy of breaking up messages may lengthen communication because the number of turns necessary to transmit and convey the same amount of information increases. However, Morrow & Rodvold (1993: 326) consider accuracy at the cost of communication time or length a *reasonable trade-off* considering the importance of accuracy to flight safety.

As regards *repetition across languages*, disturbing problems may result from bilingual interactions between pilots and pilots and controller. In one particular accident most of the people aboard died because the copilot rendered a pilot's message only conceptually to the tower instead of translating it in such a way that it would fully match his original message:

> Pilot to copilot (in Spanish): Tell them we are in an emergency.
> Copilot to controller (in English): We're running out of fuel.

The copilot's message does not make the proper degree of urgency explicit to the controller so that the conceptual repetition of the pilot's message is incorrect. Cushing comments:

> The problem is probably compounded here [...] by the fact that the language being used is a technical variant of a language other than the speaker's own, leaving him twice removed from the vernacular with which he is most familiar.
> (Cushing 1994:45)

Risky inferences can also be the result of the use of *unfamiliar terminology* as far as the addressee is concerned. This may be the case with young and inexperienced pilots and controllers, or have evolved with pilots from different cultures or simply different surroundings in which different conventions have evolved. The reason may also lie in sheer ignorance. In an example that Cushing cites, the pilot addressed was unfamiliar with an abbreviation. When the Approach Control told him

> We have the REIL [runway end identifier lights][12] lights up all the way; do you have the runway in sight?

the pilot responded after some hesitation:

> How do you tell the difference between real lights and imitation lights?
> (Cushing 1994:29)

The pilot inferred a non-existent distinction of lights right on the evidence that he was not acquainted with the abbreviation of *REIL*.

In another case, adaptation to different surroundings lay at the core of an understanding problem. The string *ladies, legal, lights, liquids* issued by the non-flying pilot were new to the copilot, so that passing through 10,000 feet on descent the aircraft fell too quickly to 8,300 feet and needed to climb back. The pilot had used the terminology of his former airline which was used to

> remind crew members at 10,000 feet to turn on the seatbelt sign, reduce airspeed to less than 250 knots, turn on the lights for recognition, and make sure the hydraulic pumps and fuel boost pumps are turned on.
> (Cushing 1994:31)

Inference is a further trouble source in aviation communication. It means that a hearer derives meaning from a sentence that is explicit in its words (*lexical inference*) or grammar (*structural inference*) (see Cushing 1994:24). More on inference and a good overview of related literature can be found in Rickheit & Strohner (1985); Rickheit & Strohner (1997). Cushing describes aviation incidents that were caused by lexical inference. In one of them, which resulted in a near miss, a captain was told twenty miles from his airport of destination "to intercept the localizer and descend to 4,000 [feet]". When the captain was five miles outside the outer marker at the commanded level the Center told him that the other aircraft on the approach in front of him had landed. The Center continued: "you are number one for the approach". These very words were interpreted by the crew as meaning *cleared for the approach*, although the clearance was not given. They reduced their flight level and two miles outside the marker, at 3,600 feet, the Center informed the crew that they were only cleared to 4,000 feet. Another aircraft was departing (Cushing 1994: 28). In another incident, the Center told the captain that he would have to be moved to either FL [flight level] 310 or FL 350. Asked which flight level he would prefer, the captain replied "flight level 350". Ten minutes later the Center enquired about his altitude and he replied "flight level 350", but was told he had not been cleared to this flight level. According to the first officer, he (presumably F/O, Cushing is not explicit about this) had received a clearance and had reported vacating FL 330 for 350. Cushing concludes that the clearance was erroneously inferred from the Center's initial question about the altitude and that the first officer's report was unnoticed (Cushing 1994: 29).

Confusion over the identity of the *intended addressee*, which often results in garbling call-signs, is a common error in aviation communication and clearly interferes with the required efficiency in information transfer. Identity garblings may occur because of technical problems such as frequency mix-ups and incomplete transmission or because of hearback errors owing to fatigue or homophony phenomena. Apart from verbally based terminology, non-verbal terminology can also be dangerously misinterpreted when unfamiliar to the addressee. A copilot pointing down and showing four fingers was taken by the pilot to confirm that the aircraft had been cleared to descend to 4,000 feet and so he left his flight level. The copilot, however, had intended to signal that the aircraft had been instructed *to park via ramp 4 on arrival* (Cushing 1994: 34). Here the problem was caused by pilots from different countries.

There is a vast range of reasons a flight crew or a controller may be diverted and hence endanger the lives of hundreds of people, which may be subsumed under the term *distractions*. For example, a pilot's personal situation may add to his exhaustion, or an overworked controller may not notice a faulty readback that, consequently, prevents him from correcting a misunderstood instruction. In general, however, according to the study of Cardosi, Falzarano, & Han (1999), it is the nature of the controller's job to plan one action while acting out another; thus it would be useless to suggest that controllers should protect themselves against being distracted during readbacks. Cardosi et al. suggest

> that controllers regard the readbacks as they would any other piece of incoming information – by using it. Actively listen to the readback and check it against the flight strips notations to ensure that the message the pilot received was the correct one.   (Cardosi, Falzarano, & Han 1999: 9)

Other distractions that are often not directly related to aviation can cause trouble as well. These distractions may include the delivery of the crew's meals, which may result in a missed frequency change. A passenger question or *excess and nonessential radio communications* might break the chain of thought and hinder the crew from concentrating on monitoring their instruments properly. A bird strike may distract the crew from changing over to tower control, and the same could happen to a pilot pre-occupied with instructing a new copilot. Often enough, the reasons a crew did not notice important occurrences such as instructions or equipment failure remain obscure (Cushing 1994: 71–74). At times, disaster is avoided thanks to technical support such as warning signals or to a controller who effectively regains a distracted crew's attention or even to chance factors.

> However, it would be foolish to count on having such good luck.
> (Cushing 1994: 74)

Despite the need for speed, which is closely related to the efficiency constraint, communication effectiveness can clearly be undermined by *impatience*. Cushing reports several incidents in which clearances and other instructions are given by controllers in too rapid a manner so that pilots have to ask for repetition. Because multiple aircraft are connected to the control tower via the same frequency, effective radio communication is impeded by traffic overload, with overlapping requests from different pilots. This situation requires a restatement of instructions (Cushing 1994: 74–75).

Another likely cause of dangerous incidents and serious accidents could be a *lack of cooperation* among the crew. Many cases involved one member wanting to get others fired from their position because of competitive job facilities. Particularly disturbing are incidents that resulted from mere *frivolousness*, e.g. from the misuse of radio frequency for messages that were irrelevant to aviation instructions and navigation matters. In an incident that resulted in a near miss, instructors of a young pilot did not handle their flight situation with adequate conscientiousness. They told jokes and conversed freely back and forth and so missed an important controller instruction that the pilot needed to turn in a certain direction immediately because of departing traffic.

Linguistic factors

Trouble sources that are of a mainly linguistic origin branch into aspects of semantics, pragmatics and surface interpretation. According to Cushing (1994:8), *ambiguity* is an ever-present source of potential misunderstandings in aviation communication. In general, ambiguity means that a sign or a string of signs (word, phrase, sentence) has more than one meaning. It can have both a lexical and a structural basis, as with sentences like "The man watched the girl with the telescope" or "She saw her duck" (Bach 2001). *Lexical ambiguity*, as the more common type of ambiguity, applies if one word has more than one meaning (Bach 2001). Consider the following example: In aviation parlance pilots use the term *PD* as an abbreviation for both of the expressions *pilot's discretion* and *profile descent*. The most devastating disaster in aviation history, the accident at *Los Rodeos Airport*, Tenerife, presumably was in part the result of lexical ambiguity (Cushing 1994:10; Aviation Safety Network 2002d:10). On March 27, 1977, a KLM Boeing 747 (Flight 4805) attempted to take off from Tenerife for a flight to Las Palmas. A PanAm Boeing 747 was still taxiing down the runway. Both aircraft collided and burst into flames. All 248 persons on board the KLM flight as well as 335 PanAm occupants died (Aviation Safety Network 2002a). The misunderstanding arose from the phrase *at takeoff*, which the pilots used to indicate that they were *in the process of taking off*, but was interpreted by the controller as meaning *at the takeoff point* (Cushing 1994:1, 7, 11). Consequently, he did not tell the pilot to abort his takeoff. The misunderstanding on the pilots' side was presumably triggered off by a prior misinterpretation of the controller's utterance:

> You are cleared to the Papa Beacon, climb to and maintain flight level nine zero, right turn after takeoff.   (Cushing 1994:7)

The wording *after takeoff* is not necessarily equivalent to permission to take off, but the pilot obviously interpreted the controller's clearance as permission to fly to the Papa Beacon, whereas the controller obviously intended to issue a subsequent command that would tell the pilot to fly to the beacon only after having received further clearance to leave the ground. Cushing concludes:

> The use of alternative unambiguous phrases for the clearance and the takeoff announcement would have enabled the controller to advise some action that might have averted the collision or prevented the takeoff roll in the first place.
> (Cushing 1994:10)

Structural ambiguity occurs when a phrase or sentence has more than one underlying structure, such as the phrase "Flying planes can be dangerous" (Cushing 1994; Bach 2001). It can be represented structurally in two different ways: in the first reading *flying* can be interpreted as an adjective to the noun *planes* in the sense that *planes that are flying can be dangerous*. In the second reading *flying* might be interpreted as *to fly planes can be dangerous*. In terms of HPSG, this fact can be stated thus: In the first case *flying* is a modifier, while *plane* is the head of the phrasal sign. In the second case, *flying* is the head, while *planes* is a complement. In both cases, of course, the NP constitutes the complement to the verb phrase so that the potential of being dangerous is predicated of the respective entity or entities. From this point of view, this type of ambiguity might be classified as a matter of syntax.

A special type of structural ambiguity leads to confusion of the speech act type that is performed in an utterance. For example, it might be unclear whether a controller utters a declaration or an instruction. Such a case is reported about a pilot who had received the following message from the controller:

> traffic at ten o'clock, three miles, level at 6,000, to pass under you

The pilot was observed descending through 6,800 feet because he had misconstrued the phrase *level at 6,000* as an instruction in the sense of *Descend to and remain level at 6,000*. The controller, however, had intended his utterance declaratively meaning *The traffic is level at 6,000* (Cushing 1994: 16).

The disambiguation of illocutionary acts figures as an essential part of the present study and will be discussed in detail in Chapter 5. Particular instances of ambiguity are indirect speech acts through which the speaker intends to express a certain communicative function by literally expressing another one.

Ambiguity in spoken language can be traced back to two main factors: *homophony*, a case in which two lexemes having the same pronunciation but different meanings, and *unspecified prosody* that leads to an indistinguishability of, e.g. speech act types.

The problems described are all of a phonetic nature such as homophony, either because of similar sounds or unclear production. In the context of aviation parlance, the notion of homophony is extended to sounds that are nearly alike. Owing to the quality of the transmission channel, some sounds that are articulatorily distinct may become auditorily indistinguishable. Not only for non-native speakers of English might homophony be a source of misinterpretation with severe consequences. A well known example of homophony that may lead to fatal consequences in aviation communication is the preposition *to* which equals the pronunciation of the numeral *two*.

Cushing reports the incident of a pilot whom the tower observed to be "somewhat higher than called for in the procedure, and flying in the wrong direction". He turned out to have misheard the clearance *a Maspeth climb* as the clearance *a massive climb*. *Maspeth* is a fix in the New York metropolitan area; however, the pilot was unacquainted with the region's geographical data (Cushing 1994: 13).

Another common mistake occurs when different aircraft whose identifications sound nearly alike are communicating with the same controller. They may have the same flight number (such as AAL 123 and UAL 123), similar sounding numbers (such as *two* and *ten*), or identical numbers in different positions (such as *four thirty-two* and *three forty-two*). The problem worsens when aircraft with the same airline name also have numbers that sound similar. The call-sign problem easily increases particularly at airline hubs, where many aircraft will have the same company name (Cardosi, Falzarano, & Han 1999: 14). In their regulation, the FAAO cater for this potential trouble source with an *Emphasis for Clarity*:

> Emphasize appropriate digits, letters, or similar sounding words to aid in distinguishing between similar sounding aircraft identifications [...].
> (Federal Aviation Administration 1995: 2.4.15)

Cardosi, Falzarano, & Han (1999) go even further in their discussion of pilot-controller communication errors and write:

> When there are similar call signs on the frequency, controllers should announce this fact; this will alert pilots and may help to reduce the incidence of pilots accepting a clearance intended for another aircraft.
> (Cardosi, Falzarano, & Han 1999: 22)

Mistakes on the suprasegmental level such as *unspecified prosody* may equally lead to similar sorts of confusion with ill effects. An incident that involves problems with intonation is reported by a flight instructor who was checking out a pilot in a small airplane. The instructor noticed considerable *power on* a few seconds before touching down. He thought he uttered the command *Back-on the power* which was interpreted by the pilot as *Back on – the power*. The utterances differ in the location of the pause (indicated by a dash) and the stress of *on* (Cushing 1994: 16). Backing off (back) means basically to go "backward" in terms of what is being done, in this situation because the power had come back on, (on the power) and was an aviation hazard.[13] In this context, Kadmon (2001: 12–13) stresses the connection between identifying the focus of an utterance and prosodic intonation patterns. For the current analysis, prosody counts as an important factor that helps determine speech act types.

The recommendation made at this point addresses the sender and advises him to clearly articulate his words and instructs the recipient to listen carefully (Cardosi, Falzarano, & Han 1999:14). Further, acoustics-related problems pertain to speech rate and human voice. Morrow & Rodvold (1998) identify as trouble sources utterances which are made in too hasty, unarticulated or low-voiced a manner. Cardosi, Falzarano, & Han (1999) comment:

> Controllers should be encouraged to speak slowly and distinctly. [...] With a normal rate of speech (156 words per minute), 5% of the controller's instructions resulted in a readback error or a request for repeat. This rate rose to 12% when the controller spoke somewhat faster (210 words per minute).
>
> (Cardosi, Falzarano, & Han 1999:22)

Instead, Cardosi, Falzarano, & Han recommend a normal, conversational tone.

Technical factors

The main trouble source of technical factors in aviation communication is radio transmission and its use. Parts of calls or responses may get lost for a number of radio-related reasons: Probably the most obvious source of miscommunication in aviation is having *no radio* at all. A predicament like this may have various causes: complete electrical failure or poor radio reception, an earpiece disconnecting from the pilot's headset or a pilot unintentionally turning down the volume on the VOR (Very High Frequency Omni-directional Range) and VHF (Very High Frequency) at the same time. Tower and cockpit losing contact just for a few seconds could lead to identifier-guessing or defective inferences and result in risky actions. In his book, Cushing lists several incidents where aircraft came close to disaster because of the absence of radio contact (Cushing 1994:63).

Non-use of radio may be purely accidental in that the pilot "just flat forgot to contact Tower" (Cushing 1994:65) or it may be motivated by absurd advice such as that of an airport manager who told a helicopter crew before flight to keep radio communication to a minimum before and after flight that "radios in many aircraft were not turned on, to save wear and tear on equipment" (Cushing 1994:67). Another important factor of non-use of radio is that the crew is not able to employ the radio because someone else in the same traffic area blocks it off by a stuck microphone, or too much radio traffic occurs at the same time because crews are transmitting on the wrong frequency. With *unclear frequency* the pilot fails to search a clear frequency when he wants to establish contact with ground control. This will probably jam the receivers of other aircraft so that their calls have to be repeated. Any interferences of this kind may impair the communication of aircraft in jeopardy (and can cost valuable seconds), let alone the situation of the current aircraft (Federal Aviation Administration 2001a). Cushing writes about an instance in which a pilot got off lightly:

> [He] finally taxied to the active runway and contacted Tower, having never gotten through to Ground, because Ground Control frequency was totally clogged with numerous aircraft trying to call at once.   (Cushing 1994:66)

He reports a separate instance in which a pilot waited for a pause in the very busy radio traffic to send his call, while several calls were cut out by people transmitting over each other. When he finally got through his call was partly deleted. The pilot concludes:

> So much confusion could be avoided if everybody would use common radio courtesy and listen before transmitting.   (Cushing 1994:67)

In some situations, pilots fail to recognise that their microphone is stuck in the transmit position, so they cannot receive instructions from the controller. This may cause *frequency blockage* for other aircraft tuned to the same frequency in the same area and result in unintentional transmitter operation. Frequency blockage may likewise be caused through inadvertent keying of the transmitter by the controller. There may be other reasons the pilot does not hear from the controller, for instance, when the volume is down, or the frequency is not the same as the controller's (Cushing 1994; Federal Aviation Administration 2001a).

> "Recurring stuck mike problems reported by an ATC facility" prompted NASA's Aviation Safety Reporting System to issue an alert in late 1992.
> (Cushing 1994:66)

Incomplete transmission applies when the pilot or controller begins to speak too early after pressing the microphone button so that the first words are not transmitted to the controller. A sender's precipitation is often based on the fact that aviation transactions are constrained by the need for speed, which seems to override the need for accuracy. The situation is worsened by outdated radio equipment that produces a time lag between the keying of a mike and the transmitter's actual output. This results in uncertain addressees owing to missing identifiers and causes many repeats which impose a load on the communication frequency and thus counteract the efficiency constraint (Cushing 1994:20;

Bürki-Cohen 1995:27; Federal Aviation Administration 2001a). An additional factor could be that the microphone is not close enough to the sender's lips.

An incident is reported involving two aircraft from different companies but which had the same flight number. They were on the same frequency while the controller was issuing commands and failed to transmit the company prefix with the identifier. The unintended addressee ended up following the controller's instructions and could only remedy his mistake by a quick return to his aircraft's prior position (Cushing 1994:20).

Conclusion

Trouble sources in aviation communication can be attributed to factors that concern the general behaviour of the persons involved and the situation they are in. It could be argued that it was preferable to assign trouble sources such as readback behaviour to the category of linguistic features. Indeed, readback largely pertains to language because participants are required to produce language; however, the difficulty often does not lie in the production of speech itself, but in the addition of a multitude of external factors. What is classified as *linguistic factors* has more to do with the structure of language than with the way in which it is used.

Some factors may overlap with the features of readback behaviour. Readback behaviour is verbatim repetition of information, while *repetition across languages* relates to the re-formulation of a message in a target language that differs from that of the source. This factor may again be categorised as a linguistic source of error, but in the example displayed here a proper translation would not have resulted in a disaster.

The subsequent order of *unfamiliar terminology* followed by *inference* is based on the fact that misinterpretation of given information is closer to correct readback behaviour than the reconstruction of missing information. The complete absence of a cornerstone that allows even for the inference of information is described in the section about *uncertain addressee*; the failure in at least perceiving given information may be caused by *distractions*. Distractions may in turn be the result of *impatience*. Non-cooperation and frivolousness deviate from the pattern. They are trouble sources that cannot standardly be traced back to the inability of using given information, but to the sheer unwillingness to do so.

Among the factors unequivocally attributable to language, ambiguity figures as a main error source. There are two sources of ambiguity: one lexically based and another with its origin in syntactic structure. With regard to speech, two central causes of ambiguity become manifest: homophony, i.e. sameness in pronunciation with different meanings, and unspecified prosody, i.e. sameness in suprasegmental properties of an utterance.

With regard to the purely technical factors that may affect aviation communication and increase the probability of accidents, the main trouble source is the unavailability or misuse of radio, which may be caused by electrical stall or an earpiece that happens to disconnect, i.e. factors which do not primarily rely on intentional behaviour, but on technical failure and accidental occurrences. A further reason may be mainly intentional, such as human behaviour resulting in the non-use or misuse of radio. The users may have been misinformed by their authorities or may not have been in a position to estimate the importance of the medium. In some cases, however, radio use was simply disregarded. Connected with the different uses of radio is the distinction between unclear and blocked frequency, which may be ascribed to the degree of the pilot's or controller's efficiency in use of radio. Blockages or unclear frequencies could result in a message not being transmitted properly and lead to misunderstandings, with hair-raising consequences. These factors doubtlessly also have a linguistic component; however, the controlling issue of the problem is technically based and overrides any linguistic behaviour.

Regarding these trouble sources, the personal and situational error factors turn out to be of highest relevance, as can be seen in Cardosi, Falzarano, & Han (1999), who list as the most important factors:

- similar call signs on the same radio channel,
- pilot expectations (cf. the case of *wishful hearing* in routine behaviour) that deviate conspicuously from the controllers' instructions and
- high controller workload.

These communication errors most commonly resulted in

- the wrong flight level (altitude deviation),
- loss of standard separation,
- pilots landing on the wrong runway and
- runway transgressions.

Linter and Buckles conclude:

> Regardless of the level of sophistication that the air traffic system achieves by the turn of the century, the effectiveness of our system will always come down to how successfully we communicate.   (Linter & Buckles 1993)

Miscommunication in aviation is well documented. Unfortunately, less is known about the reasons for these communication problems and how to avoid them (Morrow & Rodvold 1993:324). The findings compiled in this section are based on experiments and their discussion, on reporters, i.e. pilots or controllers filing an ASRS (Aviation Safety and Reporting System) report, listening sessions of radio communication and on voice recordings of tower and/or cockpit communication. The latter two, particularly the recordings found in black boxes, are of special importance for the present study.

Cockpit voice recordings (CVRs)

Large commercial aircraft and some smaller commercial, corporate and private aircraft must be equipped with two kinds of *black boxes* that record information about a flight. Both recorders are designed to help reconstruct the events leading to an aircraft accident. The one described here, the *cockpit voice recorder*, records human and technical sounds. The other, the *flight data recorder*, monitors parameters such as airspeed, altitude and heading. Both recorders are installed in that part of the aircraft least susceptible to crash damage, usually the tail section (National Safety Board 2000). Older recorders are analogue units using one-quarter inch magnetic tape. Newer recorders use digital technology and memory chips. Sounds are picked up via a system of cockpit microphones, known as *cockpit area microphones* (CAM), *public address microphones* (PA) and *radio microphones* (RDO) (Kilroy 2001).

Each recorder is equipped with an *underwater locator beacon* to assist in locating it in the event of an accident over water. A device called a *pinger* is activated when the recorder falls into water. Owing to the limited length of the recording cycle of a flight recorder, instantaneous action is mandatory to quarantine any black boxes after an incident or accident to make sure that the data are not overwritten. In fact, black boxes are painted orange to help in their recovery (Commonwealth Department of Transport and Regional Services 1999).

Following an accident, both recorders are brought to a particular institution which has the statutory power to take into custody and process any flight recorders from an aircraft that has been involved in an incident, a serious incident or an accident (Commonwealth Department of Transport and Regional Services 1999). In the United States this is the *National Safety Board* (NTSB) headquarters in Washington D.C., in Australia the *Bureau of Air Safety Investigation* (BASI). By means of computer and audio equipment, the information stored on the recorders is extracted and translated into an understandable format. This information is used to determine the probable cause of an accident (National Safety Board 2000).

The concept of a crash-and-fire protected device to record both the crew's conversation and the instrument readings was first conceived by David Warren, a young scientist at the *Aeronautical Research Laboratories* (ARL) in Melbourne, Australia (DSTO Commonwealth of Australia 1999; DSTO Commonwealth of Australia 2000). Warren was struck by the idea in the course of otherwise fruitless discussions about the possible causes of a crash of the jet-powered airliner *Comet* in 1953. The main problem was that investigation committees had hardly any clues to work with.

> There were no witnesses, no survivors, and all that was left of the aircraft were massive tangles of bent metal. [...] [Warren] reasoned that [...] there was a good chance [...] that the flight crew might have known, and it might well have been revealed in their conversation in trying to deal with the emergency.
> (DSTO Commonwealth of Australia 1999)

In 1954, Warren published his ideas in a report entitled *A Device for Assisting Investigation into Aircraft Accidents*, which nevertheless evoked little initial interest. A demonstrator unit produced in 1957 was received enthusiastically in Britain, however, where it was further developed, although the Australian aviation authorities did not approve of the demonstrator. However, following an unexplained aircraft accident in Queensland in 1960, Australia became the first country to make flight recorders obligatory in aircraft. Today, every airline in the world flies with data recorders (DSTO Commonwealth of Australia 1999; DSTO Commonwealth of Australia 2000).

The cockpit voice recorder, of course, records simply everything audible that happens in the area of the microphones. Of importance to investigators of the cockpit voice recording are engine noise, stall warnings and landing gear extension and retraction. Sounds of this sort can help deduce parameters such as engine and aircraft speed, system failures and the time at which particular events occur. Of special interest for the present analysis is the verbal information, as there are radio signals of extra-cockpit communication, intra-cockpit communication and ground or cabin crew as well as automated radio weather briefings.

In the case of an accident, the usual procedure is the following: a CVR committee is formed to listen to the recording. In the United States, for instance, this committee usually consists of members of the National Safety Board, the Federal Aviation Administration, the operator of the aircraft, the manufacturer of the airplane and the engines, and the pilots union. A written transcript is created of the tape to be used during the investigation. The transcript contains all pertinent portions of the recording and can be released to the public at the time of the Safety Board's hearing.

The treatment of cockpit voice recordings is different from that of other factual information obtained in an accident investigation. Because of the highly sensitive nature of the verbal communications inside the cockpit, the Safety Board is not allowed to release any part of a CVR tape. A high degree of security is provided for the tape and its transcript: the content and timing of release of the transcript are strictly regulated. Transcripts of pertinent portions of CVRs are released under federal law, at a Safety Board public hearing on the accident or, in the event that no hearing is held, when a majority of the factual reports are made public (National Safety Board 2000). The airlines that own the original recording are legally allowed to release it if they choose to (Kilroy 2001).

Meanwhile, many ATC/CVR-transcripts are available on the Internet (Aviation Safety Network 2000a), often in extensive extracts. Fragmented CVR tapes are sometimes also available for listening (Aviation Safety Network 2000b).

The Aviation Safety Network comments upon the value of the recordings to investigators as follows:

> Both the Flight Data Recorder and the Cockpit Voice Recorder have proven to be valuable tools in the accident investigation process. They can provide information that may be difficult or impossible to obtain by other means. When used in conjunction with other information gained in the investigation, the recorders are playing an ever increasing role in determining the Probable Cause of an aircraft accident (National Safety Board 2000).
> (see also Commonwealth Department of Transport and Regional Services 1999)

1.3 Overview of presentation

Having introduced aviation communication with its fragile system of information exchange, the analysis will now focus on the description and formalisation of linguistic features of aviation communication. Chapter 2 introduces the main theoretical background. It thereby presents approaches contributing to the understanding of discourse among which the speech act theory of Searle and Searle & Vanderveken will receive priority of discussion. Chapter 3 deals with the reasons for a formal treatment of linguistic data, and then an attribute value-based method for the analysis of aviation data is developed. Sections on creating a corpus, annotation standards and schemata refer to the methodological steps essential for the generation of an XML-based corpus of aviation data. A discussion of the concept of meta-data and current markup systems is included. Chapter 4 offers documentations of the data that had already been prepared by transcribers and about the modifications necessary to semi-automatise an XML-markup of the ATC/CVR-corpus. Furthermore, it contains comments upon phases as well as discourse control processes in aviation communication. On the whole, Chapter 4 pertains to general properties of the ATC/CVR-data, whereas Chapter 5 treats particular features of crisis talk in aviation communication. Its main purpose is to identify regularities of the speech scenario and to juxtapose aviational crisis talk with aviational non-crisis talk. One aspect of the regularities will be captured by one HPSG-sign, followed by the application and more detailed description of the formalism elaborated in Section 3.3. The glossary in Appendix A helps one to understand the most important aviation terms used in this analysis. The appendix continues with a key to the abbreviations used for the HPSG-based structures (see Appendix B) and the atomic representation of speech acts (see Appendix C) along with additional examples (Appendix D). Furthermore, background information along with the complete transcripts is given for the two sample transcripts that are investigated in more detail in the present analysis (see Appendices E and F).

Notes

1. The KWIC-(Keyword in context) concordance is a dynamic context-based dictionary that allows retrieval of a specified string in a text corpus and generating an output of the requested string framed by its immediate linguistic context.

2. This is also the case with Heydrich, Kühnlein, & Rieser (1998)

3. This property of utterances has been called *context change potential* in recent writings. Chierchia (1995:81), for example, explains the idea of dynamic semantics informally as follows: A given sentence has some kind of

> hook onto which incoming information can be hung. In this sense, [S' ∧ p] can be viewed as a representation of the options one has available as a consequence of uttering S in the initial context – that is, as the context change potential of S. [...] More specifically, a discourse, which in simple cases is built up by adding sentences one by one, will involve integrating the corresponding context change potentials.

(S' in the quoted text passage denotes the semantics of S.) Apart from Chierchia's conflating *sentences* and *utterances*, this expresses exactly the same idea.

4. This manual is published by the FAA and

> designed to provide the aviation community with basic flight information and ATC procedures for use in the National Airspace System (NAS) of the United States. An international version called the Aeronautical

> Information Publication contains parallel information, as well as specific information on the international airports for use by the international community (Federal Aviation Administration 2000f).
>
> (see also Federal Aviation Administration 2000d)

5. As cited from the FAAOs foreword:

> This order prescribes air traffic control procedures and phraseology for use by personnel providing air traffic control services. Controllers are required to be familiar with the provisions of this order that pertain to their operational responsibilities and to exercise their best judgment if they encounter situations not covered by it. (Federal Aviation Administration 2001b)

6. The *Federal Aviation Administration (FAA)* has responsibility over the

> safe, and secure use of the Nations airspace, by military as well as civil aviation, for promoting safety in air commerce [...]. The activities required to carry out these responsibilities include: safety regulations; airspace management and the establishment, operation, and maintenance of a civil-military common system of air traffic control (ATC) [...]. (Federal Aviation Administration 2000f)

7. *Clearance* is the authorisation for an aircraft to proceed under conditions specified by an air traffic control unit (Federal Aviation Administration 2000e).

8. Dave Fahrenwald, Piedmont Airlines FCIS, personal communication

9. To cite from this manual:

> This manual provides a guideline for PNNL staff and management personnel in the operation and use of leased, chartered, or PNNT-owned aircraft. The procedures and policies contained here are supplemental to Federal Aviation Regulations (FAR) and to DOE orders and PNNL policies designed to provide for safe and correct operating practices. Flight and maintenance personnel are required to become familiar with the contents of this manual and with the procedures for the planning and performance of all flight activities.
>
> Under most circumstances, this manual provides acceptable practices: all operating personnel are expected to adhere to the provisions of this manual and the applicable FARs in the performance of PNNL flight operations. However, this manual is not intended as a substitute for common sense and the sound judgment of the Pilot in Command (PIC) especially in matters that may require the modification of such procedures in the light of emergencies, adverse weather, or other extenuating circumstances.
>
> (Federal Aviation Administration 1998)

10. Doug Hoesch, personal communication

11. www.volpe.dot.gov

12. pronunciation is /riːl/

13. Kellye Je'anne Tanner in an e-mail dated April 5, 2002

CHAPTER 2

Discourse-related approaches

The underlying theory adopted in the present volume is the formal *illocu-tionary logic* of Searle & Vanderveken (1985) that developed from the prag-matist accounts of language use (cf. Austin 1962; Searle 1969; Searle 1979a; Searle 1979b). The question arises of why speech act theory was chosen as a level of modelling and why it was chosen as the only basic level although it is not as closely related to discourse as, e.g. conversation analysis. Other alternatives would have been conversational move types (CMT), which clas-sify utterances with respect to their discourse function. With an example of CMT-modelling in Section 3.3, it will become clear that an approach like this has severe drawbacks. However, the principal point is that the methodology adopted for the present investigation is committed to a *reductive* view: There is an assumption that the properties of ontologically more complex objects are constituted by the properties of their simpler components plus the rela-tions between them. This means that the features of the descriptions are also constituted by the features of the component descriptions plus rules reflect-ing the relations. As CMTs are types of descriptions richer than speech acts, an intermediate level of description would be omitted if speech act theory was ne-glected. HPSG, the grammatical theory that is the foundation of the modelling process for the current analysis, incorporates the reductive principle advocated here.

The more general aspect regarding use of illocutionary logic is that this theory is the most elaborate formal system of speech act theory. It is, however, not free from faults, as can be seen from the critical remarks in Section 2.2. The choice of illocutionary logic can be justified in two ways. First, it seems that the approach can be corrected. Second, those parts of the theory that are faulty will not be used in the present analysis. Thus the use of the theory does not affect the results given in Chapters 4–5. In order to protect the analysis against attacks, however, all of the relevant parts are understood to be conditionalised: The analysis is valid under the assumption of a valid form of illocutionary logic.

2.1 Speech act theory

Speech act theory as proposed by Austin is principally a lexical classification of *illocutionary verbs*, and was further elaborated by Searle (1969); Searle (1979a) and Searle & Vanderveken (1985), whose work is basically a classification of acts. Conditions and rules are important for determining the identity of a speech act.

Austin: A seminal work

Austin has widely been acknowledged as the founding father of the speech act theory (see e.g. Allan 1998). Austin distinguishes two types of sentences[1] and calls them *constatives*, which have truth values, and *performatives*, which do not. Austin argues that with a performative utterance under the right circumstances, the speaker performs, for instance, an act of naming, of apologising, welcoming or advising.[2] These sentences all have in common the occurrence of the same type of verb, viz. a performative verb. It realises a particular action, i.e. the action that the verb labels when it is uttered in a certain context. Contexts may include the aspect of setting, physical objects, institutional identities or roles. To some extent, the context may require a specific response, such as *uptake* with respect to a bet. Apart from these *appropriate circumstances* (Austin 1962:13), performatives also require the appropriate language so that they meet certain contextual and textual conditions.

Austin identifies conditions of success which performatives have in place of truth conditions. The conditions function as templates by checking whether they allow for a performative (see e.g. Austin 1962:14–15). They include the existence of "an accepted conventional procedure having a certain conventional effect" that allows deciding whether the circumstances of the speech act and its participants are appropriate to its being performed successfully (Austin 1962:26, 34). Allan identifies this as *preparatory condition* (Allan 1998:929). Further on, they include "the correct and complete execution of a procedure" (Austin 1962:36), and "certain thoughts, feelings, or intentions". If all the relevant conditions are fulfilled for the utterance in question, Austin judges it *happy* or *felicitous* (Austin 1962:14). If one or more conditions were not satisfied, Austin describes it as *unhappy*. He also notices nuances in the classification of unhappy acts: They can either *misfire*, i.e. not go through at all, or go through in a way that is not completely satisfactory.

All utterances are performances of speech acts that consist of a locutionary act (what is necessary when someone makes an utterance), whose components are the *phonetic act* (the act of uttering certain noises), the *phatic act* (the act of uttering certain vocables or words within a certain grammatical construction) and the *rhetic act* (the act of determining a certain meaning or reference and predication (Austin 1962:92)). In addition, an utterance also includes the performance of an *illocutionary act* (the "performance of an act *in* saying something as opposed to performance of an act *of* saying something" (Austin 1962:99)) and a *perlocutionary act* (the effects on the emotions, thoughts and actions of the hearer, (Austin 1962:108)). The idea of *perlocutionary act* will not be pursued in the analysis.[3]

In combination, the different acts form a *total speech act* which must be studied in the total speech situation. For a critism of this see Allwood (1977:54). A postulate like this prompts Austin to insist that not the sentence needs to be studied but "the issuing of an utterance in a speech situation" (Austin 1962:138). Within the framework of a context-dependent analysis of speech acts, Austin stresses the relation between speaker and hearer. One purpose of speaking is to cause an effect on the hearer, which Austin describes as *securing uptake*. A characteristic consequence of missing uptake is

> [...] the doubt about whether I stated something if it was not heard or understood.   (Austin 1962:138)

According to Austin's theory, securing uptake is a precondition for the performance of the respective speech act. Uptake-securing is an essential aspect of Searle's felicity conditions which, however, he abandons in his later work. Lyons points out that Austin, like Wittgenstein, emphasises the importance of relating the functions of language to the social contexts in which languages operate. The complete pragmatic context must be taken into account in order to understand what sort of illocutionary act the speaker has produced. Austin further insists that the philosopher should be concerned not only about descriptive, but also non-descriptive utterances (see Lyons (1977:728) and also Wittgenstein's *Sprachspiel*, Wittgenstein (1961) and Lewandowski (1990:425)).

Searle: An elaboration

In 1969, seven years after Austin, Searle published his book *Speech Acts* building upon Austin's ideas by developing a systematic framework with the goal of incorporating speech acts into linguistic theory.

Searle agrees with Austin in claiming that "the speech act is the basic unit of communication" (Searle 1969:21).[4] Searle splits utterances into four speech acts:

The utterance act: the production of words (morphemes and sentences) (Searle 1969). The utterance of an expression (Searle & Vanderveken 1985:9). It is performed in the utterance of a sentence of the form *f(p)* (Searle & Vanderveken 1985:10). There may be utterance acts that are not speech acts, i.e. those that lack the *p*.

The propositional act: constituted by reference and predication (Searle 1969). If the utterance act fulfills particular conditions the speaker will have expressed the proposition that *P* and thereby a propositional act is performed (Searle & Vanderveken 1985:10).

The illocutionary act: what the speaker is doing with words in relation to the hearer (Searle 1969). If further conditions are satisfied, the speaker will have expressed some proposition *P* with the illocutionary force *F*. Thereby the illocutionary act of the form *F(P)* is expressed. Illocutionary acts are central to Searle's theory. He defines five elementary classes of illocutionary act *assertives, directives, commissives, expressives* and *declaratives*.

The perlocutionary act: the consequences of illocutionary acts such as the effects on actions, thoughts or beliefs of hearers (Searle 1969). They may be achieved intentionally, for instance when a speaker gets a hearer to do something by asking him to do it. They may be unintentional, for instance when a speaker annoys or exasperates his audience without intending to do so (Searle & Vanderveken 1985:12). In Searle's work, perlocutions are of secondary importance.

Table 2.1 illustrates the differences between Austin's and Searle's approach to speech act theory. Searle keeps Austin's structure of locution, illocution and perlocution, summarising the phonetic and phatic act under the heading of an *utterance act*, while splitting the rhetic act into the components *reference* and *predication*. It is possible to perform the same illocutionary act in the performance of two different utterance acts, for example, as by saying *It's raining* in English and *Il pleut* in French, or by using synonymous sentences in the same language, as in *Mary loves John* and *John is loved by Mary*. This will be important in the context of ATC/CVR-transcripts, which are only available in their English translation. In turn, it is possible that one utterance act can occur in the performance of different illocutionary acts. This is the case with two different persons saying *I am happy*. The difference between the two utterance acts lies in their different denotations and hence in the proposition they convey. Within the framework of aviation communication, this may lead to misunderstandings (see the error sources in Section 1.2). An utterance act is performed *without* an illocutionary act, for example, when a person voices a word without intend-

Table 2.1 Types of acts performed in the utterance of a speech act. The structure of speech acts as analysed by Austin (1962) compared to the structure envisaged by Searle (1969). This table is taken from Bußmann (1990:727); my translation.

	Simultaneous partial aspects				
	Utterance of speech signals	Utterance of words in a specific grammatical structure	Saying something about something	Specifying the performative use of the proposition	Intended effect of the speech act
Austin (1962)	Phonetic act	Phatic act	Rhetic act	Illocutionary act	Perlocutionary act
Searle (1969)	Utterance act		Propositional act	Illocutionary act	Perlocutionary act
			Reference	Predication	
			Referring to the "World"	Saying something about the "World"	

ing it to mean anything (Searle & Vanderveken 1985:9). Illocutionary acts are related to *understanding* and thus can be conventionalised.

> It is in general possible to have a linguistic convention that determines that such and such an utterance counts as the performance of an illocutionary act.
> (Searle & Vanderveken 1985:12)

Perlocutionary acts, by contrast, are related to *subsequent effects* and consequently they cannot be conventionalised.

> There could not be any convention to the effect that such and such an utterance counts as convincing you, or persuading you, or annoying you, or exasperating you, or amusing you.   (Searle & Vanderveken 1985:12)

Simple vs. complex illocutionary acts
With respect to the complexity of speech acts, Searle distinguishes the following types:

Simple illocutionary act: consisting of a simple sentence *(F(P))* such as *I state that you are standing on my foot.*

Complex illocutionary act: consisting of simple illocutionary acts which by using *illocutionary connectives* such as *and* or *but* are conjoined in one utterance. They come in forms such as $F_1(P_1)$ & $F_2(P_2)$, which is a particular case called *illocutionary conjunction*. Example: *He promised to phone me tonight, but will I be here?* Not every pair of sentences grammatically admits every illocutionary connective (Searle & Vanderveken 1985:4). For example, the use of the conjunction *and* in *When did John come and I order you to leave the room?* is syntactically ill-formed. Similar conditions hold for *illocutionary denegation* and *conditionals* (Searle & Vanderveken 1985).

Searle proposes that "speaking a language is engaging in a highly complex rule-governed form of behaviour" (Searle 1969:12). As Schiffrin[5] puts it:

> A methodological consequence of this is that linguistic characterizations do not report "the behaviour of a group". Rather, they describe aspects of speakers mastery of a rule-governed skill (p. 12) that can be obtained by relying heavily on the intuitions (and linguistic characterization) of native speakers (p. 15). What such intuitions can provide are "idealized models" (p. 56) of the conditions that are necessary and sufficient for the utterance of a given sentence to be a successful, non-defective performance of a given act.
>
> (Schiffrin 1994:55)

From these *felicity conditions*, as they are called, rules are generated. Searle terms *constitutive* the rules that apply to speech acts. They "create or define new forms of behaviour" (Searle 1969:33) and are opposed to *regulative* rules that govern "[antecedently] or independently existing forms of behaviour" (Searle 1969:33). The forms of the two types of rules reflect their different status: regulative rules are expressed or can be paraphrased as imperatives, while constitutive rules are more definitional, e.g. *X counts as Y in context C* (Searle 1969:35). The two types of rules can also be applied to aviation communication. Regulative rules play a role insofar as aviation communication is a controlled language and each deviation might be sanctioned by adverse effects. Constitutive rules are violated in the case of deviations from the controlled language, in particular with regard to crisis talk.

As in Austin (1962), Searle's conditions and rules draw upon both context and text. They also elevate intentions and other psychological states and conditions that enable a speech act by assigning them their own type of rule. Also, in accordance with Austin, Searle classifies conditions and rules according to their importance for the act. In contrast to Austin, Searle classifies different kinds of conditions and rules according to what aspect of text and context is focussed on in the condition or rule. It may happen that different conditions overlap with the different components of a speech act.

Searle notes analytic connections between speaker meaning, sentence meaning and speaker intention.[6] He argues that an analysis of illocutionary acts must capture "both the intentional and the conventional aspects" of meaning and more crucially, "the relation between them" (Searle 1969: 45), i.e. a relationship that is sensitive to the circumstances of an utterance. Here again, certain linguistic elements are viewed as *illocutionary force indicating devices* that provide conventional procedures by which to perform a given act. Particular features conventionally go along with the performance of a particular illocutionary act. The features which help identify its force are Searle's *illocutionary force indicating devices* (IFIDs):

> Any element of a natural language which can be literally used to indicate that an utterance of a sentence containing that element has a certain illocutionary force or range of illocutionary forces we will call an illocutionary force indicating device. (Searle & Vanderveken 1985: 2)

As mentioned above, Searle distinguishes the illocutionary force of an utterance and its propositional content: F(P) where F is a variable for illocutionary force indicated by IFIDs and P stands for *proposition*. For instance, in the sentence *I promise that I will come*, *I promise* is an IFID indicating its force and (*that*) *I will come* its indicator of propositional content or proposition (Searle 1969: 30). In Searle & Vanderveken (1985), the authors are more explicit about the use of variables, a notation which will be applied in the course of this analysis:

f(p): the general form of simple sentences used to perform elementary speech acts

f: indicator of illocutionary force

p: propositional content

F(P): logical form of the illocutionary act itself

F: illocutionary force. *F* is a function of the meaning of *f* (Searle & Vanderveken 1985: 10).

P: logical form of the propositional content (Searle & Vanderveken 1985: 8). The proposition is a function of the meaning of *p* (Searle & Vanderveken 1985: 10).

Semantic rules

For the use of IFIDS, a set of rules is generated from a set of conditions. Central to Searle's theory are verbs and their semantic rules:

The *propositional content rule* refers to the *differences in the propositional content*. The type of force F generally controls what can occur in the propositional content P; i.e. it imposes certain conditions on P. Example: the content of a promise must be that the speaker perform some future course of action, while reports can be about past or present. This rule is derived from the "propositional content conditions 2 and 3" (Searle 1969:57; Searle & Vanderveken 1985:16).

The *preparatory rule* refers to the "differences in the way the utterance relates to the interests of speaker and hearer", to what is "good or bad for them". Example: in promising something, the speaker presupposes that he can perform the promised act and that it is in the hearer's interest to do it. Likewise, a speaker who apologises presupposes that what he apologises for is bad or reprehensible (Searle & Vanderveken 1985:17). This rule also refers to the "differences in the status or position of speaker and hearer".[7] Example: When a general asks a private to clean up his room this is a command or an order; if a private asks a general to clean up his room this is a request or a suggestion (Searle 1969:57). Generally speaking, the preparatory rule "tells us (at least part of) what [the speaker] *implies* in the performance of the act." These states of affairs have to obtain in order for the act to be successful and non-defective. This rule is derived from the "preparatory conditions 4 and 5" (Searle 1969:65). That the features determining the preparatory conditions are internalised by speakers and hearers and that the rules are reflected in their psychology should not lead to the inference that the preparatory rule is about the psychological states of speakers or hearers. This, however, is the case with the following *sincerity* rule (Searle & Vanderveken 1985:17).

The *sincerity rule* refers to the "differences in the expressed psychological states", e.g. assertives express a belief, directives a desire, commissives an intention. In general, in performing an illocutionary act with a propositional content, the speaker expresses[8] some attitude to that propositional content. Searle and Vanderveken claim that

> whenever one performs an illocutionary act with a propositional content one expresses a certain psychological state with that same content. [...] The propositional content of the illocutionary act is in general identical with the propositional content of the expressed psychological state.
>
> (Searle & Vanderveken 1985:18)

A psychological state can be expressed even if the speaker is insincere; in an insincere statement (a lie) the speaker does not believe what he says, in an insincere directive the speaker does not have the desire that the hearer do what he orders (Searle 1969:61; Searle & Vanderveken 1985:18). See the *sincerity condition* (Searle 1969:60). A further feature, which is treated separately in Searle & Vanderveken (1985:19–20), marks "the characteristic degree of strength" by which the same psychological state can be expressed. It is defined for each type of illocutionary force F whose sincerity condition requires that it be achieved with a certain degree of strength. For instance, in contrast to begging, imploring or beseeching, to make a request is to express relatively weakly that the hearer carry out the act in question.

The *essential rule* refers to the "differences in the point or purpose of the type of act", which is also called *illocutionary point* (Searle 1969:60). The point of a type of act is that purpose which is essential to its being an act of that type. The illocutionary point, for example, of an apology is to express the speaker's remorse or regret for having done something. In the performance of an act $F(P)$, the illocutionary point is distinct from the propositional content, but it can be achieved only as part of a total speech act. In this speech act, the propositional content is expressed with the illocutionary point; i.e. the "illocutionary point is achieved on the propositional content" (Searle & Vanderveken 1985:14–15). This rule is derived from the *essential condition* (Searle & Vanderveken 1985:15). Like the sincerity rule/condition, the essential rule has the addition of *the characteristic degree of strength* of illocutionary point of F. Both pleading and ordering are stronger than requesting. The greater strength of pleading derives from the intensity of the desire expressed, whereas the greater strength of ordering has its reason in the greater authority the speaker has over the hearer (see *mode of achievement*).

Searle's additional conditions and rules pertain to pragmatic aspects: They refer to differences in the relations to the rest of the discourse including performative verbs and discourse particles marking coherence, to acts requiring extra-linguistic institutions, to acts whose illocutionary verb has a performative use and to the style of performance. Furthermore, Searle mentions the IFIDs *punctuation* and *prosodic contour* that belong to the surface-realisation as well as *word order* and *mood of verb* which are syntactic features. He exemplifies the syntactic IFIDs by *(1) Will you leave the room?, (2) You, leave the room!, (3) You will leave the room, (4) If only you would leave the room!* Preceding or subsequent utterances may also count as IFIDs. Searle only gives a brief account of surface and syntactic IFID features as he analyses word order and constituents of utterances and determines their deep structure (Searle 1979a:21).

A speech act may be unsuccessful, i.e. a complete failure because none of the conditions and rules obtain for the intended act, it may be successful but defective, because the conditions and rules have several faults, or it may be the ideal case, i.e. successful and non-defective, because all necessary conditions and rules obtain. Searle finds that some conditions or rules are more crucial to the non-defective performance of an act than others. The essential condition, for instance, is critical as it determines the others (Searle 1969:69; Searle & Vanderveken 1985:14). More than this condition is needed, because different illocutionary forces can have the same illocutionary point. However, they differ in other respects, as it holds for the pairs order/request, assertion/testimony. The other components of illocutionary force are modifications, specifications or consequences of the illocutionary point (Searle & Vanderveken 1985:14). While each condition or rule is individually necessary for the successful and non-defective performance of a given act, it is the set of conditions or rules that is collectively sufficient for such a performance (Searle 1969:54). In the later development of illocutionary logic that will be introduced in Section 2.2, the illocutionary force is consequently regarded as a septuple consisting of the conditions. There are various kinds of illocution defects, but not all defects are sufficient to vitiate an act in its entirety.

The *propositional indicator* comprises features that help identify the nature of predication and reference. Before moving on to this aspect of speech act theory, the scope of the term *proposition* and its relation to illocutions need to be clarified. Searle distinguishes between the illocutionary act and propositional content of the illocutionary act. The independence of the two can be demonstrated by using their identity conditions:

> The same propositional content can occur with different illocutionary forces and the same force can occur with different propositional contents.
>
> (Searle & Vanderveken 1985:8)

Examples are: In performing the utterance acts *(1) Will you leave the room?, (2) You, leave the room!, (3) You will leave the room, (4) If only you would leave the room!*, the same propositional act occurs, since reference and predication are the same. The illocutionary forces differ in that (1) is a request or an exhortation, (2) a command, (3) a statement, which, however, has some directive air and (4) a wish. Different propositional acts can be performed with the same illocutionary force if, for example, a directive is paired with a different reference and predication as in *Leave the room!, Close the door!*
Certain kinds of expressions, when uttered, are recognisable by their characteristic forms: The form of the illocutionary act is the complete sentence. The

form of the predication is the grammatical predicate, and the noun phrases, containing proper names or pronouns, are used for reference. The latter two are said to combine to form propositional acts. Thus, the simple $F(P)$ is extended into $F(RP)$, whereby R stands for reference and P – in the revised version – for predication (Searle 1969).

Propositional acts are inseparably bound to the performance of illocutionary acts. They are an abstraction from the total illocutionary act, since one cannot simply express a proposition and nothing else.

> Syntactically this fact is reflected in natural languages by the fact that *that* clauses, the characteristic form of isolating the propositional content, cannot stand alone; they do not make complete sentences. One can say *I promise that I will leave the room*, but one cannot say simply *That I will leave the room*.
>
> (Searle & Vanderveken 1985:9)

There may be types of illocutionary forces that permit a content that has an incomplete proposition consisting only of a reference. This is true for the utterance of *Hurrah for Hollywood!* Utterances of this kind have the form $F(R)$ instead of $F(RP)$.[9] Searle defines R as pertaining to "some entity of the universe of discourse" (Searle & Vanderveken 1985:9). Other exceptional cases are utterances that are simply of the form F. They permit only the existence of an illocutionary force and no propositional content, e.g. *Hurrah, Ouch* and *Damn* (Searle 1969; Searle & Vanderveken 1985:9).

Apart from ifid which shows how the proposition is to be taken, i.e. what illocutionary role the utterance takes, there is the *propositional indicator* (PI) (Searle 1969:30). The construction of conditions and rules for reference and predication is parallel to those which are applied to illocutions, i.e. rules are generated from conditions.

The input-output condition

One condition that is self-evident for the successful performance of speech acts is likely to escape general attention. Nonetheless, it marks an important notion in the present analysis: the *input-output condition*, a pre-requisite for every kind of speech act which pertains to "intelligible speaking" and "understanding" (Searle 1969:57).

> The conditions for correctly understanding an utterance normally involve such diverse things as that the hearer must be awake, must be paying attention, etc.
>
> (Searle & Vanderveken 1985:21)[10]

The input-output condition refers to what Austin called *illocutionary uptake* or *uptake securing* (Austin 1962), thereby including the understanding of the force and the content of the utterance by its addressees (Austin 1962:116). The *securing of uptake* is an essential aspect of crisis talk as it is a most sensitive aspect. Particularly in extra-cockpit communication the input/output condition would not be fulfilled if radio communications were interrupted (see Section 1.2). Gibbon has developed the phatic model of *uptake loops* which – when they abound – can be judged as symptomatic of communicational problems and communicational skills alike (Gibbon 1976; Gibbon 1981; Gibbon 1985).

Before the discussion of *uptake securing, indirect speech acts* will be introduced. They add a considerable degree of complexity to speech act theory and mark a vital step towards its application to context and, at the same time, its relation to discourse.

Indirect speech acts

Searle makes the critical point that in many cases a speaker performs more than one illocutionary act in the same utterance; i.e. he performs one act "implicitly by way of performing another illocutionary act explicitly" (Searle & Vandervcken 1985:10; Scarlc 1969; Scarlc 1979b). In this way, utterances carry multiple functions. For example, the utterance *Sir, you are standing on my foot* has the explicit or non-literal primary speech act of an assertion that is used to perform the implicit or literal secondary speech act of a directive. The latter is called *indirect speech act*. Understanding is generated by virtue of background knowledge, on which the speaker relies, as well as mental capacities that he has in common with the hearer.

The conditions underlying speech acts (see IFIDs) provide an analytical resource for indirectness. They have this analytical function because they play a critical role in the interlocutors knowledge of speech act types. If utterances of multiple functions are performed, the conditions for the multiple speech acts nevertheless bear a systematic relationship to one another.

> Thus, it is relationships between underlying conditions that allow utterances to do more than one thing at a time.   (Schiffrin 1994:60)

2.2 An illocutionary logic: Searle & Vanderveken

Linguistics has adopted two directions of philosophy of language: One can be termed the Fregean school of formal languages from which the model-theoretic truth conditional systems evolved. With this concept, names ranging from Montague to Cresswell are associated. It branches to the dynamic semantics of e.g. Heim (1983); Groenendijk, & Stokhof (1991); Kamp & Reyle (1993). The second direction is the "notably informal school of ordinary language philosophy" (Allan 1998: 935) that generated speech act theory. To formalise speech act theory means to bridge the gap between the two schools. According to Allan, the agenda behind the formalisation is to extend the formal semantics of sentences of the Fregean tradition. To attain this goal, a formal theory of illocutionary types is added to a characterisation of illocutionary success and satisfactory correspondence between utterances and states of affairs in the respective world. In the following, the approach by Searle & Vanderveken (1985) will be described.

Searle & Vanderveken (1985: 7) deplore the inadequacy of existing semantic theories, as these only content themselves with assigning propositions or truth conditions to sentences and cannot assign illocutionary forces to a given sentence for each of its possible contexts of utterance. With the goal of extending intensional logics such as that of Montague (1974), Searle & Vanderveken offer the foundations for a formal theory of illocutionary forces. They sum up:

> The task of illocutionary logic, [...], is to study the entire range of possible illocutionary forces; however, these may be realized in particular natural languages. In principle it studies all possible illocutionary forces of utterances in any possible language, and not merely the actual realization of these possibiblities in actual speech acts in actual languages. Just as propositional logic studies the properties of all truth functions (e.g. conjunction, material implication, negation) without worrying about the various ways that these are realized in the syntax of English [...], so illocutionary logic studies the properties of illocutionary forces [...] without worrying about the various ways that these are realized in the syntax of English [...] and without worrying whether these features translate into other languages. No matter whether and how an illocutionary act is performed, it has a certain logical form which determines its conditions of success and relates it to other speech acts.
>
> (Searle & Vanderveken 1985: 1–2)

Searle's five classes of illocutionary acts are represented by the form $i\Pi_F P$. It reads: the illocutionary point F is achieved on a proposition P in context i. Π_F is defined as being assertive for $F = 1$, commissive for $F = 2$ and so on.

Illocutionary logic is in the process of development. According to Allan (1998:937), it is not yet integrated into theories of lexical meaning and sentence meaning. Within the field of artificial intelligence there is an independent development of formal theories of communicative intentions that go beyond single utterances (Cohen, Morgan, & Pollack 1990).

> Just as indirect speech acts are quite pervasive in real life, so in real life illocutionary acts seldom occur alone but rather occur as parts of conversations or larger stretches of discourse.   (Searle & Vanderveken 1985:11)

With this statement, Searle emphasises the necessity to rid oneself of traditional linguistics that has a tendency to confine itself to a speaker's linguistic competence as an ability to produce and understand sentences. What is more, traditional speech act theory sees illocutionary acts as isolated units. By contrast, Searle claims that illocutionary acts have to be treated in context as they occur in conversations:

> [...] we will not get an adequate account of linguistic competence or of speech acts until we can describe the speaker's ability to produce and understand utterances, i.e. to perform and understand illocutionary acts in ordered speech act sequences that constitute arguments, discussions, buying and selling, exchanging letters, making jokes, etc.   (Searle & Vanderveken 1985:11)

To understand the structure of discourse, it is important to understand that each illocutionary act potentially creates a finite and generally quite limited set of appropriate illocutionary acts as responses. They may be highly constrained as in question and answer sequences, or more open as in casual conversations that have free movements between all kinds of topics (Searle & Vanderveken 1985:11). These aspects are reminiscent of what has been analysed from such diverse perspectives as that of conversation analysis, a discipline complementary to speech act theory which has the discourse as basic unit of research, or rhetorical structure theory (see Mann & Thompson 1988 and Asher & Lascarides 2003 as well as Section 4.5.) Another approach that seems even closer to Searle's postulate, especially to his idea of finite and limited sets of illocutionary acts, is *discourse analysis*. Discourse analysis and *conversational analysis* will briefly be reviewed in Section 2.4.

Different conditions and rules place different constraints on dissimilar types of utterances. These constraints assign specific features to particular utterances. They serve as an approach to an unequivocal identification of the speech act, viz. its illocutionary force, performed through the utterance in question. This is the basic idea behind the design of a taxonomy of speech acts.

Searle & Vanderveken (1985) propose an elaborate taxonomical system that is put forth in a logical form. They argue that illocutionary force is a component of meaning because it provides illocutionary aspects of sentence meaning. The mere assignment of propositions or truth conditions to sentences would not be sufficient:

> In order to assign illocutionary acts to sentences an illocutionary logic would need first to provide a semantic analysis of illocutionary verbs and other illocutionary force indicating devices found in actual natural languages.
>
> (Searle & Vanderveken 1985:7)

In this book, the existing formal approach will be applied and extended. Particularly the pragmatic features will be stressed, which in Searle's theory form a component of an extended semantics (see Sections 3.3 and 5.3).

Searle and Vanderveken repeatedly stress the relevance of syntactic analysis for the recognition of IFIDs, but offer no syntactic interface themselves. Neither do they consider which kind of grammar would be acceptable or preferable from their point of view.

2.3 An alternative: Ross's performative analysis

An approach to speech act theory that persisted throughout the 1970s was brought forward by John Robert Ross (Ross 1970), who proposed the *performative analysis* in transformational grammar. Although this approach is not applied in the present analysis it is worthwhile considering it, since it caters for a syntactic treatment of speech acts. The critique that is launched against Ross's approach will carry over to the alternative analysis in Section 3.3. According to Ross's theory, the illocutionary force can be accounted for as one of the higher clauses in the deepest phrase-marker underlying a sentence:

> [...] every deep structure contains one and only one performative as its highest clause.   (Ross 1970:261)

The illocutionary force was construed as a property of sentences rather than utterances. In order to identify the illocutionary point of a sentence, Ross proposed that the highest clause of the deepest phrase marker underlying a sentence is performative, no matter whether the surface sentence contained a lexical performative. According to Allan (1998:935), Ross was proved wrong for his hypothesis and also for his claim that a sentential phrase marker can contain not more than one performative. Allan substantiates this rebuttal by means of the following example which dispels both of Ross's claims: *I say (that) I promise to be home by eight*. The performative component *I say* is the highest clause, but the embedded performative *I promise* indicates the illocutionary point. As most surface sentences do not have a performative verb, the one that Ross presumes is abstract, and he considers abstract verbs to be results of the linguist's imagination. By definition, abstract verbs are not manifest in the surface but in the deep structure, and must be argued for on circumstantial evidence, a step which complicates the grammar. An additional complication is that a deletion rule must be postulated to remove the abstract verb from the phrase marker at a particular point in the progression from deep structure to surface structure. Within the framework of Ross's approach, Fraser (1974) shows that it would be difficult to define a performative deletion and, in fact, none till now has been defined (Allan 1998:935). What remains of Ross (1970) – including his arguments in support of the claim that the highest clause of every declarative sentence is a performative verb of stating – has been refuted by Anderson (1971); Fraser (1974); Harnish (1975); Allan (1986) and Allan (1998).

Apart from this critique, Ross's approach will not be included in the present analysis for a simple reason. It is rooted too deeply within the framework of transformational grammar to be restated in terms of computationally more tractable grammars. In the present analysis, HPSG will be used for a variety of reasons, and the head-drivenness of HPSG would make deleted performatives, which had to be frequent, an unbearable complication. For a comparison of transformational grammar and contraint-based grammar see Sag & Wasow (1999:412).

2.4 Approaches to discourse structure

Speech act theory does not treat sequences of utterances, which would be the minimum requirement for a theory of discourse. As it is the goal of the present analysis to investigate a special kind of discourse (viz. crisis talk), speech act theory alone does not suffice. It is now time to discuss possible extensions of the theoretical framework of this analysis which make possible the desired treatment of discourse.

It is probably not feasible to analyse discourse sufficiently by one discipline alone (see also Schiffrin (1994)). Although the present analysis focusses on Searle's speech act theory, it is necessary to extend the analysis to other approaches. Pragmatic aspects must be fully integrated into the identification

of illocutionary acts. With the principle of speech act theory alone, albeit enhanced with Searle's postulate to foster an intensional semantics (e.g. to look at
what speakers *and* hearers do) it would be of no help for a satisfactory analysis of utterances such as Levinson's exemplary *For whom* (Levinson 1983:332).
And even with Searle's and Vanderveken's logical form for illocutions (Searle &
Vanderveken 1985) one could not do Levinson's example justice, since the logic
they put forth is still idealised. A discipline that complements speech act theory
is *conversation analysis*, which practically takes the discourse as the basic unit of
language usage (Lewandowski 1990:607). It will be the topic of this section followed by and juxtaposed to *discourse analysis*, which has a closer relationship
to speech act theory than conversation analysis. Speech act theory is normative
and axiomatic (and, since Searle & Vanderveken (1985), axiomatised), whereas
conversation analysis is descriptive, generalising, and built around the *token*.
Conversation analysis, and possibly to some extent also discourse analysis, may
in turn be a helpful approach to derive a classification of the data found in
natural discourse from Searle's and Vanderveken's illocutionary logic. Conversational analysis is certainly of greater importance to the current analysis to
compensate for the lack of descriptive adequacy[11] in the work of Searle and
Vanderveken.

Conversation analysis is rigorous, empirical, and formal (Schegloff & Sacks
1973:289–290) and seeks to reveal the methods by which participants in everyday conversations create strategies of social order (see for instance Coulon
(1987:70)). The term *conversation* is interpreted as relating to every kind of
verbal communication whose contributions are not pre-formed (Bange 1983;
Gülich 1990). The guiding interest of conversation analyis concentrates primarily on sociological aspects with language being only of secondary importance:

> [...] suffice it to say that this is not because of a special interest in language,
> or any theoretical primacy we accord conversation. Nonetheless the character
> of our materials as conversational has attracted our attention to the study of
> conversation as an activity in its own right, and thereby to the ways in which
> any actions accomplished in conversation require reference to the properties
> and organization of conversation for their understanding and analysis, both by
> participants and by professional investigators.   (Schegloff & Sacks 1973:290)

Conversation analysis inherited a suspicion of *premature theorising* and *ad hoc
analytical categories* from ethnomethodology. Consequently, it tries to avoid
unsubstantiated theoretical constructs and intuitions that may function as a
guide of research but are never to be used as an explanation of findings. Thus,

conversation analysis puts emphasis on the data collected from interactions and the patterns they reveal (Levinson 1983: 287, 295). A general principle of conversation is the *speaker change*, which is constituted by active listening and continual uptake securing (see Section 4.5).

Data are usually captured by tape-recordings (visual and/or auditive) of naturally occurring discourse from which transcripts are created, which embrace verbal and often also non-verbal signs of interaction such as gesture and gaze. Recordings have the great advantage of making the data of research retrievable and reproducible so that it can be studied repeatedly and made available and evaluable for others (see Sacks (1984: 26)). This constitutes enormous progress in comparison to ethnomethodology, which based its procedures on handwritten notes.

Aspects of contextual properties, such as whether the participants are close friends or of different social status, are only integrated if participants "can be rigorously shown to employ such categories in the production of conversation" (Levinson 1983: 295).[12]

Both domain and method of study are inseparably combined with each other and the method itself, which is developed from the domain, is reflexive. According to Bergmann (1981), who proposes three steps for the analysis of data, conversation analysis does not stress the interactional order per se, but rather the structures of the techniques through which an ordered conversation is produced and construed as such by the participants. Next, the topic that causes the generation of the aforementioned structures and regularities is reconstructed. In a third step, of particular interest is the description of the mechanisms that allow the permanent re-creation of new structures of order and which enable the participants to master their problems of discourse organisation.

It is essential in conversation analysis to interpret each problem as an individual matter and as a result of social cooperation. The data are to be treated with careful consideration, which is to say that interactional behaviour is not derivable from norms (see Lewandowski (1990)). To some extent, discourse analysis shares properties with conversation analysis, as both are concerned with the analysis of discourse organisation. At the same time, the style of analysis of each approach is distinctive and to a great extent incompatible with the style of the other (Levinson 1983: 286).

While Austin developed the concepts of *speech act* and *illocution* to be able to investigate and define the scope of functional meanings of utterances, a wide range of segmental models of dialogue behaviour have been put forth by researchers such as Sinclair & Coulthard (1975) and Edmondson (1981) for the special case of classroom interaction and by Ehlich & Rehbein (1977); Stubbs (1983) and Stenström (1994) for more general cases. Such studies of discourse analysis have often assumed that dialogues "can be exhaustively segmented into units, and that these units can be reliaby assigned a particular functional interpretation" (Gibbon, Mertins, & Moore 2000: 54).

Along with the segmentation goes the view (of at least some of them) that just as syntax has a hierarchy of units, e.g. word, phrase and clause, an analogous hierarchy of units can be stated for dialogue acts, the smallest functional units of dialogues. They are utterances corresponding to speech acts (Gibbon, Mertins, & Moore 2000: 6, 56). Hierarchical taxonomies of dialogue acts have proven helpful as foundations in general studies of dialogue analysis and play an important role in language engineering, such as automatic speech processing (see e.g. VERBMOBIL (Jekat et al. 1995; Alexandersson et al. 1997)). Hence, methodological steps mainly include the "isolation of a set of basic categories or units of discourse [and the] formulation of a set of concatenation rules stated over those categories" (Levinson 1983: 286).

Well-formed sequences of categories, i.e. coherent discourse, are separated from ill-formed categories, i.e. incoherent discourse (Levinson 1983: 286). According to Van Dijk (1972) and Labov & Fanshel (1977: 72), discourse analysis allows intuitions about the classification and circumscription of dialogue data; i.e. pre-constructed models and theories are permitted.

The basic unit of discourse analysis is the turn constituted by at least one speech act. Optionally, the researcher may depart from pre-defined kinds of speech acts and check their possible realisation, which may be of a direct, explicit, sequential or associative character, or, alternatively, the analysis may be structured towards a particular speech act (see Lewandowski 1990: 230). In this way, a theoretical framework that allows an *a priori* categorisation of data is backed by the analysis of discourse sequences, which are frozen by semi-interpretative transcriptions. It is, moreover, important to integrate contextual facts in order to assign the observed phenomena properly. Unlike conversation analysis, discourse analysis may be based on single texts allowing for small sets of data.

While conversation analysts may be criticised for being most inexplicit about the theories and conceptual categories they use for their approach, discourse analysis theorists may be accused of premature formalisation that leads them to largely ignore the nature of their data. The strength of discourse analysis, however, lies in its combination of linguistic results of intra-sentential organisation with the structure of discourse. Conversation analysis, on the other hand, offers methods that have proven to supply into discourse organisation substantial insights of a depth that for a long time remained unrivalled (Levinson 1983: 287).

Notes

1. At the beginning of his book, the terms *sentence* and *utterance* are used interchangeably, while later his focus of attention is on "the issuing of an utterance in a speech situation" (Austin 1962: 139).

2. At this stage, the intricate relationship between performatives and indirect speech acts will not be taken into consideration. For that purpose, see the section on indirect speech act later in this chapter in which the literal vs. indirect readings of an utterance are discussed. The investigation concentrates on the Searlean framework. An in-depth analysis of these phenomena would go beyond the scope of the exposition of Austin's theory.

3. Doubtlessly, perlocutions also play a role in aviation communication. For example, illocutions of type *assertion* which are interpreted as *directive* sometimes lead to severe effects. A near miss resulted from a crew interpreting the controller's assertion "you are number one for the approach" as a directive to reduce their flight level. In fact, what the controller meant was that the crew was the first in the queue waiting for the permission to reduce the flight level. Despite their role in linguistic research, perlocutions will be ignored with regard to present purposes as these centre on an HPSG-based formalism that is extended by the illocutionary logic of Searle & Vanderveken (1985), who do not cover this type of act.

4. Searle and Vanderveken put forward a refined definition: "the minimal units of human communication are speech acts of a type called *illocutionary acts*" (Searle & Vanderveken 1985: 1).

5. Schiffrin's comment is the basis for the distinction of professional and non-professional communication in aviation parlance (see Section 4.5).

6. In connection with Grosz & Sidner (1986) whose paper will be revisited in Section 5.5, one might refer to Grice (1957); Grice (1969), who advocated a similar view. His work on the meaning of meaning has gained considerably more attention than Searle's notes.

7. This feature refers to Searle's and Vanderveken's *characteristic mode of achievement*, which they list as a separate condition. The *characteristic mode of achievement* and the *degree of strength* can be interdependent (see sincerity rule and essential rule). For example, two utterances of the same illocutionary point can be differentiated "by way of invoking the position of authority of the speaker" (Searle & Vanderveken 1985: 15–16).

8. Searle and Vanderveken point out that the verb *express* is ambiguous in that a speaker in one sense expresses propositions and in another his feelings and attitudes such as fear, belief and happiness. With regard to sincerity conditions and rules, it is used in the second sense. They are confident that its use in the other sense is transparent from the context (Searle & Vanderveken 1985: 19).

9. For reasons of consistency, the notation in this section follows Searle (1969); in Searle & Vanderveken (1985), the notation was different, taking u instead of R, and P instead of RP.

10. Clark also seems to have ignored this condition. This condition in particular disproves Clark's criticism of Searle: He claims that Searle's terms "speech acts, illocutionary acts, and perlocutionary acts describe what speakers do, but there are no comparable terms for what listeners do – as if their actions were irrelevant" (Clark 1996: 137).

Clark states that for Searle the unit of linguistic communication is not

> the symbol, word or sentence, but rather the production or issuance of the symbol, word, or sentence, in the performance of a speech act. For him, linguistic communication is like writing a letter and dropping it in the mail. It doesn't matter whether anybody receives, reads, or understands it.   (Clark 1996: 137)

Searle, however, stresses that the illocutionary act has to be considered within a context, which does include (potential) hearers. As will become obvious from the discussion of illocutionary logic, Searle does not live up to his plans in the formal development.

11. This refers to the second of Chomsky's levels of success for grammatical description. It relates to a grammar that assigns to each string a structural description and reveals kinds of possible deviations. It describes the linguistic intuition or competence of an ideal or idealised speaker so that it significantly corresponds to the speaker's intuition and thereby formulates essential generalisations on regularities on which a given language is based.

12. Whether these data are meta data in the sense of Section 3.4 is controversial.

## CHAPTER 3

Linguistic and corpus methodology

Given that the notion of *method* pertains to the way of dealing with a problem, the methodological part of an analysis may be expected to state in what way the goal of this analysis is to be achieved. This lies at the core of the present section.

According to Searle (1969); Searle (1979a) and Searle & Vanderveken (1985), the syntactic and semantic features of an utterance provide essential information about its illocutionary force. With Searle's work, an important foundation for further research is supplied. To make his results and extensions to his research efficiently processable, a formalism is required. By means of the formalism, syntactic, semantic, pragmatic and surface features of utterances should be implementable and expressible, thereby setting the ground to (semi-)automatically annotate the corpus of ATC/CVR-data.

3.1 Formalisms, methods and linguistic theory

A theory itself does not directly approach the observables in an empirical domain. Instead, it talks about or is interpreted by modelling structures. The predictive power of a theory arises from the correspondence between the model and the empirical domain. An *informal* theory discusses the model in a natural language, that is, an interpreted language whose interpretation is implicit. Since natural languages contain ambiguities, which can make it impossible to decide whether a given argument is valid (Gamut 1991:26), and since theories become more complicated and empirical consequences less straightforwardly apparent (as is also expected for this analysis) a *formalism* is required to make the theory clear and precise. It can be seen as a *prism* that helps to understand the *empirical world* (Peregrin 2000:80) and which is used to reconstruct its regularities explicitly (Peregrin 2000:82). Peregrin characterises the empirical world as things and events whose forms or structures can be found and described, "but which are essentially vague and fuzzy and lack a pure mathematical structure." Nothing that has to do with this world (for Peregrin *The Realm of the Natural*; i.e. Plato's *Becoming*) can be proven in the mathematical sense. By contrast, the formal world (Peregrin's *The Realm of the Formal*; i.e. Platonic *Being*) consists of entities that are "precisely defined and sharply delimited; things are stipulated and facts about this world can be unambiguously proved" (Peregrin 2000: 81).

To work with a theory of determinate empirical consequences, satisfaction of the following criteria is required (as taken from Pollard & Sag (1994: 7)):

- explicitness as to what sorts of ontological categories of objects are assumed to form part of the empirical domain
- mathematical rigour as to what structures are used to model the objects
- a precise characterisation of the modelling structures that are regarded as admissible. The empirical hypotheses must in principle be capable of being rendered in a formal logic.

Pollard and Sag claim that unless these requirements are met, an "enterprise purporting to be a theory cannot have any determinate empirical consequences." Hence, they advocate the necessity for a formalised linguistic theory in accordance with Chomsky, whom they quote as follows:

> Precisely constructed models for linguistic structure can play an important role, both negative and positive, in the process of discovery itself. By pushing a precise but inadequate formulation to an unacceptable conclusion, we can often expose the exact source of this inadequacy and, consequently, gain a deeper understanding of the linguistic data. More positively, a formalized theory may automatically provide solutions for many problems other than those for which it was explicitly designed. Obscure and intuition-bound notions can neither lead to absurd conclusions nor provide new and correct ones, and hence they fail to be useful in two important respects. I think that some of those linguists who have questioned the value of precise and technical development of linguistic theory have failed to recognize the productive potential in the method of rigorously stating a proposed theory and applying it strictly to linguistic material with no attempt to avoid unacceptable conclusions by ad hoc adjustments or loose formulation.
>
> (Chomsky (1957: 5) cited in Pollard & Sag (1994: 7–8))

The advantages of a formalism lie in its precision and its clarity. Furthermore, it allows theories and theorems to be checked.[1] A formalism for an empirically oriented researcher is not an end in itself, rather it is part of a method: It does not bear an immediate increase in knowledge insofar as its application has to be preceded by comprehension. An increase in knowledge can in turn ensue from the process of formalising (Lewandowski 1990) in which the formalism is employed.

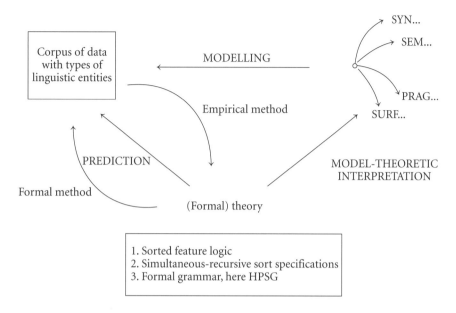

Figure 3.1 Three-way relation connecting theory, model and empirical domain of natural language combined with the relation of interdependence of method, domain and theory.

Figure 3.1 displays the three-way relation connecting theory, model and empirical domain of natural language combined with the interdependence of method, domain and theory. It follows Pollard & Sag (1994), but is slightly modified in that their unilateral *prediction* relation that connects the formal theory with the data is complemented by a backlash of the data on the theory. In this way, it can be ascertained that theory in scientific practice is informed by the empirical work, as detailed in the discussion of regressive deduction in Section 3.1. Other modifications of the original figure are marginal. According to the semantic view of theories, a theory consists of theoretical models and the empirical hypothesis that says models mirror reality in that they represent structural similarities. A *model* is defined as a set of entities in combination with a set of relations that exist between them so that the theory propositions represented by the model are true. If this is the case, provided an approximating representation of reality has indeed been achieved; i.e. the model matches the data, the theory explains what happens in the empirical domain and the theory is supported by the data (Rosencrantz 1977; Lambert & Brittan 1991).

A theory is created by virtue of the perceived reality (cp. the arc labelled *empirical method* in Figure 3.1), i.e. the domain, in the present analysis crisis-talk in the form of ATC/CVR-data. The domain is modelled by means of cognitive and linguistic interpretation, which in turn is dependent on aspects such as cultural experience. It is the method that constitutes the domain *crisis talk* as a social, conventionalised system that has to be reconstructed. From a given set of features a subset is isolated according to specific criteria. They reflect implicit theoretical assumptions and represent the object of research through reduction and idealisation. The model-theoretic interpretation is provided by a feature-structure that in the course of this analysis will be described by attribute-value matrices based on the HPSG-formalism. An *interpretation* is construed as a "mapping of a system of items (expressions) onto another system of items (denotations, meanings)." Within logic, semantic interpretations of the aforementioned kind are analysed by model theory. Model theory refers to the interpretation of a formal language; in the present analysis, this is done within Peregrin's *Realm of the formal*: it addresses mappings of certain kinds of formal structures ('formal languages') onto another type of formal structures ('model structures') (Peregrin 2000:93). Through the formal theory, whose development is an important goal of the present analysis, predictions about the domain can be made. This corresponds to the arc labelled *formal method* in Figure 3.1.

The analysis adopts a deductive approach, proceeding from formal language to formal modelling. There is reason to doubt the applicability of an inductive method.

Deduction

According to the deductivist's view, generating a theory is a method of cognition (Lewandowski 1990). Deduction means to derive complex sentences from elementary sentences, to derive sentences or thoughts from preceding sentences, or to develop thoughts according to the rules of logic (e.g. *modus ponens*[2]). Deduction is a form of thinking or reasoning or drawing inferences in which there is a transition from given sentences or hypotheses to further statements via rules. It is a form of concluding from a set of premises in the context of formal logic.

Deduction (also called *hypothetico-deductive method*) takes as its starting point the formulation of principles and the definition of terms that are related to a small number of observations or data and that are modified by additional observations, data and, to some extent, knowledge. The generation and deductive operating of appropriate hypotheses may lead to theoretic sentences or propositions with the requirement that they be explanatory. Given idealised conditions, basic definitions and particular abstractions, the deductive method leads to a theory. The theory's validity depends on supporting experience (pursuant to the framework of critical rationalism). According to Hempel (1974), no comprehensive, simple and reliable principles for the explanation and prediction of observable phenomena can be achieved by summaries and the inductive generalisation from findings alone. A procedure of observation which is hypothetico-deductive is more appropriate to attain this goal. In order to describe the observational data, the researcher has to invent a collection of terms and hypotheses, i.e. theoretical constructs that have for the time being no significance that is based on experience. Good constructs, however, must allow for explanatory and prognostic principles (Lewandowski 1990: 412–415).

Deduction is called *progressive* if first the axioms and rules (an axiomatic system) are determined and the theorems are stated subsequently or if there is progress from fixed propositions to the conclusion. It is called *regressive*[3] if one departs from a conclusion that still has to be proven. First the claim is set up and then the arguments important for proving the claim are stated. In everyday life, the conclusions are often formulated *a priori* and only later is their explanation given (Bochenski 1970). But progressive deduction also has an important role in modern sciences. The significance of regressive deduction lies in the fact that new thoughts or theorems are often intuitively postulated and afterwards regressively proven or explained.

A progressively derived sentence can be complicated or not immediately comprehensible. In order to facilitate understanding of it, the respective derivational steps must be reconstructable.

Induction

Induction means to gain knowledge from the particular about the general through specific regularities, analogies or invariants and by generation of hypotheses about the general case (Mortimer 1988). In the empirical sciences, it is a synthesising procedure: the progression from the knowledge of a finite set of elements to the class, the generalisation of empirical data by virtue of sameness and relations, the transition from positive singular cases to general (*enumerative induction*). Induction is further characterised by abstraction (isolation, typification, idealisation), generalisation and generation of hypotheses by means of fantasy and intuition (Wunderlich 1976). In practice, induction and deduction are often interwoven (logical deduction/derivation of singular hypotheses): Induction is a heuristic procedure, a creative discovery of possible general sentences whose theoretical status must be validated empirically on the basis of (deductive) conclusions. A logical and epistemological problem is the transition from partial hypotheses to theories or from singular propositions to (theoretical) generalisations, because every kind of observation presupposes (theoretical) terms, while theories contain terms which determine the direction of induction (see also observations that are made as planned perceptions, cases in which the observation is preceded by a question or a problem (see Popper 1971 and Percival 2000 for a more up-to-date discussion of the status of theoretical terms). There is no way to get from terms alone to hypotheses (Lewandowski 1990: 180)).

Theories in the empirical sciences contain universally quantified empirical sentences of which true observational sentences about data are instances: Theories are always underspecified by data. They cannot be derived or concluded (inductively) from the data itself. With deduction the content of the conclusions is not stronger than the content of the premises (implication, inference), whereas with induction the content of conclusions is stronger in the sense of being more general. With regard to "inductive inferences", validity of the conclusions is not guaranteed, but this is the case with *inductive probability* (cp. Stegmüller (1975)). According to Carnap, only within the framework of a theory of subjective probabilities can inductive principles be treated logically as an interpretation of a probability calculus: The conclusions are thus not proven, but are sentences about conditional probabilities (Kutschera 1982: 462). Inductive reasoning is dependent on *a priori* probabilities which cannot be made explicit as subjective *a priori* probabilities; however, they can become evident as expectations, which lie at the heart of every inductive process. Expectations are generated by personal experience and through the respective culture. Operative procedures of segmentation and classification of descriptive structuralism are considered *inductive methods*. The controversy between generativism and taxonomic structuralism is to be considered as a methodological controversy between the inductive and deductive method.

It would be begging the question to claim that empirical methods are inductive throughout. Hjelmslev (1969) stresses that empiricism is not the same as inductivism in the sense of an incrementation from the particular to the general, from the element to the class, and so on. According to Hjelmslev, this procedure shows clear drawbacks, e.g. in the grammatical terminology. The principle of induction does not achieve a simple description free of contradictions either. The opposite procedure would be required: to proceed from the text *in toto* to system-generated components.

An inductive method is a systematically generated class of conclusions which lead from real presuppositions to real conclusions under a particular probability (Essler 1970: 10). It enables the formulation of something new or of states of affairs that surpass the contents of the presuppositions, i.e. of what is already known or proven. For a compatible view see Spohn (2003). The deductive method, on the other hand, i.e. the totality of possible conclusions from particular presuppositions, is a procedure that leads to order, systematicity and straightforwardness in representation with regard to theories. As a result, theories can more easily be checked for contradictions. A deductive conclusion is necessarily valid with regard to the premises, with the contents of the conclusion not surpassing the contents of the presuppositions. The deductive method, however, does not allow a transition from what is known to what is not known. The creative options of the inductive method lie in the design of logically consistent theories that can be supported and ameliorated empirically. These conclusions have led to the present investigation relying on a deductive method.

Conclusion

In the case of the present investigation, the rejection of inductive methods means that conversation analysis as a methodological option has to be precluded. This is not to say that insights gained by conversation analysis are neglected if they have proven useful and can be recast in terms of discourse analysis.

This is the general strategy in the present investigation: the theoretical framework that is given *prior* to or at least *independently* of the empirical data is set up and then evaluated against the data. If it turns out that there are connections between results from neighbouring disciplines to the results obtainable from the theoretical framework, these results will be explained by the theoretical terms used in the theory without adding new vocabulary.

3.2 Dialogues and theories: Some general considerations

Traditionally, there exist two complementary ways of thinking about dialogues. The first way is to consider a dialogue as a *sequence of utterances*: This is the perspective that complies most with speech act theory. The strength of this view becomes obvious from the degree of meticulousness to which the properties of utterances have been studied. This strength is certainly inherited from a long tradition of studying the *propositional content* of utterances as expressed by sentences. This tradition goes back to Aristotle (e.g. Aristoteles 1975) and was extended notably by Frege (1969); Frege (1971); Montague (1974); Kripke (1977); Kripke (1980) and Lewis (1998).

An obvious weakness of speech act theory is that there is hardly any account of the relations between – in contrast to the properties of – utterances. Endeavours have been undertaken to remedy this problem, as exemplified by Asher's *Segmented Discourse Relation Theory* (SDRT) (see, e.g. Lascarides, Asher, & Oberlander 1992; Asher 1998; Asher & Lascarides 2003). These endeavours, however, do not go so far as to propose a solution to the problem.

A second drawback is that for the purpose of linguistic analysis the works of Austin (1962); Searle (1979b); Searle & Vanderveken (1985) offer no sufficient treatment of the propositional content.

For the first of the problems, an alternative has arisen that at the same time characterises the second way of thinking about dialogues: Clark (1996) proposes a perspective on discourse which focusses primarily on the *joint projects* that speaker and hearer pursue in a dialogue. This account essentially relies on the presence of a small set of mechanisms for establishing common ground, backchanneling, uptake securing and a limited number of other pragmatic factors. It certainly has its strengths concerning the explanation of the complexity of spontaneous speech: its richness in overlap, signals of metalinguistic communication and so forth. However, it is notoriously unclear how this account could be formalised and unified with common linguistic theories. This is certainly the minimum of what has to be done to attain the goal of this analysis.

To sum up: viewing discourse as a sequence of utterances requires strong idealisations. On the other hand, however, it has the advantage of being computationally tractable in clear contrast to trying to come to grips with a holistic account of discourse. For the present analysis, the investigation is restricted to idealised data in the sense that it does not consider overlapping utterances, and that the relations between utterances are kept simple.

As mentioned previously, the second weakness of speech act theory is its unsatisfactory treatment of the propositional content of an utterance. Searle repeatedly stresses that an analysis of the propositional content is required for a complete picture of pragmatics. However, his ideas on this matter remain implicit (e.g. Searle & Vanderveken 1985: 31). For speech act theory, propositions and the sentences which express the propositions are unanalysed. This approach cannot be sustained if the purpose of the present analysis is to be achieved: Here, an analysis of the syntactic features of sentences (the bearers of the propositional content) must be added to the description of the non-

propositional component of the utterance, its illocutionary force. Searle moti-
vates by his own statements, as he explicitly claims that *inter alia* constituents
of sentences as well as the surface order of the words function as *illocutionary
force indicating devices*. In order to use these devices, one has to go beyond the
descriptive level of the sentence and look into its syntactic constituents.

Hence, speech act theory has to be strengthened by a second component.
This component should be an analytic device that is capable of treating sentences below the level of the sentence node and able to deliver a result that contains an interface between speech act theory and the aforementioned analytic
device.

In this book, *theory* stands for a set of sentences with certain properties.
Not details but an intuitive notion is given here of what constitutes the sentences of a science. A theory, then, is a set of sentences such that all objects,
properties and relations in the *domain* of a theory are completely and correctly
rendered. The domain of a theory depends on the purpose for which the theory is built. For example, if a theory pertains to subatomic particles, its domain
consists of this sort of particles (plus their properties and so on).

The sentences of which theories are made are called *theorems*. Due to their
logical relations, parts of the theorems are distinguished. Theorems which form
a subset of a theory so that other theorems can be derived from them are called
axioms. A single theory can possibly be constructed from different *axiomatic
bases*. This means that from time to time different selections from the set of
theorems can be made in such a way that the other theorems can be derived
from them. This is called *dependency*: Not all theorems are included in the
axiomatic bases.

An explanation like this shows what it means to unify theories. Its fundamental postulate is that the respective sets of sentences are combined via union
($\cup$). It is certainly a necessary feature of the resulting theory that it contains
the sentences of the initial theories, but this might not be sufficient. One would
probably refrain from calling a theory the result of combining two theories if
there were no interesting connection between the united sets of sentences. For
example, the theory of subatomic particles united with a theory of lunar motion will not be a theory of subatomic particles and lunar motion unless one
can state how the respective theorems are related. Usually, the connections are
established via Nagel's bridge laws or something similar. The means by which
the connections are established are called the *interface* between the component
theories.

Luckily, the aspect of compatibility is not a serious problem for the present
project (hence the interface does not consist of a high number of bridge laws

or translation rules): Both theories, speech act theory and the syntactic theory, are located within the common domain of linguistics, and it will become clear how they (and their expressions) are connected. An important requirement, however, is that the two theories do not become *inconsistent*. That two theories are inconsistent means that the union of the set of sentences cannot be satisfied in any model. On the level of theorems of the union of the theories this means that two of them are the negation of each other.

This does not pose a problem for the present project, though, because the two theories in question are distinct enough not to contradict each other: speech act theory does not comprise the properties of sentential constituents and the grammar does not have parameters that relate to the illocutionary component of utterances. The point where both of them come into contact is the set of Searle's illocutionary force indicating devices. Now the question arises what sorts of properties a grammar needs to have so that it can adequately complement speech act theory.

As stated above, the objective of this volume is to provide foundational research for the – at the present stage – remote goal to (semi-)automatically identify speech acts. With this, the principle of annotation comes into play. Within the context of this analysis, *annotation* is defined as using attribute-value structures for the tagging of parts of texts, in order to assign an interpretation to a stretch of signs (for a more detailed definition of *annotation* as opposed to *representation* see Section 3.5). Given that it should be as easy as possible to transform into attribute-value structures the structures that are allowable within the constraints imposed by the grammar, it is the action of choice to select a grammar that also operates explicitly on attribute-value structures.

A traditional form of representation for grammars is the tree-structure, for example, and it is easy to see that every tree can likewise be transformed into an attribute-value structure. Thus the requirement that the grammar of choice generate attribute-value structures does not greatly restrict the number of candidates. As a second requirement, however, the grammar must be able to represent pragmatic features of sentences, such as the speaker's and listener's dependence on meaning. This requirement is not easy to meet.

Here the candidate of choice will be a version of HPSG, enriched by certain attributes that are not as yet common in HPSG grammars. What is necessary, of course, is to state how the new attributes interact with the more traditional ones. As the present analysis is *inter alia* concerned with the application of such a formalism to natural language expression, the application will function as a test for the compatibility of the resulting formalism.

The requirement of being both compatible with speech act theory and attribute-value annotation imposes constraints on the choice of the grammar that can be used for sentential analysis. As stated more informally in Section 2.3, this is the reason for rejecting Ross's account.

3.3 Head-driven phrase structure grammar (HPSG) for illocutionary acts

There are many introductions to HPSG. For this reason, the present section offers a concise overview of the main rules and principles of the theory. HPSG is a constraint-based, lexicalist approach to grammatical theory, which seeks to model human languages as systems of constraints on typed feature structures (Sag 2001). With these properties in mind, HPSG will be characterised in more detail with regard to its basic principles, particularly with regard to formal issues and syntactic principles. These are most important for the current analysis.

HPSG is a declarative grammar that provides a uniform representation of different features of linguistic signs and bears different levels of descriptions, such as syntactic, semantic and contextual dimensions in parallel order. These levels do not have a derivative relation to each other in that the parallel representation does not induce an order. Furthermore, HPSG is *mono-stratal*; i.e. there is only one stratum about which grammatical constraints are formulated. On this level, syntactic, phonological and semantic properties are represented. None of these levels has been derived from another level nor does it filter representations that are analysed as grammatical on the other levels.

HPSG is special as a declarative grammar because syntax is only regarded as one aspect of a sign. Thus, to determine the grammaticality of sentences, their semantic (phonological, morphological) representations are also taken into account. Kiss (1995: 14) emphasises that, according to the parallel order of the syntactic level to the other dimensions of analysis, syntactic regularities can refer to the semantic features of a sign (cf. Searle's IFIDS).

The modelling domain in HPSG is a system of sorted feature structures that are intended to stand in a 1:1 relation with types of natural language expressions and their subparts (Kiss 1995). HPSG structures are *sorted*: each node is labelled with a sort symbol that tells what type of object the structure is modelling. In other words, there is one sort symbol for each basic type (ontological category) of construct. For notational ease, the sort symbol that labels a node in a feature structure will often be deleted when it can be recovered from the context. The *finite* set of all sort symbols is assumed to be *partially ordered*: the sort symbols correspond to more inclusive types lower in the ordering.

HPSG feature structures are required to be *well-typed*: What kind of attribute or feature labels may appear in a feature structure is determined by its sort. Which attribute an empirical object can have depends on its ontological category. Likewise, a value of that attribute must also be of a kind appropriate for that sort and attribute label. In a completely formalised HPSG grammar, it must be stated explicitly what the sort symbols are, how they are ordered and what the appropriate attribute labels and value sorts are for each sort. Feature structures that serve as models of linguistic entities are required to satisfy further criteria of completeness: They are *total* models (not merely partial models) of the objects that they represent. Thus, they are required to be *totally well-typed* and *sort-resolved*:

– *Totally well-typed*: the feature structure is well-typed and for each node every feature which is appropriate for the sort assigned to the node is actually present.
– *Sort-resolved*: every node is assigned a sort label that is maximal (=most specific) in sort ordering.

For some sorts no attribute labels are appropriate: these are atoms.

A final basic principle of HPSG methodology is *structure sharing*. According to this principle, two paths share the same structure as their common value. This involves *token identity* of values, not just values that are a structurally identical feature structure (that would be a case of *type identity*; cf. Pollard & Sag 1994: 17–21).

Conjunctive, disjunctive and implicative descriptions of the feature structure together with the concept of typification constrain the set of permissible feature structures and thus the set of permissible language expressions. Descriptions are partially grouped and by virtue of their informational content ordered in a type hierarchy. The objects described are total models of language expressions. The description is typed so that conjunctive and disjunctive descriptions only capture objects of the same type. The maximal sorts of a sort hierarchy correspond to the types of the feature structure.

The format of feature representation in HPSG stems from the generative tradition (Chomsky & Halle 1968; Chomsky 1970). However, since HPSG is a declarative grammar, its interpretation is different: Here, feature representations and the feature structures described by the representations are not to be confused. And while features in most generative approaches do not have complex values, i.e. while no feature bundles are present, feature bundles are one of the basic concepts in HPSG (and other declarative grammars).

A declarative grammatical theory such as HPSG operates on lexicalisation; i.e. lexical units are interpreted as complex entities whose features are an expression of linguistic properties (compare categorial grammar, $\bar{\mathrm{X}}$ theory). To these properties rules and principles refer by which information is projected from the lexicon into syntax. Two of the most central principles are:

- *Subcategorisation Principle*: in any headed structure, the SUBCAT value is the list obtained by removing from the SUBCAT value of the head those specifications that were satisfied by one of the complement daughters (Pollard & Sag 1987: 71). In other words, the principle validates the subcategorisation requirements of the lexical head as they become satisfied by the complement daughters of its phrasal projections. This works in much the same way as cancellation in categorial grammar (Pollard & Sag 1994: 34).

- *Head-feature Principle (HFP)*: the HEAD value of any headed phrase is structure-shared with the HEAD value of the head daughter (Pollard & Sag 1994: 34). This principle is a reformulation of the Head Feature Convention of Generalised Phrase Structure Grammar (GPSG) (see also Pollard & Sag 1987: 58 and Sells 1985).

HPSG further incorporates the requirement of monotonicity: In the case of a derivation, information is added to a structure. Already existing information can only be extended, but not changed. Order in the application of the constraints makes no difference in the well-formedness of the structures.

The present section addresses the extension of an HPSG-formalism to the description of illocutionary acts from spontaneous speech. According to Searle, the syntactic and semantic features of an utterance provide essential information about its illocutionary force (see, e.g. Searle & Vanderveken (1985)). To make linguistic features of this sort explicit, an HPSG-formalism is employed because this allows a detailed description of the syntactic structure of sentences and also their semantic treatment (see Pollard & Sag (1987); Pollard & Sag (1994)). However, the scope of Pollard and Sag is narrower than what a description of utterances would require. And although they extend their formalism by the context-attribute CONX (Pollard & Sag 1994), which allows integration of features such as pragmatic agreement and background conditions, further extensions are necessary.

A modified formalism

Different illocutionary forces are constituted by different features. Searle's *conditions of success* are indicators that help to disambiguate the type of illocutionary force that underlies an utterance. Furthermore, the conditions of success are useful in deciding whether an illocutionary act of an utterance has been performed successfully or unsuccessfully. In addition to these conditions, which are based on an extended semantics, there are conditions of syntactic relevance and those that relate to surface features of language expressions. They jointly function as *illocutionary force indicating devices* and thereby contribute to the determination of the illocutionary force of the utterance. HPSG supplies a formalism that allows a detailed description of the syntactic structure of sentences and also their semantic interpretation (Pollard & Sag 1987; Pollard & Sag 1994). However, the HPSG rules and principles do not go beyond the structure of the sentence, let alone a dialogue, i.e. linguistic signs produced by more than one speaker, and even though Pollard & Sag (1994) introduce the CONX (=context) attribute[4] it does not serve as an adequate linguistic description. What is more, natural language expressions can hardly be modeled by a feature-structure that accords with the rules and principles of HSPG, since HPSG is oriented towards the ideal speaker/hearer as proposed in the Chomskyan paradigm and not tuned to imperfect beings. Consequently, the HPSG formalism needs to be extended. At least with regard to the syntactic features that they call *parts of speech*, Pollard and Sag point out that their list of sorts "is not intended to be exhaustive" and that they "leave open the question of the precise inventory" (Pollard & Sag 1994:22). Thus, they allow an extension of their formalism at least on a syntactic level. In this analysis, the HPSG-methodology is applied conservatively with regard to current usage (Pollard & Sag 1987); the HPSG-application, however, is used non-conservatively: the formalism is employed to a large extent free from its original interpretation. Hence, the approach is HPSG-*based* and deviates from the traditional conventions in the following respects:

HPSG rules are applied to tokens[5] of spontaneous speech instead of the traditionally analysed abstract sentences (see Searle & Vanderveken 1985). Thus, the HPSG-based structure proposes a solution to the problem of how Searle's $f(p)$, i.e. natural language expressions, can be translated into a logical form $F(P)$. This is a problem that Searle and Vanderveken consider but do not pursue, since they limit their model to idealised data. The ensuing context-dependence treated in the current analysis is captured by an extended set of types of HPSG-entities to the semantic attribute. Different substructures are added, which have been adopted from Searle's *conditions of success* (Searle & Vanderveken 1985).

In the resulting HPSG-based entry, the semantic attributes of *illocutionary force* and *proposition* together form the semantic attribute of a complex sign which has a four-dimensional structure ⟨SYN, DTRS, SURF, SEM⟩ with two *compositional* and two *interpretative* dimensions. The compositional dimensions refer to the syntactic features of the sign such as its distribution in the immediate linguistic context (SYN) and to the internal components of which it is constituted (DTRS). The interpretative dimensions stand for its surface representation (SURF), including aspects of orthography and word order (also its phonetic and perhaps gestural realisation), and for its semantic (SEM) features that include contextual properties (cf. Gibbon & Sassen (1997)).

The *head-feature principle*, which is conventionally applied to phrasal syntax, is extended to the type *illocutionary act* motivated by Searle, who argues that propositions are bound to the performance of illocutionary acts:

> In the performance of an act of the form $F(P)$ the illocutionary point is distinct from the propositional content, but it is achieved only as part of a total speech act in which the propositional content is expressed with the illocutionary point. We will say therefore that the illocutionary point is achieved on the propositional content.   (Searle & Vanderveken 1985:15)

On the evidence of some illocutions that may occur without a proposition, or at least an explicit proposition, (e.g. *Hooray for the Raiders!*), and since a proposition is derived as an abstract entity from the utterance, an illocutionary component, in the form of the illocutionary force (see Figure 5.7), is interpreted as HEAD in relation to the propositional component. This principle will be useful in modelling propositions that are distributed over the contributions, possibly of different speakers (see Rieser & Skuplik 2000 and Example (108), in this analysis). HEAD and its sister(s) are in a dependency relationship.

The HPSG-based formalism further elaborates on the idea that the conditions of success and other parameters can be construed as input to a rule whose output makes statements about the success or failure of the performance of a speech act.

In the current analysis, *conditions* are the context of utterance and conditions of success that form the illocutionary force indicating devices. They are integrated into the HPSG-based feature-structure as displayed in Figure 5.7. Here, the conditions of success formulate the parameters necessary for the successful and non-defective performance of a speech act from which

the rules are generated. They are necessary to be able to unequivocally identify the type of illocutionary force that is expressed by a particular utterance. The conditions of success form a septuple of elements, which are determined in a principled manner. It consists of the *illocutionary point*,[6] *mode
of achievement of the illocutionary point, degree of strength of this illocutionary
point, propositional content conditions, preparatory conditions, sincerity conditions* and the *degree of strength of the sincerity conditions*. Unlike other elements,
the *input-output*-condition does not figure in Searle & Vanderveken (1985),
but has been deliberately adopted from Searle's earlier work (Searle 1969;
Searle 1979a). The input-output-condition pertains to the uptake relation of
the communicative channel between speaker and hearer (see also Austin 1962;
Searle 1969), whereas in the latter work Searle puts most emphasis on the
speaker.

   Rules are derived from the conditions that are integrated into the HPSG-
based feature-structure (see Figure 5.7). Unlike conditions, rules are stated
externally to the HPSG-based feature-structure. To validate the attribute-value
matrix, the argument-slots of the rules are filled with the parameters of the
feature-structure. The totality of the rules' output pertains to the illocutionary
force of the token at issue. The combination of conditions and rules results in
a structural description of the utterance.

   The idea to identify the illocutionary force of an utterance and to determine its success or failure in the performance of a particular speech act through
a rule is expressed by the definition below. It determines the appropriate logical form of utterances in context. In other words, it assigns each utterance in
context its relevant logical form $\boxed{R(\langle i, f(p) \rangle, \langle F(P) \rangle) = 1}$
Description of the rule definition:

- The rule R is constituted by one or more elements of a *context of utterance*
  i, the natural language expression (or token) $f(p)$, and its formal description $F(P)$, i.e. the illocutionary force indicating devices which include the
  conditions of success of every type of illocutionary force. F and f stand for
  the illocutionary force indicating devices and P and p for the propositional
  content of an utterance.
- *Context of utterance* refers to a set of contingent features, here applying to
  the contextual features of $f(p)$: speaker, hearer, time, location and framing
  utterances.
- $i, f(p)$ and $F(P)$ mark the input of the rule. If $f(p)$ together with its i
  matches a particular set of templates (rules generated from $F(P)$), the output applies to the successful performance of a speech act, hence the value

1. If at least one component of i or $f(p)$ does not match the templates, the output of some other value indicates failure in the performance of a speech act.

The rules derived from the conditions are listed below for the illocutionary force of the type *directive*. For reasons of focus the present analysis will leave aside the other types of illocutionary point (*assertives, declaratives, commissives* and *expressives*), and limit itself to brief rule definitions.

The following semantic rules are derived from Searle's conditions of success. As the inventory of Searle's and Vanderveken's propositional logic is too limited, some signs had to be added to formulate the rules for the attribute value matrix (see Figure 5.7).

A speaker a_i succeeds in achieving the directive *illocutionary point* (Π_3) on a proposition P in a context i (for short: $i\Pi_3 P$, where the index marks the directive) iff in that context in an utterance he makes an attempt to get the hearer b_i to carry out the future course of action represented by P (Searle & Vanderveken 1985:39). The second part of the rule can be re-written for this context as an action/attempt (A) by the speaker (a_i) to elicit (elicitation = E) an action from the hearer (b_i), hence

$$\boxed{i\Pi_3 P \text{ iff } A(a_i)\,E(b_i, P)}$$

A speaker a_i in the context i achieves the directive illocutionary point on P by invoking his position of authority over the hearer b_i, hence

$$\boxed{\mathrm{mode}(||command||)(i, P) = 1}$$

Since the *mode of achievement* of a command restricts the conditions of achievement to its illocutionary point, it is a *special mode of achievement* (Searle & Vanderveken 1985:40).

A speaker a_i in the context i achieves the illocutionary point Π on the proposition P with the *degree of strength* k: $\boxed{i\Pi^k P}$ with $k \in \mathbb{Z}$ (Searle & Vanderveken 1985:41). In the attribute value matrix of the current investigation, however, k obtains the value $||command||$, since no comparative value is part of the present discussion, hence

$$\boxed{i\Pi_3^{||command||} P}$$

Some illocutionary points like directives place restrictions on *propositional contents*. Searle and Vanderveken introduce the function Θ_{fut}, which pertains to temporal relations and associates with each possible context of utterance i a set of all propositions that are future with respect to the moment of time t_i

(Searle & Vanderveken 1985:43). From this results the temporal relation between the utterance time (t_i) and denotation time (t_{denot}). For this analysis they are defined as

(t_i): the time interval during which an utterance is produced. It is expressed by information from the time line of the CVR transcript.

(t_{denot}): the time interval or point of time during which something that is referred to is the case.

$$\Theta_{fut}, t_i \prec t_{denot} \Rightarrow \text{Prop}_{||command||}$$

The *preparatory rule* specifies for each context of utterance i and proposition P, which states of affairs the speaker a_i must presuppose to obtain in the world of the utterance w_i if he performs the illocution $F(P)$ in i (Searle & Vanderveken 1985:43). The issuance of a command requires three rules:

(a) The speaker a_i be in a position of institutional authority (Aut) over the hearer b_i: $\Sigma_{||command||}(i, P) = $ [the proposition that a_i at time t_i is in a position of authority over b_i with regard to $P \cup \Sigma_1(i, P)$] (Searle & Vanderveken 1985:201) rewritten as:

$$\Sigma_{||command||}(i, P) = \text{Aut}(a_i, b_i, t_i, P)$$

(b) The hearer b_i is capable (Cap) of carrying out the future course of action (A_{fut}) represented by P:

$$\text{Cap}(b_i)\, A(b_i, P) \Rightarrow \text{DIR, command}$$

(c) It is not obvious, i.e. common knowledge (C), to both speaker a_i and hearer b_i that b_i will perform the action at t_i without being commanded:

$$\neg\, C(a_i, b_i)\, A(b_i, P) \Rightarrow \text{DIR, command}$$

The *sincerity rules* of an illocutionary force F are defined by specifying for each context of utterance i and proposition P which psychological states the speaker a_i expresses in the performance of $F(P)$ in i. A speaker who commands a hearer to do something is sincere iff he wants (W) him to do it (Searle & Vanderveken 1985:45):

$$\Psi_{||command||}(i, P) = [W(P)]$$

Depending on the type of illocutionary force, psychological states are expressed in speech acts with greater or lesser strength (η). For most illocutionary forces F, their *degree of strength* of illocutionary point and of sincerity conditions are identical, though in the case of commands this may be different (Searle & Vanderveken 1985:45):

$$\boxed{\text{degree (F)} > \eta}$$

Searle mentions word order as another illocutionary force indicating device that pertains to the linear ordering of syntactic constituents. The *word order* rule focusses on the position of the verb within the utterance in question. In commands such as the token at hand, it appears in first position of the utterance:

$$\boxed{\text{VF}_{utt} \Rightarrow \text{DIR}}$$

In the HPSG-based representation model (see Figure 3.2), the illocutionary force and proposition jointly function as a semantic attribute of a complex sign. The composite entry for the lemma *token*, which pertains to the *whole illocutionary act* (see Searle & Vanderveken (1985:8)) consists of two parts: first, an item of type *F* with *head*-features, second, an item of type *P* with *complement*-features. In the context of type *F(P)* under the SEM-attribute, the operator ⊔ is interpreted as unification of two SEM-attributes, e.g. A⊔B. The item of type *P* corresponds to a traditional HPSG sign, the item of type *F* is derived from by the extended HPSG formalism. An elaboration of the general model shown here will be given in Section 5.3.

An alternative solution

Ginzburg, Sag, & Purver (2001) propose a model that likewise aims at integrating an analysis of utterances into an HPSG-framework. However, Ginzburg, Sag, and Purver work with conversational move types (CMTs) rather than speech acts. Their way of integrating CMT information into grammars is to adopt a multi-dimensional type hierarchy. Apart from classifying phrases in terms of their phrase structure schema or X̄ type, they introduce a further informational dimension of CLAUSALITY. This results in a division of clauses, for example, into declarative clauses denoting propositions, interrogative clauses denoting questions, exclamative clauses denoting facts and imperative clauses denoting outcomes.[7]

In the model, each maximal phrasal type can inherit from both these dimensions. Thus, the classification allows a specification of systematic correlations between clausal construction types (cf. the SYN attribute of the proposition *P* in this analysis) and types of semantic content (cf. the SEM attributes of the illocutionary force *F* and the proposition *P* in this analysis). Starting from

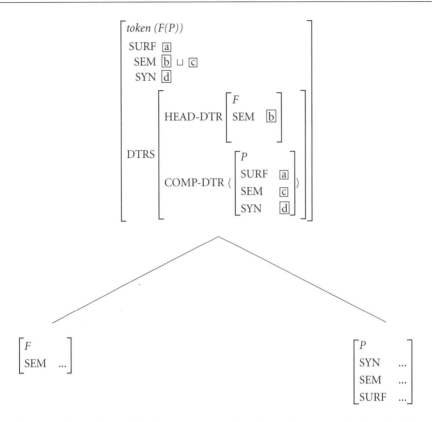

Figure 3.2 An underspecified tree structure of an illocutionary act that has the *illocutionary force* F as head-daughter and *proposition* P as the head-daughter's sister.

a situation theoretic ontology, Ginzburg, Sag, & Purver (2001) posit as a minimal ontology a 1–1 relationship between the "content of the sign" (entities of type *message* such as *proposition, question, outcome, fact*) and CMTs[8]. Propositions are associated with the CMT of asserting, which bears the illocutionary relation type *assert-relation*, whereas facts and exclaiming, e.g. generate the *exclaim-relation*. The critical point, however, is that the relationship between message types and CMTs constitute a construction which Ginzburg, Sag, and Purver themselves circumscribe as a default.

To give an example of application: the approach of Ginzburg, Sag, and Purver concerns *inter alia* the analysis of words such as *hi, thanks* and *sorry* which may stand on their own as complete utterances lacking a descriptive content. To handle utterances like these, Ginzburg, Sag, and Purver suggest associating them with a CMT for representation in the lexicon. To assume a null-descriptive content for the utterance *hi*, e.g. would lead to a problem with *bye*, which equally lacks a descriptive content. Thus, postulating underspecification would result in the "unintuitive expectation that *hi* and *bye* potentially allow for multiple CMTS" (Ginzburg, Sag, & Purver 2001:48).

This would mean that *hi* and *bye* could not be distinguished by the formalism, no matter how refined the classification of CMTS.

To compare the two approaches: In the speech act-based proceeding the semantics of utterances in context are not determined via CMTS, but via the functions which each speech act has. On the evidence of IFIDS, the semantic function is derived for each speech act. Having achieved this, the speech acts will be considered within the format of a dialogue, i.e. sequences of utterances. Ginzburg, Sag, and Purver, by contrast, who integrate many features of *Rhetorical Structure Theory* (RST) into their work (see e.g. Matthiessen & Thompson 1987; Mann & Thompson 1988), elaborate on the assumption that the discourse functions of particular syntactical structures are already given, and hence do not elaborate an analysis of their semantic functions. The comparison is illustrated in Figure 3.3.

The proposal by Ginzburg, Sag, and Purver cannot rely on a derivational connection between, e.g. syntactic features and discourse function. In any case, the question remains unanswered as to which discourse function a sentence with verb-first ordering has. On the other hand, they cannot profit from work on the connection between speech act type and discourse function, as their approach completely lacks the former notion. Asher and Lascarides (see e.g. Lascarides 2001) have recently made progress in that area of research. The ap-

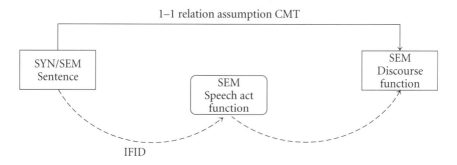

Figure 3.3 Comparison of the two approaches intended to analyse conversational interaction. The solid line depicts the solution favoured by Ginzburg, Sag, & Purver (2001), the dashed line the solution proposed in this analysis.

proach favoured in the present investigation can use both of these resources via IFIDS and the exploitation of the SEM attributes.

3.4 Creating a crisis talk corpus

Now that with HPSG a grammar has been found that meets the expectation of being compatible with speech act theory and attribute-value annotation, this grammar needs to be implemented in a form that is typical of corpus (an)notation: A notation system is necessary that allows a system-independent display of the attribute-value pairs. What is more, the attribute-value pairs along with the HPSG rules and principles need to be integrable into a corpus of ATC/CVR-data. And as in the development of *integrated resources for spoken and written language* (see Gibbon, Mertins, & Moore 2000: 3) the integration of lexical (here super-lexical or discourse) information as a common resource relating to both spoken and written language is required, there is also the need for resources like lexica (here: HPSG) and corpora to be "consistent with one another so that information can be easily exchanged between them. Similarly, tools should be capable of processing data in terms of the representations used for other resources" (Gibbon, Mertins, & Moore 2000: 3).

A suitable annotation system for this purpose is the *extensible markup language* (XML) that has widely gained popularity within the last ten years and is on the verge of becoming the markup standard of the *World Wide Web*.

This chapter will outline the steps which have to be taken for creating a corpus, in particular an XML-corpus of ATC/CVR-data, while the theoretical framework will be cemented, taking into account the earlier approach of the *Text Encoding Initiative* (TEI) to spoken language data. In addition, a current annotation-representation system will be discussed that primarily focuses on the logical structure of data, i.e. the *annotation graphs* of Bird & Liberman (1999b). In Chapters 4 and 5, I will show how to apply the theoretical background to real data. In Section 5.4, I will demonstrate how the HPSG-formalism can be mapped into an XML-markup.

Corpus design pertains to technological criteria which help define the domain (e.g. spoken language vs. written language and participants' characteristics). With linguistic discourse data, corpus design usually refers to the prerecording phase of speech. For the present analysis recorded data and also their transcripts already existed. The transcripts were created by transcribers designated by the particular governments. The steps of classifying the corpus during this post-recording and post-transcription phase, however, remain identical with those of a pre-recording phase; viz.

– specifying the linguistic content of the corpus
– defining the application of the corpus
– specifying the number and type of speakers and further details.

The resulting dialogue typology (see Section 4.1) will be expanded for special purposes that do not match any of the existing criteria. According to the EAGLES (Expert Advisory Group on Language Engineering Standards) project, there is no complete or systematic dialogue typology, so the catalogue of dialogue properties recommended by this project is applied as a guiding list (see also Gibbon, Mertins, & Moore 2000: 1.2).

Corpus collection applies to the technology that helps compile the ATC/CVR-corpus data. With regard to the current analysis, statements can only be made about the post-recording and post-transcription phase, since no technical details about the recorders were available: All ATC/CVR corpus files were located on the *World Wide Web* (Ladkin 1999; Landsberg 1995–2000; Aviation Safety Network 2000a; Aviation Safety Network 2000b). Seventy-seven transcript files and five sound files were available for this analysis. The sound files are only fragments of poor quality with a maximal duration of 30 seconds.

Efforts were also undertaken to get access to the original recordings in order to check them against the transcripts available on the web or, if necessary, to prepare new transcripts. Owing to legal issues, all institutions contacted were highly protective of their data.

Corpus representation refers to all steps involved in processing and organising the data. Organising implies the design of categories, sorting data for databases and linguistic processing. Linguistic processing with regard to dialogues branches into *dialogue representation*, i.e. the orthographic transcription of a dialogue, giving basic information, e.g. on contents, participants, and *dialogue annotation*, i.e. additional levels of linguistic information which are added to the orthographic transcription (also known as markup, tagging, Tree-banks, Time-stamps). It also pertains to the analysis and categorisation of the data with respect to their outer form. These facets will be taken into account in the following chapters. Linguistic processing, however, covers only dialogue annotation, as orthographic transcriptions already exist. Chapter 4 addresses the remaining task of category design and the process of sorting data that are interlinked in this special case with a modification of the order of the data. In this way, the data are pre-formatted for the KWIC-concordance and a subsequent XML-markup whose procedure will be documented in Section 4.3 and be taken up again in Chapter 5. An enhanced markup will be presented in Chapter 5.4. Markup pertains to the large area of *meta data*. Meta data are defined as a structured set of elements which describe a resource. In this way, people can search for electronic information more efficiently (ServiceTasmania Online 2000). Meta data have been understood as data about data. This becomes obvious from examples such as a library catalogue that contains information (meta data) about publications (data) or a file system that maintains permissions (meta data) about files (data). Thus, meta data describe other data and consequently, the meta data of one application are the data of another application so that meta data can themselves be described by meta data. However, that does not make the latter meta-meta data (see Miller 1999).

Applications of meta data are manifold: They can be used, e.g. for the cataloguing of items in a collection, resource discovery, electronic commerce, intelligent software agents, digital signatures, content rating, intellectual property rights or privacy preferences and policies. With regard to item and collection cataloguing, meta data describe individual resources such as documents, pages, images or audio files. They describe the content of collections that, e.g. contain websites, databases and directories. They further define the relationships among resources which can be found in tables of content and chapters and images in a book, and they can be found, e.g. in site maps (Miller 1999). The *Tasmanian Meta Data Guidelines* add:

> Resource description is essentially about describing information resources using a standard framework or set of principles. A resource can be anything from a web page to a bottle containing the preserved remains of a thylacine, although usually they will either be information documents or public services. Meta data describe information resources so those resources can be found, accessed and used.   (ServiceTasmania Online 2000)

Meta data are most important for the retrieval of particular data so that search engines can (better) parse the contents of a particular page, which results in a more accurate search, as the additional information aids precision. All in all, meta data make it possible to automate searches because less manual "weeding" is needed to process the search results. Within the area of electronic commerce, meta data can be used to encode at all stages required information that pertains to locating a seller or buyer and product. This is often related to searching the yellow pages, to agreeing on terms of sale such as prices, terms of payment, contractual information, and finally to transactions such as delivery mechanisms, dates and terms. With respect to intelligent agents, meta data support the representation and sharing of knowledge for knowledge exchange and modelling, they assist in specific types of communication, i.e. user-to-agent, agent-to-agent, agent-to-service exchanges, and they are essential to resource discovery as they give web-roaming agents the ability to "understand" their environment. Meta data are furthermore an ideal means of generating digital signatures which are the key to building the *Web of Trust*. Signatures are required by agents, electronic commerce and the collaboration of the web users. RDF (resource description framework) is a way to encode digital signatures on documents and on statements about documents. Content rating empowers users to select what kind of web content they wish to see or what kind of web content they do not want others to see, as in child protection. In this context, the W3C PICS (*Platform of Internet Content Selection*) working group in 1996 inaugurated the *US Communications Decency Act* and provided a simple meta data architecture. It was the precursor to RDF. Other applications of meta data include privacy preferences and policies by which the user's willingness or reluctance to disclose information about himself is described as well as a site administrator's desire to gather information about visiting users. Moreover, intellectual property rights such as contractual terms related to usage and distribution rights to a document are accounted for by meta data (Miller 1999).

Meta data records should be quick and easy to create, functional and productive for retrieval purposes and consistent across similar sectors. To create quick and easy meta data records, there are specific recommendations (see ServiceTasmania Online 2000; Dublin Core Metadata Initiative 2002). However, they are not employed for the crisis talk corpus because the main focus is on the annotation of object data. Meta data requirements develop from the fact that the web is machine-readable, but not machine understandable. Unlike the catalogue card and book, however, meta data must be updated when the resource is changed. Some resources may have an expiry date (e.g. election information), others may be added to regularly, while others may rarely change at all. Including administrative meta data in a meta data record will assist in maintaining currency (ServiceTasmania Online 2000).

3.5 Linguistic annotation: Standards and schemata

The term *linguistic annotation* covers any descriptive or analytic notations applied to raw language data. The basic data may be in the form of time functions such as audio, video or physiological recordings. Alternatively, they may be textual. The added meta data (notations) may include trancriptions of every kind, from phonetic features to discourse structures, part-of-speech tagging, sense

tagging, syntactic analysis, *named entity* identification or co-reference annotation. This is the definition that is given, e.g. in Bird & Liberman (1999b: 1).
The EAGLES-guidelines assign the term *annotation* a different twist in that they
conventionally distinguish between *annotation* as opposed to *representation*.
Representation stands for the orthographic transcription of the dialogue and
generally provides basic information about what was said and by whom, either as ASCII text or in a particular mark-up system (e.g. SGML-based TEI see
Burnard (1991), Sperberg-McQueen & Burnard (1994)). The term *annotation*
applies to additional levels of linguistic information such as morphosyntac-
tic, syntactic and semantic levels by which the orthographic transcription is
extended. The EAGLES guidelines make the critical point that for written text
corpora the distinction between *representation* and *annotation* does not pose
a problem; with regard to orthographic transcriptions of spoken dialogue,
though, the representation does not have "the same status of basic representation of the data, being itself a level of linguistic abstraction from the speech
signal" (Gibbon, Mertins, & Moore 2000: 1).

Therefore, the EAGLES guidelines outline the term *transcription* with regard to
representation "in the sense that an orthographic transcription, say, undertakes
to represent, as a verbatim record, what was said by the speakers in a dialogue"
(Gibbon, Mertins, & Moore 2000: 1).

For the creation and annotation of a corpus a markup system is necessary.
Ideally, it is platform-independent and flexible in that it allows the inclusion of
additional elements for special applications. The SGML-subset TEI spoken dialogue transcription guidelines (Sperberg-McQueen & Burnard 1994) promise
to be a suitable starting point. They define a set of generic guidelines for the
representation of textual materials in electronic form (poems, drama, spoken
dialogue), whether as constituents of a research database or components of
non-paper publications. Since the TEI supports loss-free, system-independent
interchange, the TEI-scheme would meet the requirement of independence.
However, crisis talk scenario requirements are more demanding, and the TEI
descriptive elements (Sperberg-McQueen & Burnard 1994: 11) for spoken dialogue transcription are inadequate for crisis talk annotation. A crisis talk
markup system clearly needs considerable flexibility. Specifically, crisis talk
annotation requires detailed syntactic, semantic and pragmatic features (including deixis, anaphora, speech-act identification, disambiguation and sequencing, and theme-rheme relations). The TEI option, ad hoc modification
of the *document type declaration* (DTD), is suboptimal, as it is not easy to
handle. A DTD allows the modelling of textual structures, i.e. modelling information by virtue of strict rules. VERBMOBIL annotation conventions (Gibbon,

Mertins, & Moore 2000) allow annotation of dialogue acts and some semantic-pragmatic properties, but only cover a small range of the required features, and the notation is not standardised.

The *extensible markup language* (XML) is a subset of SGML that describes structures, in particular concrete data structures in the form of tree-graphs. Its advantage over the static SGML-based TEI is that XML is dynamic and hence allows the user to create his own document type declaration. For the present analysis, XML is used to annotate larger sections of corpora and to add special annotations to particular stretches of data. Further processing of the annotated data is possible, e.g. by data conversion, flexible navigation and viewing.

In structuring information, two levels of information units are distinguished: the level of *concrete data*, also called *object language*, and the level of *abstract units*, also called *meta language*. Abstract units assign the concrete data particular functions and categories. They are called *elements* of which the three main types are *data elements, container elements* and *empty elements*. The *data elements* immediately contain the concrete data, the *container elements* contain elements which again can be container elements or data elements, while the *empty elements* have an empty content model, i.e. contain neither data nor elements. They merely mark the occurrence of an information unit (Lobin 2000).

The relation between the two levels of information units and the distinction of meta data and object data can be characterised as follows: while object data pertain to documents, the concrete data are the contents of the documents. And while meta data relate documents to other documents, abstract units relate parts of documents to other parts of the same document. In a rough equation, this can be stated as

Meta data : Object data $\approx$ Abstract units : Concrete data

The hierarchical and sequential ordering of elements is one of the basic principles of XML. The way in which the elements are later to be applied to the document instance is specified by the DTD which may be part of the document instance or contained in a separate file. Each declaration of an element is a rule. They define the information units of an element which can go together. Every element is assigned a name so that it can be uniquely identified. The information units are grouped in a relation to each other that results in a *tree structure* or, put differently, the rules that specify the elements can be summed up as a grammar that describes trees. This is something which makes the mapping into XML particularly suitable for HPSG (see Section 5.4 and Sassen & Gibbon 2002). The nodes of the trees are labels of the type of information that is modelled, i.e. the name of the element, the strings. Furthermore, nodes may provide the concrete data of the information unit. In every tree, every information unit has a place that can be uniquely described by a path.

Attributes integrate additional information into the nodes and form *groups of elements*. They are declared for element types in attribute lists which are also part of the DTD. Every attribute is assigned a name. They allow forming sets of elements which range over several element types. Attributes may be defined as *identifiers* (see also ID/IDREF-mechanisms, Section 4.1). The value of such an attribute may be used in a different place of the tree as a reference to the element it belongs to (see e.g. Lobin 2000; Eckstein 2000; Seeboerger-Weichselbaum 2000).

The different types of information units not only assist in the construction of trees, but they also allow one to determine further processing of the tree: During conversion to a printed version it may be specified that all nodes located beneath the *content* node have a colour different from the nodes above the *content* node.

XML uses an attribute-value archiving and retrieval formalism, and is potentially flexible enough to be suitable for fulfilling crisis talk annotation requirements. For the current analysis, XML attribute-value structures will be formally defined as a denotational semantics for an HPSG-type attribute value description. XML annotation has been criticised for lacking a valid semantics. The problem will be handled by using XML simply as algebra for domain structuring in a semantic document model (see the HPSG-based structure in Sections 3.3 and 5.3) as well as its implementation in Section 5.4). This approach will be applied to the seventy-seven transcripts of the crisis talk corpus. Initially, categories will be developed heuristically during actual annotation and later formulated in HPSG-style constraints. Starting with a basic XML data annotation, and based on the attribute-value description, an extended DTD will be developed and the basic dialogue annotations enhanced semi-automatically (see Sections 4.2–4.3). In a sense, the procedure extends, formalises and operationalises the older TEI proposal to formulate markup in terms of feature structures.

Owing to the multitude of annotated linguistic databases that have been published within the area of speech and language technology development over the past 15 years (e.g. *TIMIT* (Garofalo, Lamel, Fisher, Fiscus, Pallett, & Dahlgren 1986), *DAMSL* (Allen 1997), *PARTITUR*, (Schiel, Burger, Greumann, & Weilhammer 1998), *CHILDES* (MacWhinney & Gillis 1998), *EMU* (Cassidy & Harrinton 2001)), Bird and Liberman propose their *annotation graphs*, which are based on acyclic digraphs. Annotation graphs are a powerful method for representing complex annotation structures incorporating hierarchy and overlap. They provide a formal framework for constructing, maintaining and searching linguistic annotations and do not center on data formats, but on the logical structure of documents. In doing so, Bird and Liberman remain consistent with many alternative data structures and file formats. Their goal is to develop a useful *interlingua* for translation among the wealth of current annotation formats and also to permit the development of new tools with a broad applicability (Bird & Liberman 1999b: 2).

Bird and Liberman's motivation for elaborating a system of annotation graphs lies in their observation of the speech transcription and annotation that is found in many existing *communities of practice*. It is characterised by "commonality of abstract form along with diversity of concrete format" (Bird & Liberman 1999a: 1).

They also note that all annotations of recorded linguistic signals demand the one unavoidable fundamental action of associating a label, or an ordered sequence of labels, with a stretch of time in the recordings. Annotations of this kind usually distinguish labels of different types, e.g. speech sounds from non-speech sounds. The problem with many annotations is that they span different-sized intervals of recorded time, often without setting up a strict hierarchy. Thus they cannot duly represent the components of a conversation that may contain overlapping turns, while the turns may contain interrupted words and the words may contain shared phonetic segments. Bird and Liberman further deplore many types of annotations that are systematically incommensurable with others. Hence, the disfluency structures of, e.g. Jackendoff (1972) and Taylor (1995) frequently cut across conversational turns and syntactic constituents (Bird & Liberman 1999a: 1).

Bird and Liberman propose a minimal formalisation of this basic set of practices in the form of a directed graph whose arcs are labelled with *fielded records* and whose nodes are labelled with optional time references. They define a minimal, but sufficient, set of fields as consisting of the elements *type*, *system* and *class*. *Type* represents a level of an annotation, e.g. the segment, word and discourse levels, while *label* is a property, e.g. a particular word, the name of a speaker or a discourse function, and *class* is an optional field which permits the arcs of an annotation graph to be co-indexed as components of an equivalence class (Bird & Liberman 1999a: 2). Further fields might be added that contain information such as comments, annotator identifications and an update history. Annotation graphs are formalised as follows:

Let T be a set of types, L be a set of labels, and C be a set of classes. Let $R =$ $\{\langle t, l, c \rangle | t \in T, l \in L, c \in C\}$, the set of records over T, L, C. Let N be a set of nodes. Annotation graphs [...] are now defined as follows: [...] An annotation graph G over R, N is a set of triples having the form $\langle n_1, r, n_2 \rangle$, $r \in R$, $n_1, n_2 \in N$, which satisfies the following conditions:

(a) $\langle N, \{\langle n_1, r, n_2 \rangle | \langle n_1, r, n_2 \rangle \in A\} \rangle$ is a labelled acyclic digraph.

(b) $\tau : N \rightarrow \mathfrak{R}$ is an order-preserving map assigning times to (some of) the nodes (Bird & Liberman 1999a: 2).

To illustrate the definition, an example was taken from Bird & Liberman (1999a) which models a dialogue fragment (see Figure 3.4).

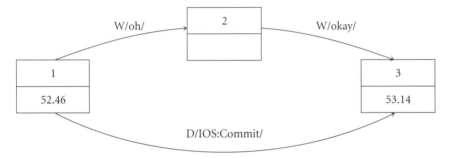

Figure 3.4 An illustration of an annotation graph that models a discourse fragment. Taken from Bird & Liberman (1999a: 2).

For better reading, the components of the fielded records which label the arcs were separated by using the slash symbol. The example consists of two word arcs and, additionally, a discourse tag which encodes *influence on speaker*. There are no class fields used and not all nodes have a time reference. The minimal annotation graph for Figure 3.4 is (see Bird & Liberman 1999a: 2):

$T = W,D$

$L = $ oh, okay, IOS:Commit

$C = \emptyset$

$N = 1, 2, 3$

$\tau = \langle 1, 52.46 \rangle, \langle 3, 53.14 \rangle$

$A = \left\{ \begin{array}{l} \langle\, 1, W/oh/, 2 \rangle, \\ \langle\, 2, W/okay/, 3 \rangle, \\ \langle\, 1, D/IOS:Commit/, 3 \rangle \end{array} \right\}$

Bird and Liberman use XML as a natural *"surface representation"* for their graphs, which to them represents a primary exchange format. Coded in XML, the dialogue fragment looks like this (see Bird & Liberman 1999a: 2):

```
<annotation>
 <arc>
  <begin id=1 time=52.46>
  <label type="W" name="oh">
  <end id=2>
 </arc>
 <arc>
  <begin id=2>
  <label type="W" name="okay">
  <end id=3 time=53.14>
 </arc>
 <arc>
  <begin id=1 time=52.46>
  <label type="D" name="IOS:Commit">
  <end id=3 time=53.14>
 </arc>
</annotation>
```

Considering the proliferation of formats and approaches as a sign of "intellectual ferment" and thus as an indication of how important the computational study of communicative interaction has become, Bird and Liberman claim that their formalism "has sufficient expressive capacity to encode, in a reasonably intuitive way, all the kinds of linguistic annotations in use today" (Bird & Liberman 1999a:1).

According to Bird & Liberman (1999a:1), the minimal formalisation also has good properties with regard to generating annotations and the retrieval of data. Apart from erasing the proliferation of cross-cutting structures, this approach has strong advantages when comparing multiple annotations which represent different purposes and perspectives. Bird and Liberman focus on the structure of annotations regardless of domain-specific concerns about permissible tags, attributes and values, since a translation into annotation graphs does not automatically generate compatibility among systems whose semantics are different. To give an example: There are many ways in which filled pauses are transcribed. Each of these will translate without problems into an annotation graph framework, however, without thereby deleting their semantic incommensurability. Nevertheless, through such an approach it is possible to focus on the substantive differences, and there is no need for taking diverse formats into consideration. Also, it is not necessary to recode annotations in an agreed, common format.

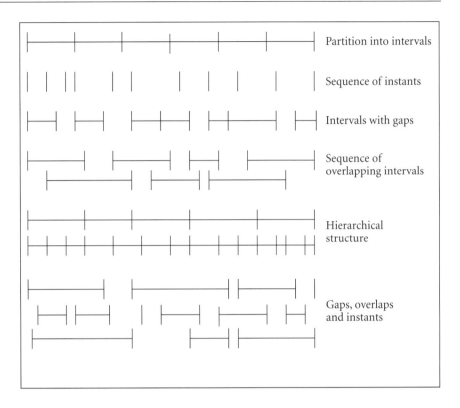

Figure 3.5 Possible structures for a single layer as taken from Bird & Liberman (1999b: 13). The figure has been slightly modified in that not all the lines of their schema were included in this figure. The principles discussed, however, apply.

In Bird & Liberman (1999a) and associated work, Bird & Liberman apply their annotation graphs to a disparate range of annotation. In doing so, they attribute logical sequence, hierarchy and co-indexing to the common and basic actions of associating labels with stretches of recorded signal data (Bird & Liberman 1999a: 9). The possible architectural issues for a single layer as taken from Bird & Liberman (1999b: 13) are visualised in Figure 3.5.

Intervals as periods of time mark the common form of annotated events. They may come in a sequence, in a hierarchy or as parallel structures if multiple nodes coincide the same point of time. Although a linguistic action might have duration, such as the attainment of a pitch target, annotation may be applied to an *instant* rather than an *interval*. The annotation formalisms *EMU*, *FESTIVAL* and *PARTITUR* serve to model instants. The alignment of instants can be investigated or exploited with respect to other instants or intervals. With the model of Bird and Liberman, instants can be treated as arcs between two nodes with the same time reference, or as short periods that are labelled as expressed in Section 5.1 or particular types of labels on periods can be interpreted as referring to the beginning or the culmination of that period (Bird & Liberman 1999b: 13). While an instant, i.e. a point, is represented as a vertical bar, an interval is depicted as a horizontal line between two points (see Figure 3.5).

Annotations are often stratified in that each layer describes a different feature of a signal. In Figure 3.5 several possibilities are diagrammed. Row number one shows a layer, which thoroughly partitions the time flow into a sequence of non-overlapping intervals. These may also be intervals overlapping just at their endpoints. The subsequent row represents a layer of discrete instants. The following two rows depict the notions of *gaps* and *overlaps*. Gaps may correspond to periods of silence or to periods in between the salient events or to periods which have yet to be annotated. Overlaps occur between turns in a dialogue or between adjacent words in a single speech stream. In the fifth row, a hierarchical grouping of intervals within a layer is illustrated. The last row has an arbitrary set of intervals and instants which Bird and Liberman adopt as the most general case for the layer of an annotation. In other words, they do not impose constraints on the structure of a layer. Furthermore, they do not treat layers specially so that they model it as the "collection of arcs having the same type" (Bird & Liberman 1999b: 14).

The principle of annotation graphs is very useful with respect to modelling multiplexed data. The term *multiplex* is defined as the combination of multiple signals (analog or digital) for transmission over a single line or medium (for further information see Webopedia (2002)). As a result, annotation graphs will be taken up in Section 5 with regard to modelling parallel events in aviation communication.

With the principle in mind of keeping every file as close to its original as possible, for an effective XML tagging and later concordancing it is nevertheless indispensible to modify and hence standardise the orthographic ATC/CVR-transcripts, which are quite diverse in their design. The EAGLES guidelines state:

> The key essentials for a good transcription system, [...], are internal consistency of practice in representing [...] and explicit documentation of the practice adopted.   (Gibbon, Mertins, & Moore 2000: 18)

This is the goal of the next chapter. Features will be discussed following the items of the *highest priority recommendations* of the EAGLES guidelines.

Notes

1. Chomsky's method is *reductio ad absurdum*. A formal way to state this is $\vdash (p \rightarrow \neg p) \rightarrow \neg p$, cf. Menne (1986:2.89).

2. To render this rule in parallel to *reductio*, fn. 1, it would have to be stated as $\vdash ((p \rightarrow q) \wedge p) \rightarrow q$, cf. Menne (1986:2.88). While *reductio* is used to disprove the possibility of some proposition, *modus ponens* is used to prove that some proposition follows from another proposition and an appropriate conditional.

3. An enlightening example of regressive deduction in the field of mathematics is the proof of conjectures in mathematics, e.g. Fermat's last theorem. It was a pure conjecture as stated in the 17th century and only proven 350 years later (Aczel 1996).

4. The CONX attribute allows the integration of features such as pragmatic agreement (Pollard & Sag 1994:92–95) and the background conditions that provide linguistically relevant information about the states of affairs of an utterance, e.g. SPEAKER, ADDRESSEE and UTTERANCE-LOCATION (Pollard & Sag 1994:332).

5. *token*: This is a term of multiple meaning. For the present analysis, it is restricted to utterances and signs in general, which uniquely and concretely occur in time and space. By contrast, a *type* is a class to which a token is assigned.

6. The illocutionary point is hence part of the definition of the illocutionary force, i.e. the illocutionary component of the utterance. The point is a finite set of illocutionary classes while there is an infinite set of forces due to the other six elements of definition, where e.g. the strength of degree of the illocutionary point marks an infinite scale of degrees.

7. Probably *propositions* is meant here in the sense of statements. Their classification leaves open some questions, e.g. whether *outcomes* and *facts* should indeed be treated contrastively rather than being regarded as terms denoting the same entity. Further, it is arguable whether *outcomes* and *facts* are the same as *propositions*. A speech act type that leads to a semantic type including temporal information would be conceivable.

8. Such an approach is problematic because it is not always the case that, e.g. directives are imperatives and that imperatives mark directives, as Lascarides (2001) points out.

CHAPTER 4

Analysis of general dialogue properties

ATC/CVR-transcripts (as released by the *Aviation Safety Net*) are purely orthographic. Ideally, they form the verbatim record of the dialogue within the crew and between crew and tower. In the transcripts, there is no information about other levels of discourse, such as the prosodic, syntactic and pragmatic level. Since recordings which underlie the transcripts are with negligible exceptions[1] not available for public or scientific use, their interpretation is problematic, because the transcripts only allow a secondary view of the linguistic and extra-linguistic actions. Detailed phonetic information such as speech velocity, speech pathologies or dialects that would be included in specifying the design of a spoken language corpus was not available for the analysis. Hence, the analysis has to rely on the transcriber's skill and accuracy.

As can be seen from the ATC/CVR-transcripts, the original language of the discourse data was not English throughout. Instead, the speaker's native language had been translated into English without including the original text. The translation can result in error sources because detailed information may have been lost. However, as the present analysis does not concentrate on the syntactic and lexical level, but on discourse structures, translations are not considered a problem under the assumption that the development of the discourse has not been changed by transcribers. Such an awareness notwithstanding, it would be more adequate from a linguistic point of view to apply the powerful instrument of HPSG-analysis to the original data.

According to the keys of the transcripts and by comparing transcripts of different origin it becomes obvious that some of them went through a process of censorship: Strings of taboo words were replaced with symbols which mark an *expletive deleted* or *non-pertinent* text. Sometimes longer stretches of discourse that did not contain any taboo epithets were substituted by the symbol for *non-pertinent* text. In other cases, transcribers found stretches of the crew's utterances unintelligible, while others did not face problems like these.[2] In this context, all transcripts taken from Aviation Safety Network (2000a) were prefixed by the warning:

> The reader of these transcripts is cautioned that the transcription of a CVR tape is not a precise science but is the best possible product from a group investigative effort. The transcript, or parts thereof, if taken out of context can be misleading. Therefore, the CVR transcripts should only be viewed as an investigative tool to be used in conjunction with other evidence. Conclusions or interpretations should not be made using the transcript as the sole source of information.   (Aviation Safety Network 2000a)

In modern language technology an orthographic transcription is no more a useful and desirable substitute for the actual sound recording, which is nowadays assumed to be available along with the transcripts of a spoken language corpus. According to Gibbon, Mertins, & Moore (2000:1), users of the transcription traditionally derived from it the wording and sense of the acoustic message.

> [...] it is assumed, with modern technological progress, that all users of a spoken language corpus will have ready access to the sound recording, which can therefore be regarded as the basic record of any spoken language data.
>   (Gibbon, Mertins, & Moore 2000:1)

Since all enquiries to access the original recordings for re-evaluation of the transcripts have been rejected, it is an unfortunate truth for the user of the ATC/CVR-corpus that

> from the point of view of speech analysis, an orthographic transcription is more remarkable for what it excludes than for what it includes.
>   (Gibbon, Mertins, & Moore 2000:1)

Consequently, to find out what kind of information is missing from the ATC/CVR-corpus' access to the sound files would be necessary. However, as more recent transcripts show, considerable energy seems to have been put into a precise and conscientious way of transcribing, which can be assumed from the various linguistic parameters (notably discourse particles) and the description (though not precise annotation) of paralinguistic parameters (e.g. loudness and velocity) integrated in the transcript. Most of these transcripts display a list of parameters that matches the EAGLES recommendations (also called EAGLES guidelines. However precise the transcripts may be, the unavailability of aviation recording data should be made explicit.

In the context of the ATC/CVR-corpus, the transcripts keep their status of *observational primacy*, which they would lose if there was ready access to the sound recordings. Furthermore, the orthographic transcription is – according to the EAGLES guidelines – the *primary level of abstraction* from the sound data "involving as little interpretation as possible" (Gibbon, Mertins, & Moore 2000: 1).

4.1 Dialogue typology

A dialogue typology serves to elaborate categories that will characterise the domain of aviation communication. The information gained in this section will partly be integrated into the HPSG-based structure introduced in Section 3.3 to make explicit contextual features concomitant with the respective token under discussion (see Section 5). The catalogue of properties as given in Section 4.2 is the result of the application of the EAGLES guidelines list to the data. Whenever appropriate, a label for the EAGLES class-identification is given. The classification proposed refers to *external* and *internal* criteria that are based on Dell Hymes' grid on the *components of speech* and *rules of speaking* (Hymes & Gumperz 1972). External criteria include situational and motivational factors, whereas internal criteria relate to formal or structural factors that allow a deeper insight into the components of dialogue such as *turns* and *dialogue acts* (Gibbon, Mertins, & Moore 2000: 6). The pertinent keywords as taken from the guidelines are set in italics.

While much research has been dedicated to dyadic dialogues (see Gibbon, Mertins, & Moore 2000: 7 about language engineering), ATC/CVR-data display exchanges that range from two to eight participants. The *number of participants* depends on the completeness of the transcript, i.e. whether intra- and extra-cockpit communication are available, and on the age of the airplane. In modern aviation, intra-cockpit communication usually takes place between captain and copilot (EAGLES A.1), whereas in older airplanes, such as the DC-10, the crew additionally consisted of first officer and an engineer (EAGLES A.2). With the disaster of SAS Flight 751 (1991), the number of participants even added up to eight because the voices of flight attendants were also recorded. Extra-cockpit communication usually takes place between captain or copilot and controller. Only in a few transcripts had the radio communication of other airplanes been included. In many transcripts, the two sorts of communication have been combined. ATC/CVR-data have to be assigned to the EAGLES category A.1 *more than two participants.*

Some of the difficulties stated in the EAGLES guidelines for dialogues of more than two participants may indeed occur in the present corpus; viz. with a growing number of participants the number of overlaps increases. This is true at least to a small extent of ATC/CVR where technical communication is subject to strict rules that may sometimes deviate from these rules. Overlap does not pose a problem for the current project, since it can be represented by annotation graphs proposed by Bird & Liberman (1999b). Moreover, modern variants of XML capture simultaneous events by means of ID/IDREF-mechanisms. Through an ID-attribute an identifier is defined for the element that contains this attribute. One can refer to this identifier by an IDREF-attribute of another element.

With regard to EAGLES' *task orientation*, the instances of ATC/CVR communication are *task driven* (B.1): Normally there is one specific task which at least one of the participants intends to accomplish with the support of the others.[3] In ATC/CVR, this is to secure uptake with the concomitant goal of preventing an aviation disaster (e.g. B.1.6.1). Tasks may informally be defined with regard to the intentions of participants, illocutionary functions of their utterances or by the end state which relates to the successful completion of the task Gibbon, Mertins, & Moore 2000:9; see also Mc Kevitt, Partridge, & Wilks 1992). The above classification follows the criterium of intentions. Gibbon, Mertins, & Moore (2000) judge the set of *task-attributes* as open-ended and hence the task to design a closed set futile.

Within the framework of *applications orientation*, most task-oriented communication fulfills a purpose that has *direct commercial* or *industrial applications* (Gibbon, Mertins, & Moore 2000:7). A concrete application can be stated for ATC/CVR-data, since an effective flow of intra- and extra-cockpit communication is considered to be essential for a successful flight. Thus, it is important for keeping the cost of commercial and non-commercial airlines as low as possible (C.1). The ATC/CVR instances are restricted to a *relatively tightly-defined domain of subject-matter* (D.1). The overall subject of ATC/CVR is D.1.1 *travel* or D.1.2 *transport* with the subclassification *air travel*. The parameters of *task* and *domain* are kept apart as a matter of sound practice (Gibbon, Mertins, & Moore 2000). If a dialogue system has to be set up for a particular application, a combination of the two parameters is necessary to specify that system. The separation of task and domain is especially useful in creating a typology of dialogues and dialogue acts, as it enables generalisations across an indefinite number of different tasks and domains that are to be integrated in the typology and in the construction of "suitably generic dialogue system software" (Gibbon, Mertins, & Moore 2000:9).

Activity types is another way of defining the category of dialogue. In a given case this is done with regard to the constraints on the dialogue roles adopted by the participants. Usually, ATC/CVR-communication has to be classified as E.1 *cooperative negotiation* in the case of *non-crisis talk*. Whenever crisis talk is at play, *problem solving* (E.3) applies to ATC/CVR. In some cases, intra-cockpit communication in particular may also fall into the category E.4 *teaching/instruction* with *teacher* and *pupil* in the instance of the crash at Nagoya, and *instructor* and *instructee*[4] as general terms for any technical stretch of discourse that relates to a flight situation with full professionals. As far as leaky points are concerned, E.6 *chatting* would also apply here.

With respect to EAGLES' *human/machine participation*, aviation communication applies to F.2 *human-human dialogue*. Due to its radio channel, extra-cockpit communication applies to category F.2.1 because of its *machine-mediated* elements, and intra-cockpit communication, which uses a face-to-face channel, refers to category F.2.2, as it displays *non-machine-mediated* elements. Thus, in an annotation of the meta data, the general dialogue type in this category is F.2.

The term *scenario* refers to any *practical conditions and attendant circumstances* which influence corpus collection. To note these conditions is important for the evaluation of the corpus "as a basis for further research and development" (Gibbon, Mertins, & Moore 2000: 10). With regard to G.1 *speaker characteristics*, they are often stored in a speaker database and relate to information such as age, gender, native language(s), geographical provenance and degree of training with regard to the communication medium or the degree of acquaintance among the participants. ATC/CVR-data are probably as diverse as its instances: At the present stage not much is known about the participants. The same goes for G.2 *channel characteristics*: in ATC/CVR-recordings, the original data were auditive. Later it was re-represented as an orthographic transcript. G.2 would also include aspects of technical problems on the channels, such as radio problems (noise) in extra-cockpit communication (see Section 1.2).

The dialogue types elaborated here will not be expressed in the form of meta data because the present analysis centers on the object data of the corpus. It would not be difficult to create meta data tags for the header. A paradigm model of meta data tags is the form in which they are annotated in HTML documents. It is only necessary to define an element META with the attributes NAME and CONTENT in which NAME can take the value EAGLES and CONTENT the possibly underspecified set of classifications of dialogue types. For example: <META NAME="eagles" CONTENT="A.2,B.1,C.1,D.1">. This would be the meta data for a crisis talk scenario with more than two participants, while nothing is said about its status, i.e. whether it is a teaching or instruction situation.

4.2 Documenting and standardising the ATC/CVR-DATA

Another recommendation in the EAGLES guidelines is to generate a common format for the orthographic representation of dialogue so as to make exchange purposes and automatic processing of the data as effective as possible. The ATC/CVR-transcripts available leave a common format a feature to be desired. A standardisation of the diverse orthographic transcripts and the way in which this goal can be attained is the topic of this section. The question will be discussed as to what extent the EAGLES guidelines can be said to apply to the source transcripts, since the ATC/CVR-transcripts do not vary so much in their basic text units. They show, however, considerable diversity in the presence, absence and encoding of the meta-information that was added to the verbatim record by the transcribers. To document this state of affairs the latent markup must be declared and explained for every transcript file. To put it succinctly, most of the transcripts contain a subset of the information that is suggested by EAGLES, yet they require an extension. This goes for the feature *translation*, which is not included in the EAGLES guidelines, and the *footer* (cf. Table 4.1), for a comparison of the EAGLES recommendations with the inventory required for the description of ATC/CVR-transcripts. To include a translation in the transcript or to replace the transcript with a translation is recommended, in order to remain as close as possible to the original data. By contrast, distributing information between header and footer or keeping everything together in the header is a question of how to organise a corpus economically. In any case, either feature can be found in the source transcripts and, hence, has to be accounted for.

The analysis will focus separately on the header of the transcripts and the transcribed body of object data. A brief remark on the footer of the files will also be included. This procedure will help generate categories for an efficient XML tagging.

The EAGLES guidelines offer valuable information on the categories that could be used for an orthographic transcription. However, essentially these are rec-

Table 4.1 A comparison of the EAGLES-recommendations with the inventory required for the description of ATC/CVR-transcripts.

EAGLES guidelines	Present analysis
Header requirements	
Body requirements	Body requirements + translation
——	Footer requirements

ommendations to be employed for an *a priori* organisation of the transcript. In the context of the present analysis, the orthographic transcription, which is a documentation of a text, has to be documented. Hence, the present corpus design is an *a posteriori* description of the organisation of a text, and the EAGLES recommendations[5] suggest parameters for the transcripts. So the latent markup is categorised and described and checked against the list of the EAGLES recommendations, which will be used as a standard for the encoding of particular meta-information. In each section, principled modifications that are necessary to achieve standardisation will be discussed.

Header of the ATC/CVR-DATA

A primary way of documenting information about texts can be attained by means of a structured header within the document containing the text itself. Every single transcript of the ATC/CVR-corpus has an in-text header, i.e. a preamble within the same file which contains information about the transcribed recording. Most of the files fulfill the bare minimum recommended by EAGLES; i.e. they include an identifier for the specific text and basic information on the speakers.[6] In most files the speaker characteristics are given in the form of a key that explains abbreviations which in turn define particular aviation roles and, in this way, the number of participants. Further data, which are supplied in the headers, are discussed below. The order of the list conforms with EAGLES recommendations. Keywords that are subsumed under specific headings are printed in italics.

Speaker characteristics
Information on the *number of participants* can only be inferred from the key of the transcript, since no header offers an explicit number. As goes for individual speaker attributes, the participants' *aviation roles* have been included in the key. Sometimes the header announces that particular text portions were translated from language X into English. Thus, the *native language* can be inferred but the header does not specify exactly who speaks which language as his mother tongue. For an instantiation of making inferences about the number of participants and their native languages see Example (7) which displays the header of the CVR-transcript of Air Algérie:

(7)   CVR transcript Air Algerie / Phoenix Flight 702P - 21 DEC
      1994 (...) Accident description (...) COV = Coventry ATC
      P1 = Captain

```
P2 = First Officer
702P = Radio contact with Coventry
Words spoken in French or Arabic are in Italic letters
```

The EAGLES guidelines also mention features such as *age* and *regional accents* on which no header of the ATC/CVR-transcripts comments. In a few cases, the sex of a person is given in the way it is done in Example (8), which displays an extract from a key.

(8)   CVR transcript Air Canada Flight 797 - 02 JUN 1983 (19)
      CAM = Cockpit Area Mike voice or sound source
      RDO = Radio Communications
      -1 = Voice identified as Captain
      -2 = Voice identified as First Officer
      -3 = Voice identified as male flight attendant ←
      -4 = Voice identified as female flight attendant ←
      -5 = Voice identified as male passenger ←

With regard to standardisation, if there was no identification of speakers these data have been reconstructed either from the abbreviations and the dialogue data in the body, or from accompanying files documenting the air disaster. Wherever possible, further information has been compiled on the individual speakers; this is not an easy task, however, since most of the data are not accessible for reasons of data protection.

Channel characteristics
Information on the *channels in use* can be inferred from the terms ATC-transcript, which pertains to extra-cockpit communication and requires the use of radio, and to CVR-transcript, which pertains to intra-cockpit communication and requires the channel of airwaves. Frequently, transcribers used the abbreviation *RDO* for radio and so explicitly state the channel in use. Wherever possible, further information has been gathered on recording details. Sources are files concomitant with the ATC/CVR-transcript. Where *recording details* are concerned, the *date* of the recording is mentioned in the header, as are *technical specifications* which often do not go beyond the name of the type of the airplane. *Time* in the transcripts refers to the time line which is applied to the text body. The key sometimes defines the time scale employed, e.g. *CST* for Central Standard Time. Wherever possible, further information has been gathered on recording details. Sources are files concomitant with the ATC/CVR-transcript.

General environmental conditions

With regard to *contextual information*, again, channel-defining terms such as ATC or CVR or the type name of the aeroplane specify the location *where the dialogues took place*. The *physical conditions* under which the dialogues were produced are generally treated in the header and by terms such as *crash, accident* or *collision* (see Examples (9) and (10), where arrows mark the line of the defining key-word), but a more precise characterisation becomes obvious from the text body.

(9)   CVR transcript United Express Flight 5925 - 19 NOV 1996 (65)
      Cockpit voice recorder transcription of the November 19,
      1996 <-
      collision at Quincy between a United Express Beechcraft 1900
      (Flight 5925) and a Beech King Air.

(10) CVR transcript Airborne Express Flight 827 (66)
      Cockpit voice recorder transcript of the December 22, 1996
      crash <-
      of an Airborne Express DC-8, Flight 827 at White River Moun-
      tain (USA).

Whenever further data could be found in the web source documentation files, they have been integrated in the corresponding transcript file. The key implicitly determines that the dialogue is *human*, in other words the communication takes place between human beings not between man and machine. As a result, the alternative features *machine* and *simulated* offered by the EAGLES guidelines do not apply here. The aspect of *matters under discussion (domain/task)* is indicated by the text identifier or the title, as illustrated by Example (11):

(11) ATC transcript Alitalia Flight 771 - 06 JUL 1962 (1)
      Air Traffic Control transcription of the July 6, 1962 crash
      of an Alitalia DC-8 (Flight 771) near Junnar, India.

In most cases, *details of the orthographic transcription* are supplied in the key. This information embraces the indication of unintelligible strings or doubtful readings of the recording as exemplified by the key of the CVR-transcript ValuJet Flight 592 below:

(12) CVR transcript ValuJet Flight 592 - 11 MAY 1996 (56)
      (...)
      Key:
      (...)
      Unintelligible word

```
@ Non pertinent word
# Expletive
( ) Questionable insertion
```

Activity type, degree of spontaneity and *details of levels of linguistic annotation* are types of information that belong to categories that are not mentioned in the header of the ATC/CVR-transcripts. *Copyright information* is sometimes supplied in the header, but mainly in the footer. *Source information* has sometimes been given for the transcripts, i.e. the document was named from which the transcript was taken by the compilers of the data, as displayed by Examples (13) and (14):

(13) CVR transcript Air France Flight 296Q - 26 JUN 1988 (27)
      Source: Final report concerning the accident which occurred
      on June 26th 1988 at Mulhouse-Habsheim (68) to the Airbus
      A320, registered F-GFKC/Ministry of Planning, Housing,
      Transport and Maritime Affairs

(14) CVR transcript United Express Flight 5925 - 19 NOV 1996 (65)
      This Cockpit Voice Recorder transcription was put together,
      using two sources: #- the Quincy Herald-Whig article "The Fi-
      nal 9 Minutes of UE Flight 5925" by #Kelly Wilson, published
      on the WWW at http://www.cis.net/~whig/Final.html (...)

Additional data have been included that pertain to *contact details for additional information* and *source information* which are available from additional files of the web source.

All further retrievable information has been included in the key. In each case, it has been enriched by an additional comment on the key as shown by Example (15):

(15) first column: transcriber's abbreviation, second column:
      explanation of abbreviation, third column: abbreviation used
      for this corpus. Parentheses mark expressions not included
      in the original key, but in the transcript. Square brackets
      mark new expressions.

Here the use of columns and brackets is explained. Further information about the key has been given under the heading of *speaker attribution*. Another text explains the organisation of the body, as illustrated by Example (16):

(16) `Transcript: first column: source of turn + turn number, time`
      `line, second column: transcribed recording`

Transcript-specific information has been added wherever necessary. To separate the header from the body for processing purposes, a hash-sign "#" has been added to the beginning of every line of the header.

Footer of the ATC/CVR-DATA

Footers have been marked consistently by the transcribers throughout the corpus. Like the headers, they have been separated in the standardisation process from the body by a hash-sign at the beginning of every line. An ascii-version of the corpus that contains comments and extra-information such as radio frequencies along with the raw transcript data is kept. This also goes for the raw transcript data ready for XML-annotation and also for an application to the KWIC-concordance program. Every modification of data is documented by the XML-annotation.

Body of the ATC/CVR-DATA

The most common text units in dialogue corpora are the *text*, and this is the same with the basic units of the ATC/CVR-transcripts. *Text* refers to self-contained dialogues, sometimes dialogue samples often with an editorial beginning and throughout all files with a technical end. The term *technical* is meant as an alternative to the EAGLES guidelines, which propose the term *natural* end, since the ATC/CVR-dialogues are terminated by the crash of the plane and/or the destruction of the recording device in the black box. Moreover, the *turn* (also called *contribution*) together with the "intuitively identified 'orthographic sentence'" (cf. Gibbon, Mertins, & Moore 2000:14) are regarded as basic text units. The *orthographic sentence* is a unit delimited by conventional written punctuation and has more of an artefact of transcription than of a real observable unit. In a narrow sense, the turn is a basic unit of spoken dialogue transcription, while the orthographic sentence is, "as a unit of written language, merely a convenient impressionistic unit providing useful preliminary heuristic input to other levels of annotation" (Gibbon, Mertins, & Moore 2000:14).

This unit features prominently, however, in the ATC/CVR-transcripts. It seems the transcribers considered the sentence to be the basic unit of spoken dialogue transcription, and this will therefore be taken into account in the tagging process.

Reference system

A *reference system* is "a set of codes that allow reference to be made to specific texts and locations in texts" (Gibbon, Mertins, & Moore 2000:14). Most ATC/CVR-transcripts have a reference system, as they are *time-aligned*. Time points can be used to refer to specific locations in the dialogue. In all cases, they occur in the left-most column of the transcribed text. While some offer a time line that labels every turn (Example (17)), others have gaps, and it is hard to find consistency in them (Example (18)).

(17)   CVR transcript United Air Lines Flight 553 - 08 DEC 1972 (9)
       APP000: 20:25:25:0 Five five three, call the tower on one
       eighteen seven
       RFO001: 20:25:28:0 Eighteen seven, five five three
       RFO002: 20:25:35:5 Midway tower, United five five three, an'
       we'r out of three for two

(18)   CVR transcript Piedmont Flight 230 - 10 AUG 1968 (6)
       08.55:00 PIC Well, looks like our altimeters were within
       reason
       COP Yeah
       PIC Yeah, I like that altimeter
       COP Boy, you know it - reads right about the middle marker
       there
       PIC Yeah
       COP I always watch that radio altimeter.
       08.55:35.3 PIC I go by this one on a field like this close
       one
       COP Yeah

Some files contained more detailed information than others. For example, File 2 (MAS Flight 511, 1964)[7] was precise about the radio frequency of the communication, about sender and addressee of messages, and provided an identification of every single turn. File 1 (Alitalia Flight 771, 1962), by contrast, did not provide any of the information quoted above and limited itself to the messages only. Fortunately, the latter case only occurred once, presumably as it was one of the earliest CVRs ever released, so conventions about notation had probably not yet been transparent or developed. Other rare cases did not have a time line (e.g. File 30 (Surinam Airways Flight 764, 1989)) and some lack a key (e.g. File 10 (Eastern Airlines Flight 401, 1972)), so the meaning of abbreviations had to be inferred from context. With a decreasing degree of completeness the preciseness of reference declines. For this reason, the time line cannot be used as a turn identification code, not even with the complete time lines, because this would make a standardised reference system impossible.

Every transcript has a *speaker attribution* which is indicated either by a letter code (usually role abbreviations, (Example (19)) or assignments of particular cockpit area microphones (Example (20)) or the name of the speaker's role, (Example (21)) fully spelt out). However, the speakers' proper names are never used. Rarely does the speaker attribution make a general reference to groups, i.e. the crew or the tower (Example (21)). The groups are usually assigned a numerical code that repeats the flight number, for instance. The speaker attribution is always without a markup delimiting notation; it can always be found on the left hand side of the transcribed recording (the object data). With bodies that have a time line, the speaker attribution is mainly in the central column (Example (20)–(21)), and in rare cases in the left-most column (Example (22)).

(19)　Air Canada Flight 621 - 5 JUL 1970
　　　Source Content
　　　CA Thirty-five flap
　　　FO Thirty-five

(20)　CVR transcript TWA Flight 159 - 06 NOV 1967
　　　23.40:15 CAM-1 See that fire in the end?
　　　23.40:15.5 CAM-?
　　　23.40:16.5 CAM-2

(21)　CVR transcript Air France Flight 296Q - 26 JUN 1988
　　　Time: Source: Contents:
　　　12.44:27 TOWER QNH Habsheim 1012 Fox Echo 9.8.4
　　　　　　 Captain OK
　　　12.44:31 Co-pilot Roger

(22)　ATC transcript Swissair Flight 111 - 02 SEP 1998
　　　Source: UTC RADIO COMMUNICATIONS
　　　SWR111 0:58:15.8 Moncton Centre, Swissair one eleven heavy
　　　good uh evening level three three zero.
　　　QM 0:58:20.4 Swissair one eleven heavy Moncton Centre. Good
　　　evening

Instances such as Example (20) in which the transcriber was not sure who was speaking are normally explicitly indicated. One of the most important and difficult issues in dialogue transcription, *speaker overlap*, i.e. "synchronous speech by more than one participant in the dialogue" (Gibbon, Mertins, & Moore 2000: 16), has only been indicated in Examples (24) and (27). While Example (23) is to some degree precise about which turns overlap, in Example (24), it is not clear at all which turns or even which parts of turns occur together. The problem is that neither beginning nor end of overlap are unequivocally determined:

> (23) CVR transcript Japan Air Lines Flight 46E - 31 MAR 1993 (41)
> 1225:30 04:14 JA42 cleared for takeoff, Japan Air forty two
> Echo heavy.
> 1225:32 04:16 CAM-3 ***** ((simultaneous with previous <-
> transmission)) after you get passed the red line. OK? - you
> gotta' get your priorities right.

> (24) CVR TRANSCRIPT China Airlines Airbus A300 at Nagoya (Japan),
> 26 April, 1994 (48)
> 49'22" F/O: NAGOYA CITY IN SIGHT, SIR.
> (OVERLAP) CAP: WOW! THE WEATHER IS EXCELLENT. <-
> HOW NICE IF (NAME OF PERSON) WERE HERE.
> F/O: HA, HA.

With regard to the layout of the transcript, overlap might occur in the utterances *Nagoya City in sight, Sir* and *Wow! The weather is excellent*, because the two are ordered in a vertical alignment, whereas the utterance *How nice if (...) were here*, which belongs to the same turn, was placed in a new line. For the standardisation, the speaker attribution has been allocated for every file in the left-most column. This task has been accomplished semi-automatically. A fully automatised solution is not possible because of the notational diversities of the different files. In line with the VERBMOBIL notation (Kohler 1994), the speaker attribution code has been changed to three letters and combined with a string of three further digits to supply a turn number. The turn numbers are used to recover gaps in the time alignment. A three-letter-code for the speaker attribution means that the speaker labels, which vary greatly, are substituted and made as consistent as possible. The goal is, however, to keep the basic role specifications assigned to the speakers: most transcribers labelled the speaker roles on the *responsibility level*, as it could be called, while the pairs *captain vs. first officer* and *pilot in command vs. copilot* apply. *Captain* in this context is parallel with *pilot in command*, and *first officer* with *copilot*.

With regard to abbreviating or encoding roles, variants can be confusing and make retrieval difficult. The role *captain* could be found abbreviated as *Capt* or *CAP* or *CAM-1* if the speaker assignment was conducted via the different cockpit area microphones, whereas *CAM-2* normally stands for *First Officer* and *CAM-3* for *Second Officer*.
The substitutions and changes have been documented in the key of each transcript as shown in Example (25):

```
(25)  CVR transcript Air Canada Flight 797 - 02 JUN 1983 (19)
      Key:

      ...

      CAM = Cockpit Area Mike voice or sound source == C-
      RDO = Radio Communications == R-
      -1 = Voice identified as Captain == -CP
      -2 = Voice identified as First Officer == -FO
      -3 = Voice identified as male flight attendant == -MA
      -4 = Voice identified as female flight attendant == -FA
      -5 = Voice identified as male passenger == -MP
      CTR = Indianapolis Center == CTR
```

In the key, the left-most column offers the code that the transcribers used for their speaker attribution. The code is spelled out in the central column, while the right-most column contains the new code that has been included for the purpose of standardisation. The standard length of the labels is three digits. A distinction has been made between *radio communications* with the basic initial letter *R*, with the dashes marking slots for the remaining two digits, and *cockpit area microphone voice* with the basic initial letter *C*. The slot for the remaining digits has been filled with one of the following two digits. *Captain* has basically been encoded as *CP* and, if he communicated via radio, the encoding has been extended to *RCP*, for intra-cockpit communication to *CCP*. Analogous extensions have been made with the other roles of the crew. The encoding has been designed to be as close as possible to the originial role names so that the levels of general roles, responsibility and functions can be preserved and are of a mnemonic quality (see Example (26)).

```
(26)  CAM000_18:48:12: [Sound similar to arcing]
      CAM001_18:48:15: [Sound similar to arcing]
      CAM002_18:51:03: [Two sounds similar to arcing]
      CCP003_18:51:04: How is your sea food, nice?
      CAM004_ [Sounds similar to arcing and snapping]
      CFO005_ It's good
```

```
CCP006_ * steak nice?
CFO007_18:51:09: Different, a little bit dry but okay
CAM008_18:51:14: [Sounds similar to arcing and snapping]
CFO009_ (What was that?)
CCP010_ #
CFO011_18:51:19: It's right here, I see it
CCP012_ Yeah
CCP013_ DC bus
CFO014_ Which one is that?
```

The components of the body will be organised in two columns: annotations of the transcribed text are located in the left column. These contain at least the speaker attribution combined with a turn reference that counts from *000* onwards. At most, the annotations may comprise one or more time lines and radio frequency. The minimal and maximal components of the left column are interlinked by an underscore and terminated by a colon. The right column contains the transcribed text of the recording. The speaker attribution of File 1 (Alitalia Flight 771, 1962) was missing and had to be completely reconstructed.

Word form

With most corpora, ATC/CVR-transcripts have in common that their transcribers use the standard (or dictionary) forms of words, regardless of their actual pronunciation. A procedure like this has the advantage that annotation and retrieval tools may be applied relatively unproblematically to speech as well as to writing (see Gibbon, Mertins, & Moore (2000)).

While in most corpora everything including numbers is typically written out in full, some transcribers use ciphers for numbers and others substitute them by a string of words. In particular, in the case of aviation disasters that are caused by linguistic problems, it would be important to distinguish different ways of pronouncing and representing the same numeral: In English there are different ways of saying the numerals of the accident flight *USAir 427*: either *four hundred twenty-seven* or *four two seven* (in the style of a telephone number), where in the latter case, it would be most interesting to determine whether the cipher *4* (phonology /fo/) had the phonetic realisation [fo:], [for], [faʊə], [faʊ'ər], or the like. The fourth alternative would perfectly meet the requirements of aviation language because this pronunciation has deliberately been determined as obligatory in order to avoid misunderstandings (see Federal Aviation Administration (2000b)). However, some pilots may not be aware of the obligatory pronunciation, owing to an inadequate training schedule or simply have forgotten about it, which means another error source (see Section 1.2).

At the stage of an orthographic transcription, some few corpora include prosodic information in the form of a brief description; this is deplorable, since prosody would be of great interest for the analysis of ATC/CVR-transcripts. Most transcribers used common merges and contractions for their orthographic representation, as displayed in Example (27):

(27)   CVR transcript USAir Flight 427 - 08 SEP 1994 (50)
       CAM-2: That sun is gonna be just like it was takin' off in
       Cleveland yesterday, too. I'm just gonna close my eyes.
       [Sound of laughter]. You holler when it looks like we're
       close. [Sound of laughter]

In other cases, dictionary forms are used, e.g. *going to* for *gonna*. Apparently, the dictionary forms have not been regarded as an authentic representative of the spoken dialogue. The EAGLES recommendations also discuss features including the transcription of compound words, the documentation of expressions that have no true dictionary form, and spelling variations. Within the framework of the current analysis, these aspects will not be taken into account because the analysis will not cover lexical or morphological aspects.

Further items that are treated under the heading of *word form* are *word fragments, orthography including punctuation, unintelligible speech, uncertain transcription* and *substitutions*.

It has not been possible to standardise merges and other special word forms, since the underlying recordings have not been available. Hence there is no way to verify whether some transcribers turned merges and contractions into dictionary forms or whether they were genuine. *Word fragments*, also known as *unfinished* or *truncated* words, occur in the transcripts that were released after 1977. Earlier ones do not show any sign of verbal truncation. It seems reasonable that in the course of time transcribing techniques have become more precise because of increased consciousness of the necessity to be as close as possible to the original data. In the transcripts available, word-initial or word-final incompleteness had been marked by a dash (Examples (28) and (29)). There were also examples of truncation which were usually indicated by a string of three dots, as in Example (30). It does not become clear, though, whether unintelligible strings and/or pauses were marked by the same code. In Examples (28)–(30) below, truncation seems to have been produced by the speakers themselves and represented by the transcribers as such.

(28) CVR transcript KLM Flight 4805 and Pan Am Flight 1736 colli-
      sion - 27 MAR 1977 (12)
      1702:20.6 APP -ird one to your left. <-

(29) CVR transcript Delta Flight 191 - 02 AUG 1985 (22)
      18.03:31 APP And we're getting some variable winds out there
      due to a sh- shower on short <-
      out there north end of DFW

(30) CVR transcript Japan Air Lines Flight 123 - 12 AUG 1985 (23)
      18:31:35 FE: What? more aft...ah...What was damaged? <-
      Where? ah...ah...ah... ah... Coat room? for rear-most, is it
      not? Understood. Ah... Coat room...general... It dropped in
      baggage space. It would be better to land.

With Example ((31)), it cannot be determined whether the speaker did indeed
not pronounce the complete word of the truncation *Sh...* (Line 12.45:39.9) or
whether this is the result of censoring an interlocutor's name or the expletive
shit. In the final phase of intra-cockpit dialogues, when the situation is usually most perilous, the crew has the tendency to use expletives; thus the latter
interpretation could be preferred. With regard to the transcription, the truncation mark of dots can easily be confused with probable deletions made by the
transcriber.

(31) CVR transcript Air France Flight 296Q - 26 JUN 1988 (27)
      12.45:39.9 Captain Sh...!

Another option is to interpret the truncation as marking a repair (see for more
information on repair Section 4.5):

> [...], word fragments may also at times serve a communicative function, in-
> dicating that the speaker has changed his/her mind about what to say next or
> how to interpret something, and expanding them may thus lead to misinter-
> pretation.   (Gibbon, Mertins, & Moore 2000: 19)

To clarify the correct reading of Line 12.45:39.9 would require access to the
original recording.

Orthography, including punctuation

With respect to the more general form of transcription, the EAGLES guidelines
judge both normal and desirable the use of a basic canonical subset of the standard orthography. For the ATC/CVR-transcripts a main type crystallises which
accords with the transcription habits of most corpora: normal capitalisation

with sentence-inital capitals and the use of full stops and other punctuation marks (Examples (32) and (34)). Other types may omit sentence-initial capitals, with otherwise normal capitalisation, and either they completely omit sentence-final punctuation or they do not have full-stops but question marks and exclamation marks (Example (33)). Commas are present in every type of transcript. Two exceptional transcripts are in capital letters throughout (see Example (24)). Standard orthography of this sort is interpretative when applied to speech but it has the advantage of improving readability for the human user and of increasing processibility for taggers and parsers.

(32) CVR transcript Lauda Air Flight 004 - 26 MAY 1991 (34)
      23.24:36 CA: OK.
      23.25:19 FO: Shall I ask the ground staff?
      23.25:22 CA: What's that?

(33) CVR transcript GP Express Airlines Flight 861 - 08 JUN 1992
      (38)
      0845:00 INT-2 five hundred to go.
      0845:13 INT-2 geese Louise.
      0845:15 INT-1 this is fun.
      0845:21 INT-1 in-range call's complete?

(34) CVR transcript Lufthansa Flight 2904 - 14 SEP 1993 (44)
      15.34:11 PNF Dreh'n weg (turn it away)
      15.34:12 PF Was? (Hey?)
      PNF Dreh ihn weg (turn it away)
      15.34:16 PF Scheisse! (shit!)

The EAGLES guidelines require of any punctuation scheme that it be explained in the text documentation. This requirement has not been met by any header of the ATC/CVR-transcripts (Gibbon, Mertins, & Moore 2000: 19–20).

Files 48 (China Airlines Airbus A300, 1994) and 62 (AeroPeru B757, 1996) differ from others in their constant capital lettering. The format has been kept, since it does not complicate concordancing as long as non-case-sensitive retrieval is executed. Orthographic errors have remained untouched unless they could unequivocally be identified as typographic errors. If errors occurred in the transcribed spoken text, they remained untouched without exception, as it could not be determined whether they resulted from a typographic error or from the transcription of a word that deviated from its normal pronunciation.

Unintelligible speech

Owing to noise during the recording, it is sometimes impossible to tell what a participant is saying. Obviously, this problem occurred frequently during transcription of the ATC/CVR-recordings, as nearly every file contains gaps. Common indicators of unintelligible speech in the transcripts were dots, but the function of this mark up was not always explained in the key. In transcript File 35 (SAS Flight 751, 1991), for instance, a distinction of uninterpreted speech had been made because of disturbances and unintelligible speech.

No indication was made about the number of *unintelligible syllables*, which is a feature suggested by the EAGLES guidelines. Cases in which it was unclear whether unintelligible sounds were marked are illustrated by Examples (35)–(37). In Example (35), the asterisks might have indeed been employed to mark unintelligible speech; however, it is also possible that they were intended to indicate censored speech. In Example (36), the use of dots remains unexplained and so do the dashes in Example (37).

(35)   Birgen Air B757 Accident Intra-Cockpit Communication (55)
       0346:07 (46:29) HOT-2 nose down
       0346:19 (46:41) HOT-2 ****
       0346:22 (46:44) CAM-3 now *
       0346:23 (46:45) HOT-2 thrust disconnect the
       0346:25 (46:47) HOT-1 auto-pilot, is autopilot disconnected?

(36)   ATC transcript TWA Flight 800 - 17 JUL 1996 (57)
       8:32:25 VIR009 Boston, Virgin zero zero nine, I can confirm
       that out of my nine o'clock position, we just had an ... it
       looked like an explosion out there about five miles away,
       six miles away.

(37)   Vnukovo Flight 2801 - 29 AUG 1996 (59)
       8:18:14 U There's no need to - here!
       8:18:16 Radio altimeter warning, duration 2 seconds.
       8:18:17 U - to descend.

In some sources unintelligible speech had been encoded through the term *unintelligible* that was inserted in the flow of the transcribed text (e.g. File 2 (MAS Flight 511, 1964)), sometimes as part of comments. Since the keys and transcription conventions of the ATC/CVR-corpus display a diverse encoding of unintelligible speech and the encoding overlaps with markers for pause ("-", "..."), break in continuity and editorial insertion (one or more dashes "-"), the encoding had to be standardised. In most sources, asterisks in different combinations were used to mark unintelligible speech. A string of three asterisks ("***") was used as encoding standard for the other files. It will simplify retrieval.

Uncertain transcription

Sometimes the transcribers guessed at what had been said. Normally, *uncertain transcription* is bracketed in one way or the other, whereby its code is different from that of *unintelligible speech*. This convention can be found in those ATC/CVR-transcripts where parentheses are used. There does not seem to be functional overlap in the use of bracketing and other indicators, although again in some instances dots were not explained and could just as easily mean uncertainty as well as unintelligible speech (see also File 36 (Air Inter Flight 148, 1992)). There is, however, a difference in treating uncertain stretches of dialogue. While in Example (39) the text which the transcriber hypothesised to hear was integrated in the transcript, the transcriber of File 37 (Trans-Air Service Flight, 1992 Example (38)) did not include his guess and reduced the questionable sections to an asterisk. Examples (38) and (39) contain quotations from the key of their transcript.

(38)   CVR transcript Trans-Air Service Flight 671 - 31 MAR 1992
       (37)
       ..(*).. = uncertain text
       8:10:03 CAM-2 Okay...(*)..now..(*).. <-
       8:10:10 CAM-2 ..(*)..(*).. <-
       8:10:31 CAM-1 Ya!

(39)   CVR transcript Japan Air Lines Flight 46E - 31 MAR 1993 (41)
       round bracket: ( ) Questionable insertion
       1230:13 08:57 CAM-3 (reports of) severe turbulence on <-
       climbout, I don't know what else is out on that galley now,
       but we're getting ready to blast off so just keep an eye out.

To simplify retrieval, codes marking uncertain transcription have been standardised. Since its original encoding overlapped with the encoding of editorial insertion ("()"), duplication has been recovered by adding a question mark after the opening parenthesis: "(?)"

Substitutions

This heading embraces aspects where words, usually proper names or four-letter words, were replaced for reasons of confidentiality or ethics. In the ATC/CVR-transcripts, proper names had sometimes been substituted by dots or initials, four-letter words by asterisks or a code (usually a hash) that indicated either an *expletive* or a *non-pertinent word*. The expression *non-pertinent word* appears to be a euphemism. Sometimes it was used in its original sense, i.e. when phrases were left out that were not directly connected to the crisis, or when very personal statements were made. Examples (40) and (41) below illustrate the overlap of codes used for non-pertinent speech and expletives alike.

(40) CVR transcript Delta Airlines Flight 554 - 19 OCT 1996 (64)
      @ - Nonpertinent word (or name)
      0440: 36 INT/PA- 4 no @ I need the ba - forward.
      0440: 37 CAM- 1 emergency power switch *.

(41) CVR transcript Fine Air Flight 101 - 07 AUG 1997 (68)
      # - Expletive deleted
      1236: 00.0 CAM- 2 what's goin' on.
      1236: 01.3 CAM- 1 whoa #.
      1236: 01.7 CAM- 1 ##.

For standardisation, the hash ("#") has been used for non-pertinent words and the "at"-sign ("@") for expletives deleted.

Speech management

The EAGLES guidelines define the term *speech management* as "the use of phenomena such as quasilexical vocalisations, pauses, repairs, restarts, and so on" (Gibbon, Mertins, & Moore 2000: 21).

Speech management is an issue for the orthographic representation of ATC/CVR-transcripts. However, sometimes phenomena of this sort are annotated at a separate level of processing instead, e.g. at the pragmatic level, but see Gibbon, Mertins, & Moore (2000: 21). In the areas of speech management, in order to preserve the possible variety of meanings that might have been intended by the transcribers, some ambiguities have not been resolved.

Many transcribers of cockpit voice recordings have taken into account the occurrence of *quasi-lexical vocalisations* in the dialogues. These are interjections and filled pauses, such as *eh, ah, uh, yeah* and *heh*. Most corpora make some attempt at standardising their transcription. From several ways suggested by the EAGLES guidelines a choice has been made not to standardise the many different forms in the present corpus, on the basis that unwanted variants proliferate and cause retrieval problems (see Gibbon, Mertins, & Moore 2000: 21). However, the original form of the data should be preserved wherever possible. Examples (42)–(43) show several forms of a discourse particle that is conventionally transcribed *ah*. Arrows mark the line with the trouble source. With

regard to the writing of the particle, some files were not consistent, but perhaps
transcribers heard a difference in pronunciation (Examples (42) and (43)).

(42)   ATC transcript US Air Flight 1493 collision - 01 FEB 1991
       (32)
       6:01:53 LC2 Calling ground say a eh tower, say again <-
       (...)
       6:02:30 USA23 Position and hold ah two four left, USAir <-
       twenty-three

(43)   CVR transcript Japan Air Lines Flight 46E - 31 MAR 1993 (41)
       1223:01 101:451 K084 Korean zero eight four, we got about a
       ten knot shear at uh, about fifteen <-
       hundred feet.

As ATC/CVR-transcripts have become more precise in recent years, they also display features such as *pauses*. It is not clear, however, whether their transcribers
referred to unfilled, i.e. perceived pauses, or silence in the speech signal, or
whether either alternative applies. With some transcripts there seems to be a
distinction between perceived pauses and silence, since pauses (presumably
perceived pauses) are contrasted with a break in continuity that may include
silence in the speech signal apart from other parameters such as lengthening of
vowels. In some files, a coding was used that overlaps with the coding of pauses,
but remains unexplained: in Example (44), the dots might be interpreted as
indicating a break in continuity of unintelligible stretches of discourse:

(44)   CVR transcript Aeroflot Flight 9981 - 08 OCT 1996 (63)
       CCO014: 1:03: No, let's...go around.
       CNA015: 1:02: Thirty.
       CCP016: 1:01: Why are we going around ?
       CNA017: 1:01: Twenty.
       CCO018: 1:00: No, no !
       CCP019: 1:00: Idle !
       CNA020: 0:57: Ten...eight...six...

The length of the pauses had not been documented in any of the transcripts.
Notation of pauses was in the form of dots, a single dash or a chain of dashes,
as illustrated by Examples (45) and (46):

(45)   CVR transcript GP Express Airlines Flight 861 - 08 JUN 1992
       (38)
       - Pause

```
0844:51 INT-2 there's our area of weather - so -.
```

(46) ATC transcript Swissair Flight 111 - 02 SEP 1998 (71)
      ... = Pause
      QM 1:14:33.2 Swissair one eleven roger ... turn right proceed
      ...uh ... you say to Boston you want to go?

Since the encoding of pauses was inconsistent and it therefore partly overlaps with the encoding of unintelligible speech ("...", "-"), break in continuity and editorial insertion ("-"), the standardised encoding is three dashes: "- - -". The encoding of *break in continuity* conflicts with the encoding of pauses, unintelligible speech and editorial insertion ("- - -"). It has been standardised by the percent sign code: "%".

Although many ATC/CVR-transcripts do take into account the occurrence of repetitions and repairs, they are not marked up, as exemplified by an extract from Files 32 and 34, Examples (47) and (48), respectively).

(47) ATC transcript US Air Flight 1493 collision - 01 FEB 1991
      (32)
      6:01:53 LC2 Calling ground say a eh tower, say again

(48) CVR transcript Lauda Air Flight 004 - 26 MAY 1991 (34)
      23.25:26 CA: Ah, you can tell 'em it, just it's, it's, it's,
      just ah, no, ah, it's probably ah wa... ah moisture or some-
      thing 'cause it's not just, oh, it's coming on and off.
      23.25:39 FO: Yeah.
      23.25:40 CA: But, ah, you know it's a ... it doesn't really,
      it's just an advisory thing, I don't ah ...

The EAGLES guidelines recommend tagging phenomena like these "with some kind of bracketing". However, in the transcripts no annotation of this sort could be found.

Paralinguistic features

According to the EAGLES guidelines, *paralinguistic features* refer to concomitant suprasegmental aspects of voice such as superimposed laughter, tempo, loudness rather than features of this kind that occur in isolation. Except for a few instances, ATC/CVR-transcripts do not usually mark features like these. In Example (49) there is an editorial comment that acts as an annotation to the object data. In Example (50), the paralinguistic phenomenon is mentioned, though no object data are present.

(49)   CVR transcript Trans-Air Service Flight 671 - 31 MAR 1992
       (37)
       1230:07 08:51 CAM-3 we're expecting a rough fide. ((yelled
       in a loud voice)) <-

(50)   CVR transcript Air India Flight 182 - 23 JUN 1985 (21)
       07.11:38 That is all right.

       -

       - (feeble words) <-

Of frequent occurrence in the ATC/CVR-corpus are isolated voiced features. In the ATC/CVR-transcripts, as is typical of other corpora, *non-verbal sounds* are transcribed in the form of a comment. Five types of non-verbal sounds are differentiated and exemplified (see Examples (51)–(56) and Gibbon, Mertins, & Moore (2000:22–23)):

Non-verbal but vocal utterances attributable to a speaker:

(51)   CVR transcript TWA Flight 800 - 17 JUL 1996 (57)
       2005:12 CAM-2 ((sound of cough)).

Non-verbal but vocal utterances not attributable to a speaker:

(52)   CVR transcript Japan Air Lines Flight 46E - 31 MAR 1993 (41)
       1226:24 05:08 CAM- ((sound of laughter))

Non-vocal noises attributable to a speaker:

(53)   Air Canada Flight 621 - 5 JUL 1970 (8)
       CCP045: Okay, thanks [apparent power increase, whistling]

Non-vocal noises not attributable to some speaker, including noises not produced by a human being:

(54)   CVR transcript United Air Lines Flight 553 - 08 DEC 1972 (9)
       0.27:10.64 CAM [Sound of landing gear warning horn begins
       and continues to end of recording]

Technical noises:

(55)   CVR transcript United Air Lines Flight 553 - 08 DEC 1972 (9)
       20.27:20.14 CAM [Sound of double click - similar to sound
       made by landing gear lever moved into up detent]

(56)   `CVR transcript American Eagle Flight 4184 - 31 OCT 1994 (51)`
       `1554: 52 CAM- [sound of click similar to shoulder harness`
       `being fastened]`

ATC/CVR-transcripts do not offer comments on *kinesic features* or *body language*, as it is sometimes informally called. To integrate information about eye contact, gesture and other body movements, a mere sound recording does not suffice, but would require the presence of a recording camera. With respect to *situational features*, several instances of ATC/CVR-transcripts offered not only basic information about the context of the dialogue in their header but, in much more detail, in their body. The EAGLES guidelines mark the body information as *more 'short-term'*, such as the arrival or the departure of a participant. They term it *editorial comment* and make a subdistinction which is, however, not applicable to the present analysis (cf. Gibbon, Mertins, & Moore 2000: 23–25). [The term *editorial comments* is an addition not made as such by the EAGLES recommendations. They mention a subset of commentaries applying to *situational features*. Editorial comments were marked by different kinds of bracketing in the ATC/CVR-transcripts, i.e. square brackets, parentheses and curly braces. The encoding has been standardised by square brackets ("[ ]").] Example ((57)) mainly applies to more short term information and is marked by round brackets, a convention often only modified by double parentheses in this corpus.

(57)   `AeroPeru B757 off Lima (Peru) 2 Oct, 1996 (62)`
       `00:42:12 (01:55) Copilot THE ALTIMETERS ARE STUCK (They`
       `observe the first instrument failure. According to the voice`
       `recording, copilot Fernandez was in command during take off.`
       `Pilot Schreiber will take command 4 minutes later)`

The aspect of *translation* has been added to the discussion, as it does not form part of the EAGLES guidelines. Not only do some transcripts include the original language of the recording but also a translation, usually into English. There were slightly different ways of marking the juxtaposition of the original language and its translation: Transcribers of File 44 (Example (58)) employed round brackets for the English translation, whereas those of File 77 (Example (59)) typeset the English text in green letters, which cannot be maintained in a text-only corpus without having a style sheet.

(58)   `CVR transcript Lufthansa Flight 2904 - 14 SEP 1993 (44)`
       `15.29:58 PF Sonst schaffe ich das nicht (otherwise I won't`

```
        manage it)
        15.30:03 PNF ... gute idee (.. good idea)
(59)  Air France Flight 4590 - 25 JUL 2000 (77)
        Key:
        green= English translation
        ...
```

Other transcripts do not offer a juxtaposition of the original language and
its translation, but were reduced to its translation. The translated parts were
marked by underscores (File 24) or by strings in capital letters (see Example
(60)).

```
(60)  CVR transcript Korean Air Flight 007 - 31 AUG 1983 (20)
        Words spoken in English are in UPPERCASE letters
        Words spoken in Korean have been translated into English and
        are in lowercase letters
        9:04 18:03:14 015 VHF CAM-1,2,3 ZERO ZERO SEVEN
        9:09 18:03:19 007 VHF 3 CAM-1,2,3 GO AHEAD
        9:11 18:03:21 015 VHF CAM-1,2,3 What are you doing
```

A third variant is a translation without any indications of where the translated
text had been inserted. Translation might be considered a special form of editorial comment. However, in the context of standardisation, it has been treated
as a feature in its own right. Its inconsistent encoding has been standardised
by using double curly braces: "{{ }}". The "(*)"-notation for translation overlapped with the code for unintelligible speech, but was also unexplained in
some files and has been changed to "%" through automatic tagging.

Some files contain an encoding that was not explained in the key. The bulk
of the disambiguated symbols were suspense dots, and often it seemed that
they were used for unintelligible text. If such a use could be unequivocally assumed, the key was extended. In cases where the use has remained obscure, a
remark about the missing definition for the symbol was integrated in the key.
With regard to XML-annotation, as is set out later in this book, the obscure symbols received extra treatment by specific tagging. For standardisation purposes,
symbols that did not overlap with the obscure symbols have been chosen.

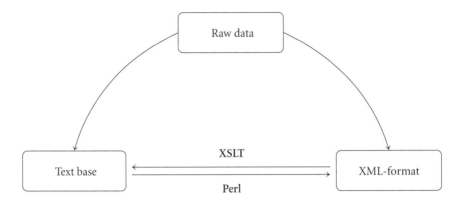

Figure 4.1 Overview of the two corpus formats generated for this analysis.

4.3 XML-markup of the standardised data

After manual and semi-automatic modification of the corpus data, perl-scripts help automatise application of the finishing touch. The scripts generate two types of data: the first, i.e. the text base, meets the desiderata of the KWIC-concordance, and the second the requirements of an XML-tagged corpus for the present study. The translation relation between the two formats is one of equivalence (see Figure (4.1)) so that one format can be translated into the other: This can be achieved either by using XSLT (eXtensible Stylesheet Language Transformations) for translation from XML to text base format or by using perl-scripts for translation from text base to XML format (see the concordancing system PAX of Trippel & Gibbon (2001) and the TASX (Time Aligned Signal data eXchange Format) annotator of Gut & Milde (2001)). For the current analysis, however, the two formats have been generated independently.

The steps necessary for the generation of different data types are listed below and summarised along with corpus file-names and examples in Table (4.2).

Stage 1.0 Input is raw data, i.e. 77 different, concatenated ATC/CVR files. The files are in ascii format and have a pre-annotation that was provided by transcribers. The files are structured into a header, a footer and a body. The body has between two and five columns, depending on its annotational details. Header and footer are commented by hashes. A separator marks the end of the previous file and the beginning of the following file. (Hashes and delimiters are important additions to further processing for the script). Example (61) displays the main pattern of a transcript that is still in its raw

Table 4.2 Summary of the steps needed in order to generate a corpus in XML-format from untagged raw data by means of Perl scripts as explained in Section 4.3

	Input			Output		
	filename	format	example	filename	format	example
	`cvrlabel5.txt`	raw data, transcriber's representation, 77 different ATC/CVR files concatenated, two to five columns	`CC0027: 8:56: Watch it!`	pattern: `cvrlabel5.\d(3)`	77 separate files, format unchanged	`CC0027: 8:56: Watch it!`
	pattern: `cvrlabel5.\d(3)`	77 separate files, format unchanged	`CC0027: 8:56: Watch it!`	pattern: `cvrlabel5.\d(3).kwic1`	77 separate files, triple+ columns turned into double columns; data for dynamic concordance	`CC0027_8:56: Watch it!`
	pattern: `cvrlabel5.\d(3)`	77 separate files, format unchanged	`CC0027: 8:56: Watch it!`	pattern: `cvrlabel5.\d(3).kwic2`	77 separate files, triple+ columns turned into double columns; source name added to every new line; data for dynamic concordance	`6_CC0027_8:56: Watch it!`
	pattern: `cvrlabel5.\d(3)`	77 separate files, format unchanged	`CC0027: 8:56: Watch it!`	pattern: `cvrlabel5.\d(3).new`	77 separate files, single to triple + columns, partly xml-tagged: sender, turn-id, time, frequency, addressee	`<sender-turn-id> CC0027: </sender-turn-id> <time>8:56:</time> Watch it!`
	pattern: `cvrlabel5.\d(3).new`	77 separate files, single, double or triple+ columns, partly xml-tagged	`<sender-turn-id> CC0027: </sender-turn-id> <time>8:56:</time> Watch it!`	pattern: `cvrlabel5.\d(3).new.xml`	77 separate files, single to triple+ columns, contains xml-tags: turn + transcription-related tags, xml-tagged comments	`<sender-turn-id> CC0027: </sender-turn-id> <time>8:56:</time> <turn>Watch it!</turn>`

form. The round brackets framing suspense dots do not form part of the corpus files, but were inserted in order to mark deleted text in the extract:

(61)
```
------------------------------------------------
# CVR transcript Air Canada Flight 797 - 02 JUN 1983 (19)
# Key: first column: transcriber's abbreviation, (...)
CAM158 [Sound similar to cockpit door]
CFO159 Okay, you got it *** (...)
CTR166 19:07:32 Three sixty two Indianapolis Center roger
PXX167 19:07:35 We'll take direct Holston Mountain if you
can do that
ANN168 19:07:41 [Recorder goes off] (...)
# Copyright © 1996-1999 Harro Ranter / Fabian Lujan...
------------------------------------------------
```

Seventy-seven separate files result from processing the script. The format of the files has remained unchanged. The files are named according to their extension type `cvrlabel5.- - -`, with the three dashes indicating that every file has a numeric extension. At this stage, the processing branches into a text base that conforms to the requirements of the KWIC-concordance and to corpus files that contain XML-tags. For each branch different scripts are used.

Stage 1.1 The core idea of the perl-script has been regular expressions that process 19 different patterns of annotational data. In order to work with data that are as close to their original form as possible, the patterns were not standardised. Input pertains to the output of Stage 1.0. Output of this process constitutes 77 new files, named according to the extension type `cvrlabel5.- - -.kwic1`. The raw data have been changed to a format that meets the requirements of the KWIC-concordance: All annotational data that contain information about the sender, the turn-identification number and, optionally, time codes and data on the radio frequency are assembled in one column by means of an underscore that fills the blank between the data blocks in question:

(62)
```
# CVR transcript Air Canada Flight 797 - 02 JUN 1983 (19)
# Key: first column: transcriber's abbreviation, (...)
CAM158_: [Sound similar to cockpit door]
CFO159_: Okay, you got it *** (...)
CTR166_19:07:32: Three sixty two Indianapolis Center roger
PXX167_19:07:35: We'll take direct Holston Mountain if you
```

```
can do that
ANN168_19:07:41: [Recorder goes off]
# Copyright © 1996-1999 Harro Ranter / Fabian Lujan (...)
```

A second file format was produced. The file-name (here the file-number) was prefixed to each line of the file in question. Each file was numbered according to its position in the input file of Stage 1.0 and the same number was taken up again, assigning numbers within every file as Example (63) illustrates:

(63) 19_# CVR transcript Air Canada Flight 797 - 02 JUN 1983
      (19)
      19_# Key: first column: transcriber's abbreviation, (...)
      19_CAM158_: [Sound similar to cockpit door]
      19_CFO159_: Okay, you got it *** 19_(...)
      19_CTR166_19:07:32: Three sixty two Indianapolis Center
      roger
      19_PXX167_19:07:35: We'll take direct Holston Mountain if
      you can do that
      19_ANN168_19:07:41: [Recorder goes off]
      19_# Copyright © 1996-1999 Harro Ranter / Fabian Lujan
      (...)

The file extension is cvrlabel5.- - -.kwic2. Except for the addition of the file-name the output is identical to that of the script above.

Stage 1.2 The next script is a modification of the script described for Stage 1.1. Its function is to tag selected variables by XML-tags, and its input is identical to the output of processing Stage 1.0. Output consists of 77 new files named according to the extension type cvrlabel5.- - -.new. The raw data have partly been changed to the XML-format: In the body, tags are inserted for sender and turn-identification (<sender-turn-id>...</sender-turn-id>), time code (<time>...</time>), frequency (<frequency>...</frequency>) and addressee (<addressee>...</addressee>). The utterance representation and the commented header and footer remained untouched.

A pretty-print format has been added, in which every type of tagged data has been written into a new line, as illustrated in Example (64):

(64) # CVR transcript Air Canada Flight 797 - 02 JUN 1983 (19)
      # Key: first column: transcriber's abbreviation, (...)
      <sender-turn-id>CAM158</sender-turn-id>

```
<time>:</time>
[Sound similar to cockpit door]
<sender-turn-id>CFO159</sender-turn-id>
<time>:</time>
Okay, you got it *** (...)
<sender-turn-id>PXX167</sender-turn-id>
<time>19:07:35:</time>
We'll take direct Holston Mountain if you can do that
<sender-turn-id>ANN168</sender-turn-id>
<time>19:07:41:</time>
[Recorder goes off] (...)
# Copyright © 1996-1999 Harro Ranter / Fabian Lujan(...)
```

With this step, a raw XML-annotation for the corpus has been accomplished.

Stage 1.3   The number of XML-tags is augmented by the substitution of the patterns that were used by the transcribers and standardised in the course of the present study. Its input is identical to the output of processing Stage 1.2. Output here comprises 77 separate files of the general type cvrlabel5.-
- -.new.xml. Any added XML-notation relates to the header and the footer where the hashes are replaced by XML-comments, and to the body which has been enriched by XML-tags that mark transcription-related problems, e.g. the tags (<unintelligible>...</unintelligible>, <questionable>...</questionable>) or conversation-related phenomena (<pause>...</pause>, <non-pertinent>...</non-pertinent>). Moreover, time tags that frame nothing but a colon, which stands for a missing time code, are substituted by an empty string. The pretty-print format has been extended by writing into a new line every new string that had been tagged (see Example (65)):

(65)   ```
<!- CVR transcript Air Canada Flight 797 (...) ->
<!- Key: (...) ->
<sender-turn-id>CAM158</sender-turn-id> <time>empty</time>
<editorial-comment> Sound similar to cockpit door
</editorial-comment>
<sender-turn-id>CFO159</sender-turn-id>
<time>:</time>
<turn> Okay, you got it *** </turn> (...)
<sender-turn-id>PXX167</sender-turn-id>
<time>19:07:35:</time>
```
```

```
<turn> We'll take direct Holston Mountain if you can do
that </turn>
<sender-turn-id>ANN168</sender-turn-id>
<time>19:07:41:</time>
<editorial-comment> Recorder goes off (...)
</editorial-comment>
<!- Copyright © 1996-1999 Harro Ranter / Fabian Lujan->
```

The DTD (document type declaration) displayed in this section relates to the corpus that has been processed by the scripts available at http://pbns. claudia-sassen.net. The following DTD applies to the present state of automatic tagging; i.e. it only tags the body of each transcript and marks the header and the footer simply by the SGML-based comments (<!-- -->) without inserting further meta data. This DTD has been validated by an nsgmls-parser.

```
<!ELEMENT transcript ((sender-turn-id)+,(addressee)*,(frequency)*,
                      (time)*,(turn))*>
<!ELEMENT sender-turn-id (#PCDATA)>
<!ELEMENT addressee (#PCDATA)>
<!ELEMENT frequency (#PCDATA)>
<!ELEMENT time (#PCDATA)>
<!ELEMENT turn ((#PCDATA),(unintelligible)*,(questionable)*,(pause)*,
                (continuity-break)*,(translation)*,(non-pertinent)*,
                (expletive-deleted)*,(meaning-obscure)*,
                (editorial-comment)*)*>
 <!ELEMENT unintelligible (#PCDATA)>
 <!ELEMENT questionable ((#PCDATA),(meaning-obscure)*)*>
 <!ELEMENT pause (#PCDATA)>
 <!ELEMENT continuity-break (#PCDATA)>
 <!ELEMENT translation ((#PCDATA),(unintelligible)*,(questionable)*,
                        (expletive-deleted)*,(meaning-obscure)*,
                        (editorial-comment)*)*>
 <!ELEMENT non-pertinent (#PCDATA)>
 <!ELEMENT expletive-deleted (#PCDATA)>
 <!ELEMENT meaning-obscure (#PCDATA)>
 <!ELEMENT editorial-comment (#PCDATA)>
```

4.4 Phases in aviation communication

Phases in the development of a crisis

No typical development of phases that lead to a crisis can be observed in the transcripts available. As can be judged from the documents, some crews did not suspect at all that anything was going wrong, as nothing apparently unusual was happening. Only a few seconds later, their plane would hit ground. This was, for example, the case with *American Flight 383*, dated November 8, 1965. Example (66) displays the complete transcript of the *American Flight 383* incident. A turning point from crisis to non-crisis is not obvious, but may tentatively be stipulated for Turn CWR010 in which the crew realises that they were having problems with the runway.

(66)   CWR000: Cincinnati Tower *** we're six miles southeast and
        ** control VFR.
        TWR001: Runway 18, wind 230 degrees, five knots, altimeter
        30.
        CWR002: Roger, Runway 18.
        TWR003: Have you in sight - cleared to land.
        CWR004: We're cleared to land, roger. How far west is that
        precip line now?
        TWR005: Looks like it's just about over the field at this
        time, sir. We're not getting anything on the field however
        *** if we have a windshift I'll keep you advised as you turn
        on to final.
        CWR006: Thank you - we'd appreciate it.
        TWR007: We're beginning to pick up a little rain now.
        CWR008: OK.
        TWR009: Have you still got the runway OK?
        CWR010: Ah *** just barely *** we'll pick up the ILS here.
        TWR011: Approach lights, flashers and runway lights are all
        on high intensity.
        CWR012: OK.

A clear transition from one phase to the other can be observed with the *Birgen Air B757 Accident* (6 February, 1996): in the first phase the crew noticed a problem with the flight altimeters. This happened in a phase of non-crisis (see Example (67)).

(67)   HCO000 0341:40 42:02: have a nice flight
        HCO006 0342:23 eighty knots
        HCP007 0342:24 checked
        HCP008 0342:26 my airspeed indicator's not working
        HCO009 0342:28 yes
        HCO010 0342:29 yours is not working
        HCO011 0342:30 one twenty

```
HCP012 0342:32 is yours working?
HCO013 0342:32 yes sir
```

The second phase, still before the crisis, was dominated by the crew negotiating and testing solution strategies (see Example (68)):

(68)
```
HCP056 0344:54 let's check their circuit breakers
HCO057 0344:55 yes
HCP058 0344:57 alternate is correct
HCO059 0344:59 the alternate one is correct
HCP060 0345:04 as aircraft was not flying and on ground
something happening is usual
HCP061 0345:07 such as elevator asymmetry and other things
HCP062 0345:11 we don't believe them
HFE063 0345:23 shall I reset its circuit breaker
HCP064 0345:24 yes reset it
HFE065 0345:25 to understand the reason
HCP066 0345:27 yeah
CAM067 0345:28 [sound of aircraft overspeed warning]
HCP068 0345:30 okay it's no matter
HCP069 0345:39 pull the airspeed we will see
```

After every strategy had failed, the third phase, i.e. the crisis, was entered and the flight resulted in a crash. Example (69) illustrates the final transition from non-crisis to crisis. The first signs of a crisis could be assigned to Turn HCP089 when HCP runs out of ideas and asks his crew for help. Reactions of panic become evident in Turn HCO095 and subsequent utterances in which iterations prevail. Furthermore, emotional questions which refer to the obscurity of the situation are frequent.

(69)
```
HCP085 0346:25 disconnect the auto-pilot, is autopilot
disconnected?
HCO086 0346:25 already disconnected, disconnected sir
HCP089 0346:39 not climb? what am I to do?
HCO090 0346:43 you may level off, altitude okay, I am
selecting the altitude hold sir
HCP091 0346:47 select select
HCO092 0346:48 altitude hold
HCO093 0346:51 okay, five thousand feet
HCP094 0346:52 thrust levers, thrust thrust thrust thrust
HCO095 0346:54 retard
HCP096 0346:54 thrust, don't pull back,
```

```
       don't pull back, don't pull back, don't pull back
       HCO097 0346:56 okay open open
       HCP098 0346:57 don't pull back, please don't pull back
       HCO099 0346:59 open sir, open
       HFE101 0347:02 sir pull up
       HCP102 0347:03 what's happening
       HCO103 0347:05 oh what's happening
       GPW105 0347:09 [sink rate whoop whoop pull up warning starts
       and continues until the end]
       HCO106 0347:13 let's do like this
       ANN108 0347:17 [end of recording]
```

Having reviewed phases in the development of crises in aviation communication on the macro-level, I will now turn to its micro-structure.

Conversational phases

Face-to-face communication displays basically three conversational phases: opening, medial and terminal. In the literature, characterisations of the *opening phase* usually refer to a functional rather than a structural level. Rintel and Pittam make the structurally related observation that to begin an opening phase requires participants to walk toward each other to come within earshot just as it would be necessary in phone conversations to have a dialling process (Rintel & Pittam 1997:529). Literature about conversational openings in general mirrors the essential items that Laver lists in his article on phatic communion (Laver 1974). House, for instance, highlights its interpersonal phatic function (see House 1982:53). According to Halliday (1973) and Laver (1974:3), the smooth transition from a state of *non-talk* to a state of *talk* is stressed, while the "availability to talk" (Schegloff 1972) is signalled with each other (Goffman 1963:102). In conversational openings, the frequency of conventionalised utterances is high.

The transition from the opening to the *medial phase* is overt in gestures such as lifting one's head in order to establish eye-contact on the same level as well as in linguistic markers like *Well...* or *What I came to see you about was...* or *Well, what can I do for you?* (see Laver 1974:4 and also Kendon & Ferber (1973)). Because of its topic talk, House calls the medial phase "the informative core of the encounter" which has mostly an ideational function (House 1982:53). The frequency of stereotypes is less than in the marginal phases. Length and complexity of utterances is generally growing, although they may be interspersed with brief utterances. Speaker change is not conventionally governed; instead it relies on a complex system of signals that can be modelled by an approach through a set of rules (Sacks, Schegloff, & Jefferson 1974).

According to House, the *terminal phase*, also called *closing*, represents the inversion of the opening phase in that it catalyses the transition from *talk* to *non-talk* and lets the *availability to talk* expire. The transition is accompanied by gestures and facial expressions along with expressions such as *Well,...,* or *Mustn't keep you*, whereby the former may also occur during the transition from the *opening phase* to the *medial phase*. From time to time, the agreements created in the medial phase are summarised as *position statements* (Laver 1974: 10). In general, the term *closing* stands for leaving the medial phase and introducing the *terminal exchange*, which is characterised by a high frequency of stereotypes. Schegloff and Sacks point out that loops may develop from *closings*: "one can close a conversation by closing a section which has as its business closing a conversation" (Schegloff & Sacks 1973: 322).
In other words, within a phase that aims at the termination of a conversation, there may be a recursion to the medial phase as a result of *reopening topic talk*. The next attempt at terminating the conversation is not executed by a mere insertion of a *terminal exchange*, but by the initiation of another *closing* in which eventually a *terminal exchange* is placed.

Theories about face-to-face conversation have discussed many scenarios of communication including service encounters, doctor-patient talk and school conversation. However, discussions have not branched to aviation communication, which will be done to some extent in this section where the available ATC/CVR-data were checked against features of conversational phases.

Cockpit voice recorders contain an endless tape, or microchips that are reset every 30 minutes (Beveren 1995). As a result, only a small segment is extant of the complete dialogue that may have lasted for several hours. For this reason, there was no transcript that matched the model of three conversational phases for intra-cockpit communication as introduced in this section: A greeting formula, being typical of the opening phase, was probably exchanged outside the plane or during moments that were not recorded. Farewell formula that indicate the closing phase could be found in the transcripts, although in aviation communication closing phases are very special cases of normal farewell behaviour. The medial phase that is characterised by topic-related talk was overt in every transcript. Intra-cockpit communication is an instance of face-to-face interaction. Thus, the three conversational phases of face-to-face interaction can also be presupposed for intra-cockpit communication. On the other hand, extra-cockpit communication, which is directed to many different controllers during a flight, develops over a shorter time span and thus, in most cases, exposes all three conversational phases (see Example (70)):

(70)   RFO017: Good evening Rome, Itavia 870.
        RCC018: Good evening to you too, 870. Squawk 1136. Cleared
        to Palermo, via Bolsena, Puma, Latina, Ponza, Amber 13
        RFO019: 1136 is coming and 870 is cleared to Palermo via
        Bolsena, Puma, Latina, Ponza, Amber 13 and we're approaching
        190...
        RCC028: 870, call Rome 125.5. Bye.
        RFO029: 125.5.

In Example (70), the turns RFO017 and the first utterance of RCC018 pertain to the opening phase, while the following utterances of RCC018 until RCC028 are topic talk. The remaining part of the extract refers to the farewell, which, as is sometimes also the case with initial greetings, is not bilateral.

From the cvr-transcripts there is evidence that at least (the medial phase of) intra-cockpit communication may have two different kinds of topic: professional communication on technical matters of aviation as opposed to *leaky points*, i.e. non-professional communication within a professional setting (see Section 1.2). According to Cushing (1994), extra-cockpit communication also displays the two ranges of professional and non-professional conversation topics.

4.5 Discourse-control processes

For *discourse-control processes*, Gibbon (1985) distinguishes three types of processes of functional overlap: first, *topic processes* which determine goal-oriented progression of information exchange in discourse; second, *uptake processes* which provide error-control strategies in support of them, and third *framing processes*, defining orientation points within the structural and semantic development of discourse (Gibbon 1985:404).[8] Framing processes cater for the internal organisation of a conversation and make it coherent in the sense of Grice's *maxim of manner*. Framing processes are constituted by *adjacency pairs* and *conditional relevance* (see e.g. Sacks 1971; Schegloff & Sacks 1973; Levinson 1983; Schegloff 1992; Schiffrin 1994; Clark 1996) as well as by the strategy of *coherence marking* that subsumes the strategy of turn-framing, i.e. speaker change and allied signals (see e.g. Yngve 1970; Duncan jr. 1973; Sacks, Schegloff, & Jefferson 1974; Duncan 1974; Duncan & Niederehe 1974;

McLaughlin 1984; Duncan & Fiske 1985; Willkopp 1988 and Stenström 1994). In addition, discourse-control processes subsume the principle of *uptake*.

For speaker change, Sacks, Schegloff, & Jefferson (1974) propose the following recursive principles, which become active in the medial phase of conversations, while conversational openings and closings are conventionally regulated. For the present analysis, the principles are cited from Murray (1989: 326):

1. Completion of a turn unit (e.g. sentences, clause, phrase) constitutes a potential transition to another speaker; and
2. Turn allocation operates because the current speaker can

    (a) *select the next speaker, or*
    (b) *let another speaker self-select, or*
    (c) *continue.*

Further turn-allocation techniques identified by Sacks, Schegloff, & Jefferson (1974) are *tag questions* as exit cues and sets of adjacency pairs. The model has been criticised as being basic and a *local management system* that only locally controls the order of speaker turns and thus operates turn-by-turn. It does not determine the quantitative distribution of turns, their length or aspects with respect to structure or content. Duncan & Fiske (1985) establish a more differentiated model that bears four categories of cues signalling either *turn-seizing, floor-holding, turn-yielding* or *backchanneling* (see also e.g. Duncan jr. 1973; Duncan 1974).

In the literature, few references to turn-framing in ATC/CVR are available. Hints can be found in the FAAO 7110.65, written specifically as the governing document for air traffic controllers with regard to procedures and phraseology. Further information can be located in the AIM which is written for pilots, giving direction on what to expect from ATC and what ATC expects of them. The FARs (Federal Aviation Regulations) with additional requirements for pilots also contains brief information about turn-taking.[9] These documents only refer to highly rule-governed communication such as the performance of a checklist. A closer look will be taken at the ATC/CVR-corpus data to understand the structure of turn-framing and in particular uptake securing, both in professional and non-professional communication of which the latter is also known as *leaky points*. As explained by Clark and Gibbon, uptake securing effects communication to switch from the object level to the meta level. Framing processes are important, since they are essential for the reconstruction of multiplexed transcripts; however, they will not be discussed to an extent comparable to that of the central uptake-related topics.

Uptake processes are a vital means relating to the successful unfolding of conversation in crisis situations. The principle of *uptake* goes back to Austin, who claims that an illocutionary act can only be executed if neither are there acoustic problems nor insecurities exist regarding the meaning of an utterance. Thus, *uptake* is the prerequisite of every speech act (cf. Austin 1962:115; Gibbon 1985:409, see also Jakobson 1960 and especially Searle 1969:57). Clark points out that uptake is evidence of understanding (Clark (1996:200), see also Bodenheimer (1992:7)), and hypothesises that whenever something is produced on the object level (Clark's *track 1*), its initiator is directly or indirectly asking a question in the sense of *Do you understand what I mean by this?* on the meta-level (Clark's *track 2*). He expects his respondent to take him up, i.e. to signal that he hears the initiator and that he understands what he means (Clark 1996:243). It is important to note that uptakes of this kind, which often occur in the backchannel, are not to be confused with a simultaneous indication of agreement, as is made explicit by Allwood (1997:1). Its recursive and iterative features make *uptake processes* distinctive, while framing and topic processes are limited to linear and hierarchical structures.

Characteristic of uptake processes are optional *uptake loops*. These consist of verbal feedback between interlocutors and may be the components of a *functional cycle*, which is a temporally based adaptive process with the *adjacency pair* as its minimal unit:

> [...] a development process in discourse in which current indexically valid feature specifications (e.g. concerning noise, [...]) are continually checked and logged at turn boundaries.   (Gibbon 1985:408)

An uptake loop is a rule about a sequence of components, which Gibbon derives from instances of international radio amateur talk:

...(<DISCONFIRM REQUEST, REPLY>)$_i$, CONFIRM...,

where *DISCONFIRM* stands for negative *uptake*; i.e. one participant signals to the other that he did not understand, and by a *REQUEST* appeals for repetition, clarification or substantiation (Stenström 1994:106) of the utterance containing the trouble source to which the other reacts with a *REPLY*. The index *i* is a variable for the number of repetitions. This pattern, which is the core uptake loop, may be followed by a superordinate positive *uptake* by which the speaker signals understanding, here called *CONFIRM*. *Uptake loops* may be repeated as often as necessary for securing understanding (see Gibbon 1981:36; Stenström 1994:106). A complete breakdown of communication would trigger a concomitant excessive use of uptake loops. Its occurrence within conver-

sations is "free[ly] after turn-switches, either as the next exchange or initiated inside a longer contribution; distributionally, uptake loops may thus be
seen as transaction-level parallels to contribution-level parentheses" (Gibbon
1981:37).

The canonical form of an uptake-securing process can be rephrased by
WHAT? – THAT! – OH...

Repair is a conversational mechanism that refers to iterative problems with
regard to speech production, acoustic perception and semantic comprehension
(cf. also Edmondson & House 1981; Stenström 1994). It remedies these problems in favour of an undisturbed conversation. *Correction* and *repair* are often
used as parallel terms; however, Schegloff & Sacks (1977) understand *correction*
as a special case of *repair*, since *repair* captures "the more general domain of
occurrences" (Schegloff & Sacks 1977:363). They develop a multi-faceted concept of *repair* that ranges from difficulties in finding the appropriate lexeme,
modifications of utterances that in fact would have been devoid of obvious
mistakes or errors[10] to actual corrections by *error replacement*. The component
of a turn that needs modification is called *repairable* or *trouble source*. Two
main sorts of *repair* can be distinguished: first, *self-repair*, when the originator of the *repairable* carries out the *repair* himself, and second, *other-repair*,
when an interlocutor carries out the *repair*. Motivation for a *repair* may result
from two different aspects: from *self-initiated repair*, when the originator of
the *repairable* himself initiates the *repair* and from *other-initiated repair*, when
somebody apart from the originator of the *repairable* initiates the *repair*. In
general, there is a preference for self-repair, which is not triggered by a face-
saving motivation of the speaker, but by immediacy: self-repair is easier to
realise than other-repair:

> For example, 'dispreferreds' are structurally delayed in turns and sequences,
> and are (or may be) preceded by other items; [...].
>
> (Schegloff & Sacks 1977:362)

Possible *placements* of self-initiated repair and their identifiers occur within
the same turn as the *repairable* ($=T_R$). These are indicated by disruption of
words or utterances, prolongations or signals such as *uh*, in the *transition
space*[11] ($=S_T$) of the turn containing the *repairable* or in the turn subsequent
to the one which follows the turn containing the *repairable* (Schegloff & Sacks
1977:367). Other-initiated repair typically only occurs within the consecutive
turn to the turn containing the trouble-source (Schegloff & Sacks 1977:367).
It is indicated by a group of *turn constructional devices* such as *Huh?*, interrog-
atives like *What?*, *Who?*, *Where?*, or the partial repetition of the trouble-source

turn, including an interrogative such as *The what?, To a where?* as well as the sequence *Y'mean* with a concomitant possible interpretation of the previous turn. These devices are also often referred to as *check* (Stenström 1994: 107). Although self-initiation and other-initiation of repair are different mechanisms of conversation, they are not independent of each other.

Discourse-control processes in professional communication

Unlike extra-cockpit communication, intra-cockpit communication generally mirrors a considerable range of spoken language behaviour. Many instances contain features of discourse-control processes such as turn-framing and repair behaviour, which may be exemplified by markers including the discourse particle *uh*. Example (71) shows an instance of turn-seizing, where speaker KLM makes use of the particle *uh* at the beginning of Turn KLM093:

(71)   CVR transcript KLM Flight 4805 and Pan Am Flight 1736
        collision - 27 MAR 1977 ()
        CCP090: Maybe he, maybe he counts these are three.
        CXX091: Huh.
        CXX092: I like this.
        KLM093: Uh, the KLM ... four eight zero five is now <-
        ready for take-off uh and we're waiting for our ATC
        clearance.

Example (72) is an instance of floor-holding, indicated by the particle *uh* in medial position of Turn APP076:

(72)   CVR transcript Eastern Air Lines Flight 401 - 29 DEC 1972 ()
        APP076: 23:37:48 Eastern, uh, 401 turn left heading two
        seven zero <-
        RCP077: 23:37:53 Left two seven zero, roger

Example (73) instantiates self-repair introduced by the phrase *I'm sorry* in medial position of Turn CFO015 where the communication shifts from the object level to the meta level:

(73)   CVR transcript Surinam Airways Flight 764 - 07 JUN 1989
        CFO015: One oh three I'm sorry one oh four. <-
        CCP016: Okay.
        CFO017: One oh four.

The following can be stated in relation to the topic of conversation: During professional communication, the highly restricted exchanges between pilot and copilot, as well as between pilot and controller, mostly follow the pattern of adjacency pairs. Furthermore, they show a high degree of turn-seizing by other selection and/or many responses remaining in the backchannel which – in crew communication – is sometimes non-verbal. Turn CXX156 of Example (74) shows such a non-verbal cue that is concomitant with verbal feedback during a checklist.

(74)   CVR transcript Avianca Flight 052 - 25 JAN 1990 (31) CFE150:
       2119:41 Speed brake lever.
       CCP151: 2119:42 Full forward.
       CFE152: 2119:43 Spoiler switches.
       CFO153: 2119:45 On.
       CFE154: 2119.45 On.
       CFE155: 2119:46 Engine start selectors on.
       CXX156: 2119:50 [Engine igniter sound starts and continues
       until end of tape.]<-

In Example (75), feedback to the captain's command remains non-verbal, see Turn CAM067:

(75)   CVR transcript KLM Flight 4805 and Pan Am Flight 1736
       collision - 27 MAR 1977
       (...)
       CCP066: Weight and balance finals?
       CAM067: [Sounds similar to stabilizer, trim]. <-

The examples, however, do not indicate whether any visual and other non-verbal cues were occurring during the turn-framing processes, such as gaze away or movement of hand or body. The probability that these cues also apply here is high, since all the components that make a face-to-face communication are given.

Conversations in extra-cockpit communication unfold via radio signal. Therefore, they do not rely on visual cues but on verbal behaviour alone, as is also the case with phone conversations. The linguistic cues of discourse-control processes are analogous to those of intra-cockpit communication. Example (76) displays an instance of a clarification dialogue with an uptake loop:

(76)   RDO037: 4:08:42 Uh, Two-Forty-Two, stand by. <-
       ACC038: 4:08:46 Say again. <-
       RDO039: 4:08:48 Stand by. <-

```
ACC040: 4:08:49 Roger, maintain one five thousand if you
understand me; maintain one five thousand, Southern
Two-Forty-Two. <-
RDO041: 4:08:55 We're trying to get it up there.
ACC042: 4:08:57 Roger.
```

In Turn RDO037, the crew asks the approach control to *stand by*, while the controller requests a repetition of the crew's speech and thus enters the uptake loop. Clarification follows immediately by repetition of Turn RDO037. The controller confirms that he has now understood what the crew said and goes on with his instructions. Through the confirming utterance the uptake loop is terminated.

Discourse-control processes in non-professional communication: Leaky points

Leaky points (Gibbon 1981) deviate from the strict pattern of aviation communication and relate to whatever the participants desire. They can be related to the verbal features identified by Sacks, Schegloff, & Jefferson (1974) and Duncan & Fiske (1985) for face-to-face communication.

For intra-cockpit communication, as displayed in Example (77), the leaky point can be determined as beginning at Turn CFA004.[12] In Example (77), there are cues for all kinds of turn-framing types: While in Turn CFA004 CFA self-selects the speaker role, he then yields it by a question that marks other-selection. As no other participant seizes the turn, CFA continues with his speaker role. There are reactions in the backchannel (Turns CCP005 and CFO012) and replies which could have been limited to the functional status of feedback, but which turn out to be longer and so might be assigned the status of a turn. The frequency of other-selection in turn-framing is higher than self-selection. On the whole, there is a high preference for replies not remaining in the backchannel.

(77)   CVR transcript USAir Flight 427 - 08 SEP 1994 (50)
       CFA000: They didn't give us connecting flight information or
       anything. Do you know what gate we're coming into?
       CCP001: Not yet.
       CFA002: Any idea?
       CCP003: No.
       CFA004: Do ya know what I'm thinkin' about? Pretzels. <-

```
CCP005: Pretzels? <-
CFA006: You guys need drinks here?
CCP007: I could use a glass of somethin', whatever's open,
water, uh, water, a juice?
CFO008: I'll split a, yeah, a water, a juice, whatever's
back there. I'll split one with 'im.
CFA009: Okey-dokey. Do you want me to make you my special
fruity juice cocktail?
CCP010: How fruity is it?
CFA011: Why don't you just try it?
CFO012: All right, I'll be a guinea pig.
```

The conversation in Example (77) took place before a crisis occurred. Example (78) will illustrate the verbal behaviour of the same crew during emergency:

(78)
```
CCP089: Hang on.
CFO090: Oh, Shit.
CCP091: Hang on. What the hell is this?
CAM092: [Sound of stick shaker; sound of altitude alert]
CFA093: Traffic. Traffic.
CCP094: What the ***
CFO095: Oh ***
CCP096: Oh God, Oh God ***
APP097: USAir ***
RCP098: 427, emergency!
```

Despite the frequent occurrence of unintelligible talk the following features can be established: normal organisation of conversation is broken off. Example (78) displays a loose sequence of turns that all refer to the topic of an emergency, while there is no apparent coherence between the turns. Self-selection is preferred.

In the ATC/CVR-corpus, no data could be found that pertains to leaky points in extra-cockpit communication of non-crisis talk. It proved likewise difficult to spot leaky points in the radio communication during a crisis. In most cases, leaky talk was created by the persons directly involved, i.e. the crew. The only example where leaky talk comes from the tower is displayed in Example (79). Interestingly, the leaky points are produced by TWB, the tower background which self-selects:

(79)
```
CRW005: TWR 118.3 916 Will do.
TWR006: 917:31:00 Have you in sight. You are clear to land.
```

```
            Surface wind 030/10.
            CRW007: 917:40:00 511.
            TWB008: 919:40:00 Ooops! <-
            TWB009: 919:49:00 Wheels have fallen off. <-
            TWR010: 919:52:00 Yes, Tower. Comet *** wheels fallen off.
            Comet aircraft landing. OK. Thank you.
```

In Example (80) the captain (RCP) contacts tower to declare an emergency (see Turn RCP090). In doing so, he fails to give his flight identification, misses to segment the contents of his contribution effectively and in the end combines his declaration with a request for clarification.

```
(80)  APP087: 4:13:45 Uh, I'm not receiving it. But radar contact;
      your position is 20 miles west of Dobbins.
      CFO088: 4:14:03 Get those engines #.
      RCP090: 4:14:24 All right, listen, we've lost both engines,
      and, uh, I can't, uh, tell you the .implications of this-we,
      uh, only got two engines and how far is Dobbins now? <-
      APP091: 4:14:34 Southern, uh, Two-Forty-Two, uh, 19 miles.
```

All in all, a preference for other-selection could be observed for leaky points of extra-cockpit communication. This may be so because the participants, in particular the crew hopes to receive help from the tower.

Notes

1. Twelve fragments of poor recording quality were found on the web with a maximal duration of less than 40 seconds. Owing to their unsatisfactory quality, they were not used for the analysis.

2. Compare for example the CVR transcripts of *Delta Flight 191 – 02 AUG 1985* under http://aviation-safety.net/investigation/cvr/transcripts/cvr_dl191.shtml and http://www.airdisaster.com/cvr/dl191tr. shtml.

3. In Clark's terms, this would be expressed by saying that the relevant participant "proposes a joint project", see Clark (1996: 191)

4. In aviation communication, the terms may be paraphrased by the terminological pairs *pilot in command* vs. *copilot*, *captain* vs. *first officer*, which mark a responsibility level, not to forget the *controller*, who may issue commands to the captain. They may be opposed to terms used for a functional level, i.e. *pilot flying* vs. *pilot non-flying*. Further technical roles, which are only relevant in older aircraft, are *second officer* from a responsibility point of view, while *flight engineer* and *navigator* apply to the functional level. Exceptional roles are

those of participants that do not necessarily occur in ATC/CVR-transcripts. These are *steward, stewardess* and *flight attendant*, as e.g. in the transcripts used for the present analysis.

5. The EAGLES guidelines, in turn, refer to recommendations made by Llisterri (1996), Sperberg-McQueen & Burnard (1994) and Gibbon, Moore, & Winski (1997).

6. Unlike an external documentation, an in-text header makes it less likely to confuse texts because it can be utilised as part of an automatic analysis to provide background information as output. Furthermore, it enables quick reference, particularly if a manual, which is used as an external documentation, is not to hand. A slight drawback of in-text headers with regard to the ATC/CVR-corpus is that some information has to be repeated in the head of every transcript. However, the degree of redundancy is not so high that a reference or a link to an external documentation in the form of a manual or a database management system would be necessary (see Gibbon, Mertins, & Moore 2000:13).

7. The pattern "file information (flight name, date)" names the file and its contents as used in the ATC/CVR corpus.

8. *Topic processes* overlap with what Allwood, Nivre, & Ahlsen (1992) call "focussed or main message functions". *Uptake processes* apply to a great extent to their *speech management functions*, while *framing processes* display *interactive functions*.

9. Bryan Rife in an e-mail dated 25 September, 2000.

10. As exemplified by Schegloff and Sacks: *Ken: Sure enough ten minutes later the bell r- the doorbell rang [...]* (Schegloff & Sacks 1977:363).

11. *Transition space* denotes the location at which possible transition to a next speaker becomes relevant (Schegloff & Sacks 1977:366, ftn.12), cf. *transition relevance place*, (Sacks, Schegloff, & Jefferson 1974)

12. Whether the non-professional talk begins with Turn CFA004 or whether it also applies to the preceding turns is controversial. In this context, Turns CFA000–CCP003 have been defined as belonging to professional talk because the topic is aviation and has an immediate relevance to the flight situation. Moreover, the conversation is organised in adjacency pairs.

CHAPTER 5

Analysis of particular dialogue properties

For an analysis of crisis talk, not every ATC/CVR-transcript is appropriate. To fulfill the criterion of empirical soundness, the transcript is required to show both threads[1] of crisis talk and threads that do not apply to a crisis situation. Data of non-crisis talk may contain a *problem*. It is important that the problem is not (yet) the center of the talk. This requirement is essential for further contrastive analyses of crisis and non-crisis talk features. The other essential requirement is the criterion of empirical completeness of the dialogue. The transcript must not have gaps that distort comprehension of the ongoing action. This goes for missing words in utterances and also for unclear speaker identifications. There is, however, no need for the transcript to be a representation of the dialogue in its original language. The present analysis stresses the development of a method that allows investigation of crisis talk from a *functional* point of view, i.e. the analysis of language use. In this way, the method can be applied to various instances of crisis talk data. There is, in fact, a need for syntactic analysis, too, as it is a foundation of an automatic analysis. Automatic analysis is initiated via language data. An adequate grammar for this purpose is HPSG.

5.1 Identifying regularities

In the transcripts that meet the criteria of empirical soundness and completeness, a number of interactional patterns can be observed by which it is possible to determine whether the phase in question belongs to crisis talk or non-crisis talk.

Decomposition of the dialogue

The dialogue represented by the transcript must be decomposed by splitting it into threads. *Threads* are signal events, specifiable as sub-dialogues, viz. sequences of utterances that are thematically coherent[2] and may contain one or more types of speech acts.[3] The smallest thread is constituted by at least two turns. A turn is constituted by at least one speech act whereby a speech act is constituted by at least one utterance. As in dialogue games in task-oriented communication, coherence is manifest in speech acts that initiate an exchange such as those with the force *ask, command* or *state*, followed by responses and feedback patterns (Kowtko, Isard, & Doherty 1993). Feedback patterns are (speech) acts with the phatic function of keeping the channel of communication open (see Malinowski 1923, repr. 1969; Jakobson 1960). They do not have a function that is direct-dialogical. With its status of a sub-dialogue, a thread requires at least one speaker change, i.e. a minimum of two utterances. Each utterance, including those that cannot be assigned to a thread, will be analysed for its communicative function, which results in determining its illocutionary point and force. To consider unassignable utterances as well is highly important for the linguistic diagnosis of crisis talk. Further attention is paid to sub-sequences of threads that have the communicative function of backchannels. Communication here unrolls on the meta level, with the backchannel having a special status because it may be non-verbal. The resulting hierarchy is modelled in the tree diagram of Figure 5.1.

It is, however, controversial where to define the boundaries for the end of one thread and the beginning of the next. Keeping in mind that threads are defined as thematically coherent units of signal events, two possibilities exist: either each event of a signal source is considered as coherent for itself, e.g. the sound of the *ground proximity warning system* is one thread and the cockpit conversation is one thread, or there are cross-references between the signal sources wherever this seems adequate for the data (cf. Example (81)). Thus, a thread would, for instance, consist of a conversation of the crew members who deal with a particular topic and, as the case may be, react to a technical signal. The technical signal would then be integrated in the thread. In the present investigation the first solution has been pursued (see Figures 5.2 and 5.3).

During a flight many things – linguistic or non-linguistic – may happen. Problems in the analysis arise because the events of the transcripts are displayed as multiplex, since, for example, the utterances are not represented according to their coherence but in the order in which they were produced, i.e. several threads may overlap or interleave. In its original sense, *multiplex* means the combination of multiple signals for transmission over a single line or medium (Webopedia 2002). Aviation transcripts also conform to this definition, since speech signals from various participants along with signals from technical sources are transmitted (here: represented) over a single medium (here: the channel of graphostylistic medium).

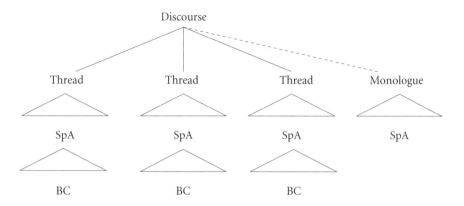

Figure 5.1 A dialogue hierarchy model and its decomposition relations. SpA=Speech Act, BC = backchannel

To illustrate this: The crews of the transcripts selected consist of three people. This alone may cause a switch in the order of the utterances that belong to a specific thread. When captain and first officer talk about a problem and the second officer announces a fact that has a different topic and the captain reacts to his announcement, and when then the talk between captain and first officer is continued, this will make reordering and reassignment of the utterances necessary. The crew's talk may also be interrupted by the controller's radio contact. Another possible case is the entrance of a third party, e.g. a flight assistant or a passenger who has a request. The request may temporarily distract the other party from the original conversational topic and initiate another thread. An analysis of the dialogues thus necessitates the reconstruction of each thread by means of extraction from the overall dialogue. Useful criteria in this respect are coreference or anaphoric relations to mark the relation between two textual elements that denote the same object. Subsequent mentioning of an entity that has already been introduced is often indicated by a particular type of noun phrase (anaphoric expression) (Mengel et al. 1999: 126).

An effective way in which the multiplexed order of threads can be untangled is depicted in Figures 5.2 and 5.3 (see also the digraphs of Bird and Liberman, who proposed the model of annotation graphs, in Section 3.4). The figures refer to the conversation of Example (81) and model the parallel threads of crew conversation, radio communication, radio altimeters, ground proximity warning system and the signal of the altitude warning horn. The difference between the figures lies in the abstraction from the concrete data in Figure 5.2 and in the application of the transcript data to the model in Figure 5.3. Parallel

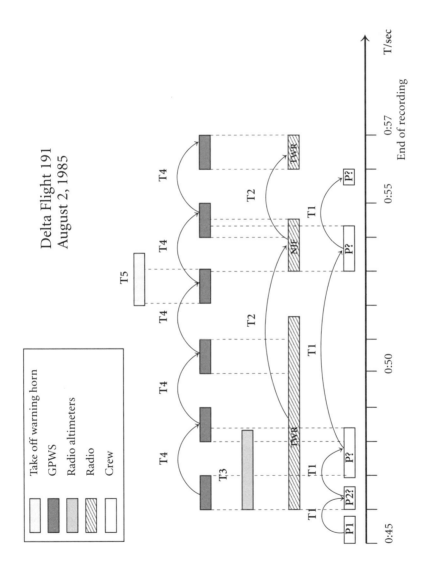

Figure 5.2 Model of the parallel events that occur during a flight. Key: T_n = thread, P_n = participant, TWR = tower, NJF = crew specification, GPWS = ground proximity warning system.

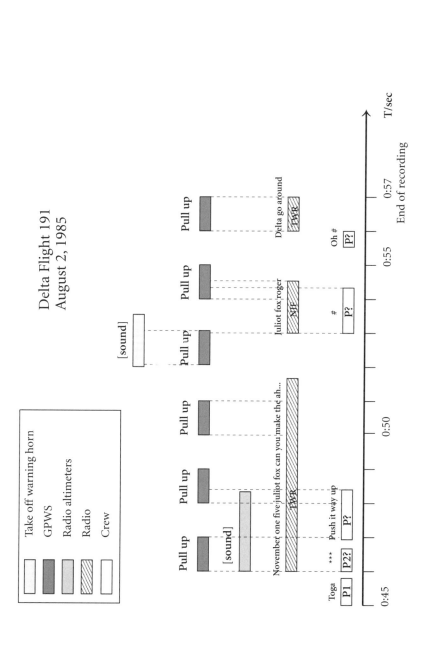

Figure 5.3 Application of the dialogue fragment (Example (81)) to the model of parallel events. Key: P$_n$ = participant, TWR = tower, NJF = crew specification, GPWS = ground proximity warning system.

events, including their points of overlap, can potentially be illustrated in much detail. Here, owing to data missing from the transcript, only the point of time at which an event begins can be detailed, the duration of the respective event under discussion runs out in an approximation.

(81)   CVR transcript Delta Flight 191 - 02 AUG 1985 (22)
CCP096: 18:05:45 Toga
CXX097: 18:05:46 ***
TWR098: 18:05:46 November one five juliot fox can you make
the ah we'll expedite down to the ah taxi thirty one and a
right turn off the traffics a mile final
CAM099: 18:05:46 [Sound of radio altimeters]
GPW100: 18:05:46 Whoop whoop pull up [sound of GPW is
distributed evenly and continously]
CXX101: 18:05:47 Push it way up
GPW102: 18:05:48 Whoop whoop pull up
GPW103: 18:05:49 Whoop whoop pull up
CAM104: 18:05:52 [Sound of noise similar to landing; sound
of takeoff warning horn: The sound continues for 1:6
seconds]
NJF105: 18:05:53 Juliot fox roger
CXX106: 18:05:53 #
CXX107: 18:05:55:5 Oh # [second impact]
TWR108: 18:05:56 Delta go around
ANN109: 18:05:57 End of recording

Figures 5.2 and 5.3 relate to the principle of annotation graphs as proposed by Bird and Liberman in that they offer a stratified representation of parallel events. Every layer describes a different kind of thread. The arcs model the respective signal events, the nodes pertain to stretches of time. The figures represent intervals of events, gaps and sequences of overlapping intervals.

Decomposition and representation of speech acts

Every speech act type, whether it is part of a thread or not, will be modelled by an HPSG-based structure. For every sequence that is modelled the explicanda are stated that qualify the respective speech acts to belong to one and the same thread. Sequences of one or more speech act types that belong to one turn or utterance will be marked. The same goes for iterated utterances, i.e. utterances in which the same speech act with the same words is repeated. The structure particularly takes into account the differences in the conditions of success of the different speech acts that are diagnosed for the dialogue. Other aspects will remain underspecified. An underspecified way of modelling a sequence of speech act types looks like this:

$$
\left\langle sa_1 = \begin{bmatrix} \text{FORCE iiT}_{point}^{force}\text{P} \\ \text{SUCCESS} \begin{bmatrix} \text{POINT} \dots \\ \text{MODE}_{POINT} \dots \\ \text{PREP} \dots \\ \text{SINCERITY} \dots \\ \dots \end{bmatrix} \end{bmatrix}, sa_2 = \begin{bmatrix} \text{FORCE iiT}_{point}^{force}\text{P} \\ \text{SUCCESS} \begin{bmatrix} \text{POINT} \dots \\ \text{MODE}_{POINT} \dots \\ \text{PREP} \dots \\ \text{SINCERITY} \dots \\ \dots \end{bmatrix} \end{bmatrix}, \dots sa_k \right\rangle
$$

For a more detailed representation of speech acts see Section 5.3. Constraints on the sequence of speech act types will be represented as regular expressions containing members of the set I, as shown in the example: $(sa_1\ sa_2)^+\ sa_3$

I is the set of all speech act types that occur in the selected dialogues of the crisis talk corpus: $I = \{\ sa_1, sa_2, \dots sa_k\ \}$

The idea behind decomposition is to make generalisations about the speech act types that formulate constraints on the sequence of speech act types which constitute the threads. The research aims at a juxtaposition of speech act sequences during crisis talk with speech act sequences before the crisis. In this way, crisis talk can be viewed in its larger context. Generalisations will be made on the evidence of selected speech act sequences, i.e. those that have the highest frequency of occurrence. The resulting constraints will be integrated as a subcategorisation list in an HPSG-based structure that models particular discourse sequences by means of one sign.

In order to find regularities in the speech act sequences of the threads, the most frequent and, at the same time, shortest sequence (a primitive) will be determined. A sequence like this corresponds to an adjacency pair that has exactly one speaker change and thus consists of two turns (or utterances). The adjacency pairs might be modified. The modifications mark an essential part of the analysis and will be considered in the overall generalisations of the development of aviation communication.

Expectable are sequences of adjacency pairs such as *question-answer* $(q_1a_1q_2a_2)$ or those of conditional relevance $(q_1q_2a_2a_1)$ if the tower interrupted the cockpit conversation (checklist); they also include saturated uptake loops that include sequences such as the speech act *state* followed by *request for clarification, clarify,* which may be concluded by *confirm*. For crisis talk, a higher frequency of uptake loops is expected and several occasions in which the loops are unsaturated; i.e. a request for clarification does not receive an appropriate response. The number of adjacency pairs that only have a first pair part is assumed to increase, the occurrence of iterated speech act types and tokens in one and the same utterance or turn will be more frequent. Politeness behaviour exemplified by acts such as *greet* and *thank* will decrease in number. There may also be instances in which the number of speech act types and tokens per turn will increase.

An alternative account of sequencing

Poesio & Traum (1997) pursue a strategy similar to the one outlined in Section 5.1. Details will be given where the two strategies diverge, and why that of Poesio & Traum (1997) was not adopted.

The analysis of Poesio and Traum, like the one in the present paper, relies on the notion of a thread, which is defined as follows:

> Much as [Grosz & Sidner (1986)] assume that discourse purposes are related to higher discourse purposes, we assume that conversational acts are related to other conversational acts, as well as to higher level actions, realised by multiple core speech acts and not associated with any utterance in particular. We call these more complex acts CONVERSATIONAL THREADS [...]
>
> (Poesio & Traum 1997:22)

Thus, conversational threads, or threads for short, are realised by conversational acts, which in turn are realised by multiple core speech acts. These latter notions will now be clarified, but it is clear that conversational acts arc not (necessarily) identical to individual utterances.

The basic notions for their theory are introduced through a table in Poesio & Traum (1997:13), which is reproduced here in Table 5.1.

The different act types that are exemplified in this table are collectively denoted by the term conversational act. The term *core speech act* is introduced as follows:

> Following the implemented TRAINS-93 system, we adopt here the multi-level CONVERSATIONAL ACTS theory, presented in Traum & Hinkelman (1992). This theory maintains the classical illocutionary acts of speech act theory (e.g. **in-form**, **suggest**), now called CORE SPEECH ACTS. These actions are, however, reinterpreted as multi-agent collaborative achievements, taking on their full effect only after they have been *grounded*, i.e. acknowledged [...]
>
> (Poesio & Traum 1997:12)

Table 5.1 The table from Poesio & Traum (1997) introducing the different types of discourse levels and their related act types. SubUU=sublexical utterance unit, e.g. turn-taking signals, UU=utterance unit, DU=discourse unit, ack=acknowledge, ReqRepair=request repair, ReqAck=request acknowledgement, ynq=yes-no question, q&a=question answer, eval=evaluate.

Discourse Level	Act Type	Sample Acts
Sub UU	Turn-Taking	take-turn, keep-turn, release-turn, assign-turn
UU	Grounding	initiate, continue, ack, repair, ReqRepair, ReqAck, cancel
DU	Core Speech Act	inform, ynq, check, eval, suggest, request, accept, cancel
Multiple DUs	Argumentation	elaborate, summarize, clarify q&a, convince, find-plan

Poesio and Traum continue to say that their Conversational Acts (CA) theory presumes that the three other types of speech acts are performed in conversation, whereby argumentation acts should be realised by more than one core speech act. Note that the reinterpretation of speech acts as relations between pairs of illocutionary acts – just like the present proposal – amounts to adopting a dynamic theory of interpretation. This is reflected in the implementation of the compositional DRT from Muskens (1994) by the authors. Now that the notion of a conversational act has been explained, return can be made to the notion of a thread, as it is used by Poesio & Traum (1997). The authors explain that it

> is a basic fact about the way humans interpret events that they tend to be grouped into larger 'stories' or, as we will call them here, THREADS [...] A thread is itself an event, that decomposes hierarchically into its constituent events (Kautz 1987). The hierarchical organization of speech acts into larger units or discourse segments (associated with more general purposes) is just an instance of this more general phenomenon of events being grouped into threads, and the relations between DSPs assumed by Grosz and Sidner are those generally assumed to hold between actions. (e.g. in Kautz's theory)
>
> (Poesio & Traum 1997:26)

It is clear that the notion of a thread as used in the current paper is identical to the notion of a thread in Poesio & Traum (1997): in both cases it is used to ascertain the fact that certain stretches of discourse form a coherent unit, or tell a single story. It is shared assumption with Grosz & Sidner (1986) that the very notion of coherence can thus be explained. But if the notion of a thread is the same, what is the difference between their account and the present one?

Remember that Poesio & Traum (1997) reinterpret as a relation what they call the classical notions of speech act theory. They take it that a speech act is uttered felicitously only if a pertinent grounding act is performed by the interlocutor of the speaker. This is a clear difference in methodology in relation to the present paper. Here, speech acts are conceived of as is indicated in the traditional literature, and the result is that the illocutionary force indicating devices (IFIDs) can be used to assign an illocutionary force to the utterances.

This feature has no place in the theory of Poesio & Traum (1997). Clearly, if the identity of a core speech act depends on the presence of a subsequent act, there is no way to syntactically, phonetically, graphematically or semantically derive the type of act present. Characteristically, there is no level of syntactic analysis in the account given by Poesio and Traum. But as it is a goal of the present book to take a bottom-up approach and to use IFIDs, the way in which Poesio and Traum construe discourse is no option.

What can be considered a strength of the account in Poesio & Traum (1997) is the opportunity to account for the multifunctionality of utterances. This can be demonstrated by one of the standard examples from the paper, viz. Example (82).

(82)   a.   There is an engine at Avon.
       b.   It is hooked to a boxcar.

Utterance (82a), issued by one interlocutor, and Utterance (82b), issued by the other, constitute some part of a thread. The contributions which the single utterances make to the thread is rendered by the following DRSs (discourse representation structures) in Poesio & Traum (1997:42):

(83)

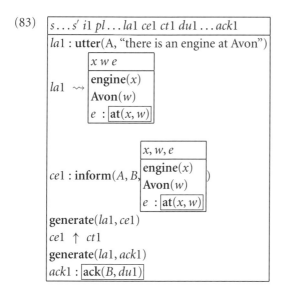

$s\ldots s'\ i1\ pl\ldots la1\ ce1\ ct1\ du1\ldots ack1$

$la1$: **utter**(A, "there is an engine at Avon")

$$la1 \rightsquigarrow \begin{array}{|l|} \hline x\ w\ e \\ \hline \textbf{engine}(x) \\ \textbf{Avon}(w) \\ e\ :\ \boxed{\textbf{at}(x,w)} \\ \hline \end{array}$$

$$ce1 : \textbf{inform}(A, B, \begin{array}{|l|} \hline x,\ w,\ e \\ \hline \textbf{engine}(x) \\ \textbf{Avon}(w) \\ e\ :\ \boxed{\textbf{at}(x,w)} \\ \hline \end{array})$$

generate($la1$, $ce1$)

$ce1\ \uparrow\ ct1$

generate($la1$, $ack1$)

$ack1$: $\boxed{\textbf{ack}(B, du1)}$

(84)

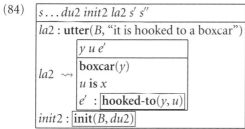

$s\ldots du2\ init2\ la2\ s'\ s''$

$la2$: **utter**(B, "it is hooked to a boxcar")

$$la2 \rightsquigarrow \begin{array}{|l|} \hline y\ u\ e' \\ \hline \textbf{boxcar}(y) \\ u\ \textbf{is}\ x \\ e'\ :\ \boxed{\textbf{hooked-to}(y,u)} \\ \hline \end{array}$$

$init2$: $\boxed{\textbf{init}(B, du2)}$

A look at the DRS in Example (83) tells us that there is a locutionary act $la1$, which is an utterance by speaker A to the fact that there is an engine at Avon. This locutionary act leads to the message expressed by the upper embedded DRS in Example (83) that there is an engine at Avon. This message, being a piece of information, realises the conversational event $ce1$. In other words, $la1$ generates the conversational event $ce1$. The latter, in turn is dominated by the conversational thread $ct1$, which lies hierarchically below and is indicated by $ce1\ \uparrow\ ct1$. Now the difficulties, however, begin.

As stated in Example (83), $la1$ generates an acknowledgement, $ack1$; this is presumably a typo. Following the logic of the paper, the relevant acknowledgement should be generated by $la2$, namely "it is hooked to a boxcar" from Utterance (82b). This would make sense, as no context is given for Utterance (82a) to which $la1$ could be an acknowledgement. Rather, the initial DRS seems to be empty. Thus, the respective line in the DRS in Example (83) should read **generate**($la2$, $ack1$). The next change, of course would have to be to turn the line $ack1$: $\boxed{\text{ack}(B, du1)}$ into $ack1$: $\boxed{\text{ack}(B, du2)}$. Having done this, it would be necessary to include the discourse referents $la2$ and $du2$ in the universe of Example (83). The resulting DRS would read

(85)

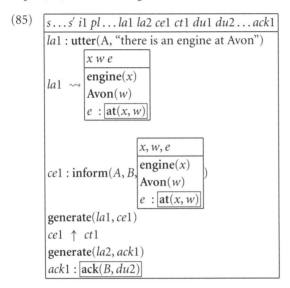

The last line in the DRS in Example (85), unlike that in Example (83), accounts for the fact that the acknowledgement by speaker B is uttered in a second discourse unit. Nevertheless, it may be questioned whether the DRS in Example (85) actually expresses what should be expressed. What the DRS states now is that, whatever utterance follows, it acknowledges the content of the previous one. This is surely something Poesio and Traum would not want to have, given the number of possibilities they enumerate as continuations for utterances that initiate argumentation acts or threads in the description of a finite state automaton (FSA). The automaton is repeated here in Table 5.2.

Table 5.2 specifies the transitions that are possible by performing utterance units: The initiating utterance unit brings the FSA from State S into State 1. Whenever it is in this state, the following utterances can be of a number of types: the current speaker can continue talking, keeping the FSA in State 1, just as if he were to repair his preceding utterance. An ensuing repair by the interlocutor, by contrast, would result in a transition into State 3. It is only an acknowledgement act by the interlocutor that leads to State F, which is the prerequisite for starting a new discourse unit.

Given that illocutionary acts can indeed realise initiations of new discourse units and acknowledgements of the current ones, it is implausible (and indeed

Table 5.2 The definition of the FSA given in Poesio and Traum (1997). The superscripts *I* and *R* refer to initiator and responder, respectively.

Next Act	In State						
	S	1	2	3	4	F	D
initiate^I	1						
continue^I		1			4		
continue^R			2	3			
repair^I		1	1	1	4	1	
repair^R	3		2	3	3	3	
ReqRepair^I			4	4	4	4	
ReqRepair^R	2		2	2	2	2	
ack^I				F	1*	F	
ack^R		F	F*			F	
ReqAck^I		1				1	
ReqAck^R				3		3	
cancel^I		D	D	D	D	D	
cancel^R			1	1		D	

excluded by Table 5.2) to suppose that all of them do so. Nevertheless, "it is hooked to a boxcar" seems to be a good candidate for an acknowledgement. The step to take is to include the utterance itself in the DRS that contains the *ack* entry, i.e. Example (85). This would lead to Example (86).

(86)
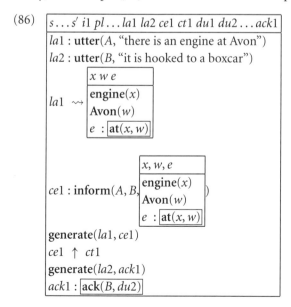

The DRS in Example (86) would now render the obtaining facts correctly, but, of course, Example (84) would have to be modified accordingly.

Whichever measures are taken to represent the structure of the discourse and the functions of the utterances correctly, there remains some point of critique: At no point do Poesio & Traum (1997) make use of the devices that are present at the surface of the discourse and that could and should be used for due explanation. This is one of the goals of the present study, and the reason that the analysis by Poesio & Traum (1997) is not an alternative for current purposes.

Specification of the selected transcripts

As a matter of fact, none of the corpus files turned out to be without gaps, i.e. without unintelligible or incomplete utterances, or utterances whose content was questionable. With some of the transcripts it was particularly difficult, as they were censored; e.g. utterances or parts of utterances were deliberately replaced with a symbol that marked an *expletive deleted* or *non-pertinent text*. There might have been additional utterances that were left out by the transcribers without being documented. It is necessary to rely on the transcriber's care and thoroughness in every respect. Two transcripts were chosen for the analysis whose gaps did not affect comprehension of the respective threads and, with this, of the whole dialogue. Some utterances do not prove unequivocally assignable because of the high frequency of pronouns in the speech. Others obviously do not have any thread they belong to, because of the crisis situation in which the normal flow of information is disrupted.

The transcripts that were selected for the analysis document the *Eastern Air Lines Flight 401, December 29, 1972* (tr1) and *Avianca Flight 052, January 25, 1990* (tr2).

The probable cause of the Eastern Air Lines crash is ascribed to the flight crew's failure to monitor the flight instruments. Thus, the crew did not detect an unexpected descent soon enough to prevent impact with the ground. The crew's attention had been distracted by the malfunction of the nose landing gear position-indicating system.

The Avianca Flight ended in a disaster probably because of a low state of fuel compounded by the engines running down. The crew had to enter three holding patterns during the aircraft's flight to New York and, while they were already running out of fuel, had to carry out a go-around as follow-up to a missed approach due to the bad weather conditions at the airport. The complete transcripts and further background information on the accidents are given in Appendices E and F.

Avianca is a Colombian airline. That the crew spoke Spanish during phases of intra-cockpit communication is highly probable. The transcript is entirely in English, though, and does not indicate whether any of the utterances were translations from Spanish. Since the major goal of the present investigation is to develop a method that allows a functional analysis of utterances applicable to various instantiations of crisis talk, a syntactic analysis and thus the original language of each utterance are of secondary importance.

The transcripts have only minor gaps, which means few incomplete or unintelligible utterances where the missing parts do not distort the overall meaning of the dialogue to a recognisable extent. Their respective length is 140 lines with 6 incomplete utterances, 5 unintelligible utterances and three instances of expletives deleted (tr1), and 409 lines with 5 incomplete utterances (tr2). While tr1 had 33 turns with an unclear speaker identity, tr2 had 6 turns which proved unassignable to speakers. In tr1, these were exclusively related to the turns aimed at the tower (abbreviated RXX, where –XX means that it is not clear whether the captain or the copilot was speaking). In tr2, unclear speakers referred to intra-cockpit speech. In either case, missing or imprecise speaker assignments did not affect the meaning of the overall dialogue or the unequivocal assignment of utterances to threads.

Linguistic coherence markers, such as anaphora, may have an adverse effect when it comes to a high frequency of pronouns in the dialogue.[4] Since the crew has the visual channel at its disposal, apart from the auditive, olfactory and tactile channel, talk may refer to context rather than to text, as illustrated in Example (87):

(87) CCP061: Now push the switches just a ... forward.
      CCP062: Okay.

In this sequence of utterances, both utterances were produced by the captain, the first being a *command*[5] and the second a *confirm* by which the captain approves of an action that the reader of the transcript cannot witness. By executing the action the other person confirms that he has understood the captain's command.

On the other hand, utterances which do not seem to pair with any other utterance and thus do not belong to a thread may have elicited a reaction on the contextual level because the interlocutors replied, e.g. by using gestures. Thus, it might be dangerous to infer that during crisis talk utterances are produced which remain unanswered. However, it appears that gesture or other contextual replies are not at issue.

For tr1, 103 threads and 461 speech act tokens were found, for tr2, 30 threads and 153 speech act tokens. In tr1, 8 of the 103 threads contain backchannel subsequences, while in tr2, 6 threads had backchannels. For both transcripts 19 speech act types could be determined, among them the acts *state, command, ask* and *confirm*. Most of the utterances contained only simple speech acts. Most cases exactly one speech act was produced via one turn. Seventeen turns of tr1 contained two different speech act types, 3 turns had two speech acts of the same type. Three turns contained 3 different speech act types, 3 turns with 3 speech act tokens contained the same speech act type twice or thrice. Two turns contained 4 speech act tokens of which one type was iterated once. Tr2 had 5 turns that consisted of two speech act tokens where one turn had one iteration of a speech act type.

Minimal sequences

For either transcript, the most frequent minimal sequence consisted of illocutions of the force *command* followed by a *confirm*. In atomic writing the sequence is abbreviated *seq → co+con*. Criteria for determining the coherence of *command* and *confirm* were in the first place coreference criteria as exemplified in Example (88):

(88) CCP088: 2111:32 Give me flaps fourteen.
      ...
      CFO090: 2111:33 Flaps fourteen.

The captain commands the first officer to set *flaps fourteen*. The latter replies to the command reading back the essential part of the captain's utterance verbatim. ATC-regulations and comparisons with other crew communication of different transcripts show that a reply of this sort usually signals *confirm*. A case may be constructed in which the first officer only accidently utters the words *flaps fourteen*; however, probability is higher that he reacted to the captain's command and indeed means *confirm*.

The high occurrence of the sequence *seq → co+con* satisfies the expectations with regard to the register and conversation structure of aviation. Giving orders and signalling understanding is vital for the successful execution of flights and is thus part of the ATC-regulations. The regulations make sure that the pilot-in-command submits orders aimed at the pilot flying and receives commands from the tower. There may be cases in which the pilot-in-command also sends out orders to the tower. While *command* applies to the object level of language, *confirm* pertains to two levels: to the meta level, because it signals acoustic and semantic understanding of the preceding speech act, and to the object level, because it usually signals that the demanded action will be carried out in the immediate context or has already been carried out. In tr1, *seq* → *co+con* occurred fifty-three times, in tr2 fourteen times.

Other salient but less frequent minimal sequences in both transcripts are built up from illocutions of the force *ask* and *confirm* (*seq* → *as+con*), often in the form of yes-no questions by which the captain mostly wants to check whether an action has already been carried out (see Example (89)):

(89) CCP246: 2124:22 Advise him we are emergency!
      CCP247: 2124:26 Did you tell him? (as)
      ...
      CFO249: 2124:28 Yes sir. (con)
      CFO250: 2124:29 I already advised him.

Other frequent minimal sequences in both transcripts consist of illocutionary acts of the force *state* and *confirm* (*seq* → *st+con*), which again is not surprising, because some of the utterances that could have been produced using a directive illocutionary role are in fact statements. That is to say, statements must be interpreted as *indirect commands* in some cases.

The checklist is a problematic case, because during this phase usually no verb is used. This is unfortunate, since the verb mood in particular is a helpful illocutionary force indicating device. Thus, it is difficult to judge whether the person in command utters a directive or an assertive. As exemplified below, the person in command simply reads out the keyword on the list while, in accordance with the ATC-regulations, his colleague(s) confirm(s) his illocution and execute(s) whatever is correlated with the keyword.

(90) CCP148: 2119:30 Mode selector approach land checklist.
      CFE149: 2119:32 Landing check.
      CFE150: 2119:41 Speed brake lever.
      CCP151: 2119:42 Full forward.
      CFE152: 2119:43 Spoiler switches.
      CFO153: 2119:45 On.

If the illocutions were interpreted as assertives, they could be further understood as indirect commands. The decision has been made to follow this idea. In the above checklist-thread, anaphoric criteria are the read back *landing check* by the flight engineer, who then seems to be in command as far as the checklist is concerned. His illocution of the force *state* prompts the captain to respond with *full forward*, a state that may be related to the state of a speed brake lever. Analogously, one of the states which spoiler switches may have is indeed *on*, as the first officer confirms, and thus indicates that the first officer reacts to the flight engineer's utterance.

The minimal sequences *seq → st+con* and *seq → co+con* are regarded as basic minimal sequences because of their status in the aviation regulations and their resulting salience in the transcripts. Other minimal sequences that can be found, e.g. *seq → as+con* (ask-confirm) or *seq → re+con* (request-confirm), rank as modifications, because the forces *ask* and *request* form part of the same illocutionary role as *command*, viz. of the *directive*.

Modifications of minimal sequences

Two categories of modifications can be established for the analysis of the transcripts: *paradigmatic* and *syntagmatic* modifications. Paradigmatic modifications apply to the type described above in which the illocutionary force is changed while the type of illocutionary point remains the same. A syntagmatic modification pertains to an alteration of the *combination* of the sequence's components (regardless of whether its components have been paradigmatically modified): The minimal sequence of the basic type *seq → co+con* may be modified by breaking up the adjacent position of the illocutionary forces. This may happen in the case of reprise utterances in which an utterance of the same illocutionary force is appended to a previous one while the utterance is repeated verbatim. Example: *seq → co+co+con*:

(91)   TWR128: 2117:42 Increase, increase! (co+co)
       (...)
       RXX130: 2117:44 Increasing (con)

The reprise utterance may originate from the same or a different participant, as in the sequence *seq → st+con+con*:

(92)   CFE152: 2119:43 Spoiler switches. (st)
       CFO153: 2119:45 On. (con)
       CFE154: 2119.45 On. (con)

While the reprise act is appended to the original act, the adjacency of the forces is not disrupted. However, disruption of the adjacency is at issue when the basic sequence obtains in its centre a chunk of text that consists of one or more points which modify the preceding point or which belong to a different illocutionary role. In Example (93), the minimal sequence *seq* → *as+con* is expanded into the sequence *seq* → *as+rfc+cl+con*, i.e. the points *ask, request for clarification, clarification, confirmation*. This sequence pertains to an uptake loop that helps secure understanding (which takes place on the meta level), where *rfc+cl* mark the core of the loop.

(93) CCP086: 23:39:37 Did you ever take it out of there? (as)

CFO087: Huh? (rfc)

CCP088: Have you ever taken it out of there? (cl)

CFO089: Hadn't till now (con)

That the sequence of four utterances belong to the same thread may be inferred from the following coherence criteria: While the captain asks about the *it* (here: the nose wheel), the first officer replies in the backchannel signalling on the meta level that he did not understand the captain's utterance. That the backchannel indeed refers to that utterance can be determined from the fact that the captain repeated the first utterance, and also by the fact that the first officer's next utterance (*Hadn't till now*) obviously answers the captain's query. If the first officer's backchannel had not related to the captain's question, he might have marked that by an utterance such as *No, I meant XY*.

A further modification comes into play when the minimal sequence is unsaturated in that the first pair part does not have a second pair part and thus does not constitute a thread. Example (94) shows an illocution with the point *ask* that occurs right before the aircraft impacts with the ground:

(94) CCP136: 23:42:09 Hey, what's happening here? (as)

CAM137: [Sound of click]

CAM138: 23:42:10 [Sound of six beeps similar to radio altimeter increasing in rate]

CAM139: 23:42:12 [Sound of impact]

Another type of an unsaturated sequence can be exemplified for an uptake loop that is not saturated:

(95) CFO133: 23:42:05 We did something to the altitude (st)

CCP134: What? (rfc)

CFO135: 23:42:07 We're still at two thousand right? (as)

CCP136: 23:42:09 Hey, what's happening here? (as)

CAM137: [Sound of click]

The first officer (CFO) states that they (probably he himself and the second officer) modified the flight level, whereas the captain (CCP) seems to refer to that statement with a request for clarification as he apparently did not understand his colleague's utterance acoustically. The second officer does not reply but launches another question (as) which is followed by another question (as) by the captain, all of which remain unanswered. The unsaturated uptake loop can be restated as *seq → st+rfc+Ø+Ø* for no clarification and, thus, no confirmation follow either.

Another instantiation of an unsaturated uptake loop, this time a more complex one, is displayed in Example (96). It is presumably the first officer (RXX), who issues a statement to tower about the current airspeed. The tower responds with a request to increase airspeed, which is followed by an emphatic command as the crew apparently failed to react. The captain produces a request for clarification, which is aimed at the crew. The person, who is presumably to be first officer, utters *Increasing*. It is yet not clear whether this utterance could be interpreted as having a double function, i.e. as a confirm towards the tower and as clarification towards the captain: The controller repeats his command to increase airspeed while the captain requests clarification (*What?*). The captain again asks for clarification but does not receive an answer. Meanwhile it seems that RXX has increased airspeed as the tower responds with an *Okay*. Finally, the captain explains why he had communication problems. The resulting sequence of the unsaturated uptake loop is *seq → co+co+rfc+Ø+Ø+con/cl+rfc+Ø+Ø* where Ø marks the gaps of the unsaturated uptake loops:

(96)   RXX123: 2117:20 Avianca zero five two, one four zero knots.
       TWR125: 2117:30 Avianca zero five two, can you increase your
       airspeed one zero knots?
       TWR128: 2117:42 Increase, increase! (co+co)
       CCP129: 2117:42 What? (rfc)
       RXX130: 2117:44 Increasing (con/cl?)
       CCP131: 2117:45 What? (rfc)
       TWR132: 2117:46 Okay (con)
       CCP138: 2117:55 Tell me things louder, because I'm not hear-
       ing it.

From the examples that were analysed, patterns as stated in Table 5.3 were derived (more examples are listed in Appendix D). This analysis is not meant to be statistical. What is important about the results is their tendency. One could describe these patterns with regular expressions; however, they would result in a complicated enumeration of patterns that are not significant. Nevertheless, the results above show that crisis talk has more patterns than non-crisis talk.

Table 5.3 Patterns of speech act sequences in non-crisis talk and crisis talk.

Speech act sequences in	
non-crisis talk	crisis talk
$seq \rightarrow$ $\begin{cases} st + \emptyset \\ st + con \\ st + rfc + cl + con \\ st + rfc + cl + el + \emptyset \\ st + st + rfc + cl + el + con/dis \\ co + con \\ co + rfc + cl + \emptyset \\ as + con \\ as + dis \end{cases}$	$seq \rightarrow$ $\begin{cases} st + \emptyset \\ st + con \\ st + st + con + con \\ st + rfc + \emptyset + \emptyset \\ st + rfc + cl + con \\ co + \emptyset \\ co + con \\ co + dis \\ co + (co) + con + con \\ co + rfc + cl + con \\ co + (co+)rfc + \emptyset + rfc + \emptyset \\ as + \emptyset \\ as + con \\ as + dis \\ as + con + con \\ as + rfc + cl + con/dis \\ as + rfc + cl + con \end{cases}$

Comparing crisis talk and non-crisis talk, the following tendencies – which are summed up in Table 5.4 – can be established: while non-crisis talk has one illocutionary act more than crisis talk, there are more patterns in crisis talk. Uptake-securing sequences with an *elaborate*[6] only occur in non-crisis talk. To elaborate on one's preceding clarification is probably too time-consuming for a situation that requires quick action. The number of politeness formulae like *thank* and *greet* decreases in crisis talk. In the remainder of this section, stress will be put on examples from crisis talk.

Expressives, particularly *curses* and *warnings* are primarily present in utterances of crisis talk, as exemplified by Example (97):

(97) CVR transcript Lufthansa Flight 2904 - 14 SEP 1993
      PNF Dreh ihn weg (turn it away)
      PF Scheisse! (shit!) <-

While non-crisis talk does have uptake securing, the number of these processes increase in crisis talk. In crisis talk, unsaturated uptake sequences are salient. *Unsaturated* means that a *request for clarification* is not followed by a *clarification*. The term *unsaturated* may also be extended to minimal sequences in that a directive or an assertive does not elicit any reaction. This is also observable for crisis talk, whereas in non-crisis talk unsaturated assertives only can be found.

In crisis talk, the number of speech act types and tokens per turn increases. Also, identical repetition of commands and questions is observable. Non-crisis talk does not display reprise utterances of this kind. Repetitions cause disfluencies in conversation, similar to unsaturated uptake loops. They can be grouped as *restarts* and *iterations*. *Restarts* mark new beginnings in the pronunciation of a word after the speech production was previously broken off, usually resulting in truncated words and/or utterances. The speaker may take up the truncated sign or utterance and re-iterate it, or he may return to an earlier thought with an extended formulation. An instance of restart after a truncated word/utterance and probably return to an earlier thought is shown in Example (98):

> (98) CVR transcript Japan Air Lines Flight 123 - 12 AUG 1985
>   18:31:35 FE: What? more aft...ah...What was damaged? <-

Restart after truncated utterance, new thought and probably return to previously truncated utterance is instantiated here by Example (99):

> (99) CVR transcript Air Canada Flight 797 - 02 JUN 1983 (19)
>   CFO120: 19:04:07 Okay I eh, you don't <-
>   have to do it now, I can't go back now, it's too heavy, I
>   think we'd better go down

Example (100) instantiates a restart with iteration of last sign of truncated utterance:

> (100) CVR transcript Lauda Air Flight 004 - 26 MAY 1991 (34)
>   23.25:26 CA: Ah, you can tell 'em it, just it's, it's, it's,
>   just ah, no, ah, <-
>   it's probably ah wa... ah moisture or something 'cause it's
>   not just, oh, it's coming on and off.

Within-turn repetitions apply to the iteration of language phenomena: On the word level this goes for discourse particles, and on the utterance level for the speech act types *directive* or *assertive*. Especially iterations of directives might be interpreted as a functional shift by which the directive obtains some qualities of an *expressive*. The same might be stated for iterated discourse particles. This observation goes back to Searle, who makes the critical point that the use of some linguistic expressions may have a semantic and functional shift when they are used in dialogue. For instance, this is the case with the English directive verb *urge*, which, according to Searle, has an assertive use, but is in the first instance a directive, and as such "to urge is simply to advocate a course of action" (Searle & Vanderveken 1985:200). Here is a within-turn repetition of directives (Example (101)):

(101)   AeroPeru B757 off Lima (Peru) 2 Oct, 1996
        CCO257: 00:52:43 (12:26) THE LOWER ONE, THE LOWER ONE, THE
        LOWER ONE, THE LOWER ONE, THAT LAST ONE... <-
        AIR DATA THERE IT IS.
        (...)
        CCP260: 00:52:52 (12:35) FUCK..!
        BASIC INSTRUMENTS, LET'S GO TO BASIC INSTRUMENTS! <-
        (...)
        ATC537: 01:11:02 (30:45) GO UP, GO UP <-
        IF IT INDICATES PULL UP <-
        CCP538: 01:11:05 (30:48) I HAVE IT, I HAVE IT!

Example (102) offers a within-turn repetition of assertives:

(102)   (7) Birgen Air B757 Accident 6 Feb, 1996
        HCP096: 0346:54 thrust, don't pull back,
        don't pull back, don't pull back, don't pull back
        HCO097: 0346:56 okay open open <-
        HCP098: 0346:57 don't pull back, please don't pull back
        HCO099: 0346:59 open sir, open <-

Example (103) contains a within-turn repetition of expressives, Example (104) an inter-turn repetition of the same speech act type:

(103)   CVR transcript United Flight 585 - 03 MAR 1991
        CAM027: 09:43:37:4 [Click sound similiar to that of a flap
        lever actuation]
        CFO028: 09:43:38:4 Oh my God... <-
        [unidentifiable click sound] Oh my God! <-

(104)   Birgen Air B757 Accident 6 Feb, 1996
        HCP102: 0347:03 what's happening <-
        HCO103: 0347:05 oh what's happening <-

And finally, repetition of discourse particles with the possible function of an expressive looks like this:

(105)   CVR transcript Japan Air Lines Flight 123 - 12 AUG 1985 (23)
        18:31:35 FE: What? more aft...ah...What was damaged? Where?
        ah...ah...ah... ah... Coat room? <-

Table 5.4 Comparison of patterns in crisis talk and non-crisis talk. An upward arrow means an increasing tendency, a downward arrow refers to a decreasing tendency.

Feature	Crisis talk	Non-crisis talk
Complexity of patterns	⇑	⇓
Additional illocutionary types	*curse*	*elaborate*
Number of uptake securing processes	⇑	⇓
Number of unsaturated sequences	⇑	⇓
Number of illocutionary types and tokens per turn	⇑	⇓
Number of reprise utterances	⇑	⇓
Number of politeness formulae	⇓	⇑

5.2 Representation of an utterance sequence as an HPSG-based sign

By way of illustration, one coherent sequence of utterances taken from the two transcripts under discussion will be featured. It demonstrates how a thread can be modelled by an extended HPSG. The selected thread revolves around the plane's nose-wheel (Example (106)):

(106) CCP086: Did you ever take it out of there?
       CFO087: Huh?
       CCP088: Have you ever taken it out of there?
       CFO089: Hadn't till now.

The captain (CCP) wants to know whether the first officer (CFO) has ever in his life taken it out of the well. The first officer obviously does not understand the captain's utterance, an illocutionary act of type *directive* with the illocutionary force *ask*, and replies on the meta level with a *request for clarification* (illocutionary act of type *directive*, force *request*). Thus he enters an uptake loop that the captain continues with the repetition of his initial utterance, albeit in a slightly different manner by a near paraphrase. He utters an illocutionary act on the meta level of type *assertive*/force *clarify*. The first officer is now responding on two levels. With an illocutionary act of type *assertive* and its force *disconfirm* he makes a remark about the content of the captain's utterance. On the meta level he produces an utterance of type *assertive* with the force *confirm* and, in doing so, completes and leaves the process of the uptake loop. Uptake securing has been successfully performed.

An HPSG-based representation is used to model Example (106) by means of one HPSG sign. The basic idea is to apply to the discourse level the HPSG rules and principles that are traditionally used on the sentence level. The model is developed on the foundation of the formalism that was elaborated for the representation of single illocutionary acts (see Figure 3.2). A new view integrated into this model is the core idea of *dynamic semantics* (see e.g. Benthem 1996). This idea can be expressed in the words of Asher, Busquets, & Le Draoulec (2001), who say that

> a theory of discourse interpretation takes into account the meaning of a discourse beyond that of its constituent sentences taken singly, in order to give an interpretation of a discourse as a whole. To do this, we need to address two questions. Firstly, how do we model a discourse context and secondly, what is the contribution of a new sentence in such a context? If we can answer these two questions, we will have a means to build up the meaning of a discourse incrementally and in something like a compositional fashion. This view has gradually become the dominant one since the early eighties in formal theories of meaning and is known as *dynamic semantics*. According to this view, the meaning of a sentence is a relation between contexts; it is a transition from the given context (i.e. the input context) to a new context in which the input context has been updated with the information contained in the sentence.
>
> (Asher, Busquets, & Le Draoulec 2001:219–220)

The main function of the model is to describe criteria for the well-formedness of dialogues. Two ideal communication methods will be identified by the model: first, a direct reply/confirm to a question (st+con) or a confirmation that follows straight on a command (co+con); second, a confirm to a command that is preceded by an uptake loop (co+rfc+cl+con).

For this analysis, the traditional HPSG principles, i.e. the *head feature principle* and its closely related *subcategorisation principle* were applied to the discourse level. The sign that results from the application of the modified HPSG-inventory is of type *thread* (see Figure 5.6) and marks the static representation of a finite-state automaton that is used to describe the ideal development of communication. The automaton is based on the idea that utterances model transitions from one state to the next. This implements the idea that underlies dynamic semantics. While the nodes mark the states, the arrows stand for the transitions (see Figures 5.4 and 5.5). The HEAD-DTR of the sign is the first utterance of the thread *Did you ever take it out of there?* that subcategorises for a further thread, here marked either by the uptake loop as explained above or by a shorter version that is filled out by one token only. Thus, the SUBCAT-list has deliberately been underspecified, since the model aims at representing two possible kinds of dialogue development for aviation communication. The dialogue thread may be represented as a regular expression in the following way: $seq \rightarrow as(rfc,cl)^* con$

The full sequence $seq \rightarrow as+rfc+cl+con$ is especially symptomatic of crisis talk in that uptake securing problems occur which have to be resolved by a communication process, uptake loops, on the meta-linguistic level. The extracted sequence $seq \rightarrow as+con$, by contrast, is the ideal way of communication in aviation (which might also be part of crisis talk). It simply consists of an illocutionary act of type *directive* either of the force *ask (for information)* or *command*, and it is saturated by an illocutionary act of type *assertive* of the force *confirm*.

Furthermore, the model elaborates on the idea that the clarification thread representing the uptake loop has the HEAD-DTR *rfc token* (rfc=request for clarification) that subcategorises for the tokens of type *clarification-token* followed by a *confirmation-token*. If one of these tokens is missing, the uptake loop is not saturated.

The sign of the lemma *thread* (see Figure 5.6) has the attributes SURF, SEM and SYN. The SURF-attribute has as value the complete thread (see Example (106)). For notational ease the value of the attribute has been abbreviated by dots. The SEM-attribute marks the illocutionary purpose of the thread, i.e. to secure uptake, to get from a state of need for information (s_1) to the state of information-saturation (s_4), which is represented by the value pair $\langle s_1, s_4 \rangle$, the overall result of the conversation. It was developed in the following way: the first utterance of the thread is a functor that is applied to the subsequent utterance, its argument. The result of this operation again is a functor which is applied to the next argument. The application can be rephrased as

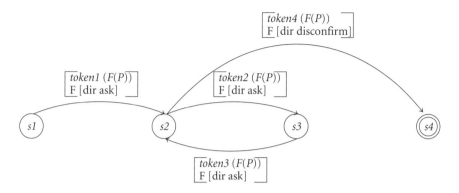

Figure 5.4 Representation of a dialogue sequence with a possible uptake loop by a transition network that models a nondeterministic finite state automaton. Two circles mark the final state.

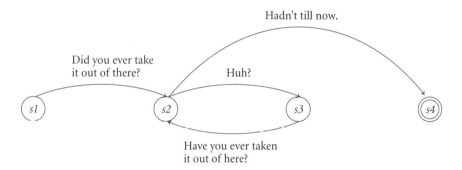

Figure 5.5 Application: the model is mapped onto a thread that contains an uptake loop.

$[[[\langle s_1,s_2\rangle](\langle s_2,s_3\rangle)](\langle s_3,s_2\rangle)](\langle s_2,s_4\rangle)=\langle s_1,s_4\rangle$, which is a concatenation of transitions represented by the pairs in angular brackets. The expressions in square brackets mark functors in relation to their respective arguments grouped in parentheses. The transition from the initial to the final state might be executed directly by a reply to the initiating *question-token*, or it might take a process of uptake securing and need a sequence of further tokens. This is modelled by the SYN-attribute that breaks down into the HEAD-DTR of type *question-token* and its COMP-DTRS of type *clarification-thread*.

   Head-daughter of the complete thread is the *question-token*, instantiated by *Did you ever take it out of there?* The utterance is the value of the SURF attribute that belongs to the HEAD-DTR. The SEM attribute has the value $\langle s_1,s_2\rangle$. The SYN-attribute bears a SUBCAT-list that has deliberately been underspecified so that it can either refer to the *clarification-thread* or to the *confirmation-token*, both of which mark the COMP-DTRS. The SUBCAT-list requires that the question token be followed at some stage by a confirmation-token. If the confirmation follows directly after the question, the confirmation-token fills out the slot in the SUBCAT-list, explicitly on the object level.

The HEAD-DTR of the lemma *clarification-thread* is the token *Huh?* The SEM-attribute consists of the value $\langle s_2, s_4 \rangle$ that results from the following: The head *Huh?* is a functor and applied to the semantics of the *clarify* COMP-DTR which in turn is the argument of the functor. The result of this functional application is again a function, which is applied to the second DTR, i.e. the *confirm*-COMP-DTR. The result is the argument of the question token.

The HEAD-DTR of the lemma *rfc-token* subcategorises for the COMP-DTRS of the lemma *clarification-token*, instantiated by *Have you ever taken it out of there?*, and of the lemma *confirmation-token* instantiated by *Hadn't till now*. If the conversation takes its path via an uptake loop, the confirmation-token fills the slot in the SUBCAT-list, explicitly on the meta-level.

An alternative representation would be to extract the confirmation-token from its nested position and to place it on the same level as the clarification-thread. In this way, the confirmation-token obtains a status as sister of the clarification-thread. At first sight, this type of restructuring appears to be a suitable means to stress the optionality of the uptake loop. However, its optionality has already been determined in the SUBCAT-list of the question-token. Besides, a re-arrangement of the clarification-token as sister of the clarification-thread does not highlight the role of the confirmation-token. Not only is the representation of the confirmation-token problematic, it is also unclear how the SEM confirm-slot in the SUBCAT-list can be filled.

5.3 Representation of an utterance-token as an HPSG-based sign

The formalism used for the purpose of modelling a token in the form of an HPSG-based sign has already been outlined in Section 3.3 and will now be extended (see Figure 5.7). The token selected is the utterance *disconnect the autopilot*, which has a directive illocutionary point with the force *command* and lacks an explicit performative verb. It is orthographically reduced to its corresponding sentence. For this analysis, a token has deliberately been chosen that is different from those in Section 5.2 so as to include an instantiation of another discourse function. The token comes from a cockpit voice recording transcript of an air disaster that took place at Puerto Plata, Dominican Repub-

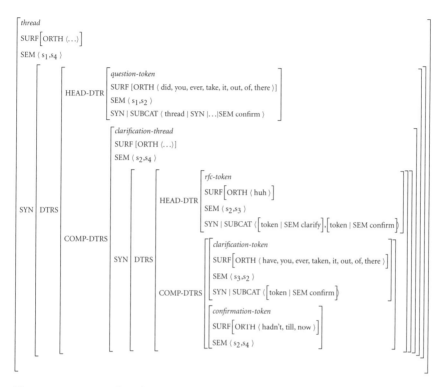

Figure 5.6 An HPSG-based sign as a representation model for a crisis talk thread.

lic in 1996 (see Aviation Safety Network 2000a). The transcript documents the crew's communication before their airplane crashes into the sea. Here is an extract from the transcript, in which the token under discussion is marked by an arrow:

(107)   Birgen Air B757 Accident Intra-Cockpit Communication 6 Feb,
        1996
        HCP085: 0346:25 disconnect the autopilot,   ←
                        is autopilot disconnected?
        HCO086: 0346:25 already disconnected, disconnected sir
        HFE087: 0346:31 ...

The topic of the conversation between Captain (HCP) and Copilot (HCO) is the autopilot. HCP commands HCO to disconnect it. In the same turn he asks whether his command has been completed and HCO confirms this, overlapping with parts of HCP's turn. The extract includes a time code whose scale is specific to the cockpit voice recorder. The numeric extensions after the speaker codes mark turn numbers.

Illocutionary force and proposition jointly function as a semantic attribute of a complex sign. The composite entry for the lemma *token*, which pertains to the *whole illocutionary act* (see Searle & Vanderveken 1985:8), consists of two parts: first, an item of type *F* with *head*-features, secondly an item of type *P* with *complement*-features. In the context of type *F(P)* under the SEM (semantics) attribute, the ⊔-operator is interpreted as unification, e.g. A⊔B. The item of type *illocutionary force* (*F*) has a SEM-attribute only because F is an operator that maps sentences onto utterances. The syntactic analysis, which is always dependent on its surface representation, is aimed at the sentence level, in other words, it refers to the utterance's propositional content. For this reason, the SYN and SURF-levels do not appear under the *F*-node. The semantic attribute contains the result of the association of the output of the individual rules derived from the conditions. The result pertains to the *illocutionary force* (FORCE) of the token (*command*) and its illocutionary point (Π_3 = directive). The SEM-attribute further includes

- the I/O-attribute that marks the input-output condition and applies to the uptake between speaker and hearer. Its value is *noise*;
- the POINT-attribute of the illocutionary point condition;
- the MODE$_{POINT}$-attribute that pertains to the mode of achievement of this illocutionary point;
- the STRENGTH$_{POINT}$-attribute of the degree of strength of the illocutionary point;
- the PREPI–PREPIII-attributes of the preparatory conditions;
- the SINCERITY-attribute of the sincerity condition;
- the STRENGTH$_{SINCERITY}$-attribute of the degree of strength of the sincerity condition.

Searle elaborates on an extended semantics that comprises features that could be termed as belonging to the pragmatic dimension. However, no distinction is made between the semantic and pragmatic dimensions: The formalism is not extended by a pragmatic attribute but, instead, by further substructures of the semantic attribute. Thus, with regard to the formal description of contextual features, the following attributes and substructures are included: the CONX-attribute (context) that breaks down into the substructures PARTIC-attribute (participant) and DISCREL-attribute (discourse relations). The former has the attributes SPEAKER/SUPERORD (superordinate) and HEARER/SUBORD (subordinate) with the values *captain* and *copilot*, respectively. With its THEME-attribute the latter refers to the preceding utterance (value: *emergency*) and with the RHEME-attribute relates to the current token (value: *disconnect the autopilot*).

Two further components form part of the CONX-attribute: the SETTINGS-attribute and the CHANNEL-attribute. The SETTINGS-attribute branches into the TIME attribute of a value that takes a time interval from the CVR transcript and the PLACE-attribute with the value *cockpit*, whereas the CHANNEL-attribute is structured more simply and only has the value *air-waves*.

Within the framework of a fine-grained differentiation of illocutionary forces, it might be wise to include a PERLOC-attribute that refers to the perlocutionary effect of an utterance. This, however, would go beyond the scope of this analysis and must be treated elsewhere.

The item of type *proposition* (P) is constituted by the attributes SURF, SEM and SYN.

The proposition bears the SURF-attributes PHON for phonology, PUNC for punctuation, WORD ORDER, and ORTH for orthography, which has as value a list of all lexical components of the token. The SEM-attribute consists of the CONTENT-attribute (propositional content) and the TEMPREF-attribute (temporal reference). The former attribute breaks down into reference (=REF) with the value *the autopilot* and predication (=PRED) *disconnect*. The TEMPREF-attribute displays as value a formula that indicates a future act. It includes the value of the TIME-attribute of the *illocutionary force*. The SYN-attribute breaks down into the attributes HEAD and SUBCAT, in accordance with the syntactic *head feature principle*. They have substructures of a conventional syntactic analysis as in Pollard & Sag (1987).

To analyse the propositional content, it is separated from the utterance context. Since this analysis requires surface information, the syntactic analysis of the utterance's constituent structure is provided in the proposition-entry. Any other token would be represented in a similar way, according to its particular conditions of success and other contextual features. Future research will have to clarify in what way restrictions on utterance sequences can be spelt out for non-controlled languages in a more principled way. Thus, it would have to fall back on theories such as SDRT (Segmented Discourse Representation Theory, see Asher & Lascarides 2003).

The modified head-feature principle will be useful in modelling propositions that are distributed over contributions, possibly of different speakers. Rieser & Skuplik (2000) address this problem and concentrate on tokens such as

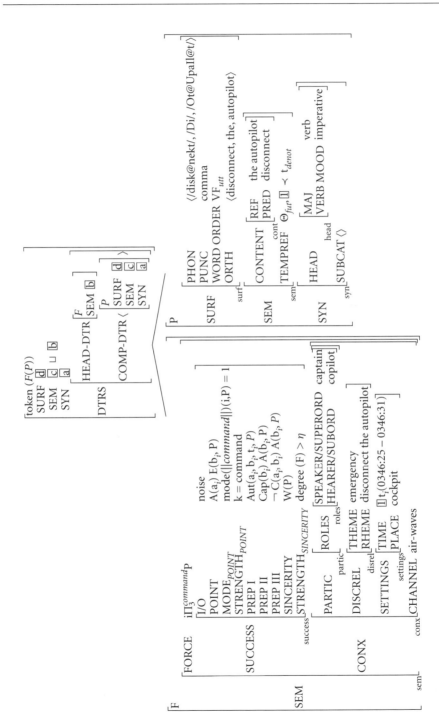

Figure 5.7 An HPSG-based structure for the token *disconnect the autopilot*.

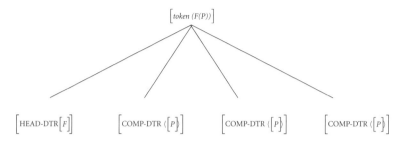

Figure 5.8 An underspecified tree structure of a proposition that is distributed over several speaker contributions.

(108) a.   A: jetzt nimmst du
     b.   B: eine Schraube
     c.   A: eine orange mit einem Schlitz

which they interpret as one turn whose propositional content, *eine orange Schraube mit einem Schlitz nehmen*, is spread over the contributions of speakers A and B. Each part of the proposition is dependent on the illocutionary force of the class *directive*. The force is indicated by the imperative mood of the verb *nehmen*, for example. As displayed in the HPSG-based feature structure, head and sister form a dependency relation. The example above is illustrated in Figure 5.8.

In this section, utterance sequences and utterance-tokens have been formally modelled in HPSG so that an adequate approach to the description of signs has been provided. Section 5.4 will clarify in what way the HPSG-formalism can be implemented in a form that is typical of corpus annotation (cf. Section 3.4). It will present a principled way in which HPSG can be implemented in XML.

5.4 Implementation: XML as a denotational semantics for HPSG-based signs

In order to implement the HPSG-based sign in XML, the token *thrust levers* from Example (109) has been chosen as the sample utterance, since it exhibits a central feature of crisis talk: It is part of a turn in which a directive is repeated.

(109)   (7) Birgen Air B757 Accident 6 Feb, 1996
       HCP094: 0346:52 thrust levers, thrust
       thrust thrust thrust <-

```
HCO095: 0346:54 retard
HCP096: 0346:54 thrust, don't pull back,
don't pull back, don't pull back, don't
pull back
HCO097: 0346:56 okay open open
HCP098: 0346:57 don't pull back,
please don't pull back
HCO099: 0346:59 open sir, open
```

As the speaker continues he takes up his directive again in a reduced form in that he iterates the indirect imperative *thrust*, which is categorised for the current purposes as a verb. The repetition is represented by the PHON-attribute as a substructure of SURF, whereby the verb is marked by a superscript as a component that occurs more than once. Like uptake loops, a repeated directive can be represented as part of a finite state dialogue model.

For the purpose of annotating the corpus with the HPSG-based structures, XML attribute-value structures have been formally defined as a denotational semantics for an HPSG-type attribute-value description. XML uses an attribute value archiving and retrieval formalism, and is flexible enough to be suitable for fulfilling crisis talk annotation requirements. XML annotation has been criticised for lacking a valid semantics: As long as the XML tags are syntactically

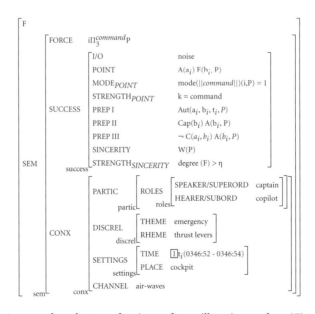

Figure 5.9 An HPSG-based entry of an item of type *illocutionary force* (F).

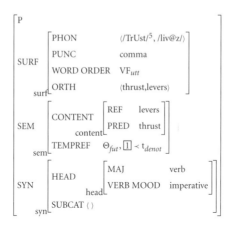

Figure 5.10 An HPSG-based entry for the item of type *proposition* (*P*). The superscript in the PHON-attribute marks the number of repetitions.

well-formed its assignment to PCDATA, arbitrary data concerning type and structure, is not semantically constrained. This problem will be handled by using XML simply as algebra for domain structuring in a semantic document model, the HPSG-based representation structure. Together with the appropriate processing mechanisms, XML also provides an operational semantics for the attribute-value description. This approach has been applied to the crisis talk corpus. Initially, categories were developed heuristically during actual annotation and later formulated in HPSG-style constraints. Starting with a basic XML data annotation, and based on the attribute-value description, an extended DTD was developed and the basic dialogue annotations enhanced semi-automatically. In a sense, the procedure extends, formalises and operationalises the older TEI proposal to formulate markup in terms of feature structures. The following exemplifies how HPSG is mapped into XML. First, an overview of the steps applied is given:

- basic XML annotation of a transcribed dialogue fragment;
- creation of the corresponding DTD;
- description of an utterance of the dialogue fragment in HPSG-based notation (see Figures 5.9 and 5.10);
- rewriting the HPSG-based sign as an XML feature structure including its DTD;
- enhancing the XML document instance and its DTD;
- validation of the DTDs.

A basic XML dialogue annotation of the transcript looks like this:

```
<?xml version="1.0" standalone="no"?>
<!DOCTYPE transcript SYSTEM "transcript.dtd">
<transcript>
    <title>Birgen Air B757 Accident 6 Feb, 1996
    </title>
    <speaker>HCP</speaker>
    <turn-id>094</turn-id>
    <time>0346:52</time>
    <turn>thrust levers, thrust thrust thrust thrust
    </turn>
    <speaker>HCO</speaker>
    <turn-id>095</turn-id>
    <time>0346:54</time>
    <turn>retard</turn>
</transcript>
```

The corresponding DTD is:

```
<!ELEMENT transcript (title,(speaker,turn-id,time,turn)+)>
<!ELEMENT title (#PCDATA)>
<!ELEMENT speaker (#PCDATA)>
<!ELEMENT turn-id (#PCDATA)>
<!ELEMENT time (#PCDATA)>
<!ELEMENT turn (#PCDATA)>
```

An enriched DTD containing the enhancements of Figures 5.9 and 5.10 is formulated as follows:

```
<!ELEMENT transcript (title,(speaker,turn-id,turn)+)>
<!ELEMENT title (#PCDATA)>
<!ELEMENT speaker (#PCDATA)>
<!ELEMENT turn-id (#PCDATA)>
<!ELEMENT turn (token)>
<!ELEMENT token (f,p)>
<!ATTLIST token surf IDREF #REQUIRED
                sem  IDREF #REQUIRED
                syn  IDREF #REQUIRED>
<!ELEMENT f (fsem)>
<!ELEMENT fsem (force,success,conx)>
<!ATTLIST fsem occ IDREF #REQUIRED>
<!ELEMENT force (#PCDATA)>
<!ELEMENT success (i-o,point,mode-point,strength-point,
                   prepI,prepII,prepIII,sincerity,
                   strength-sincerity)>
<!ELEMENT i-o (#PCDATA)>
<!ELEMENT point (#PCDATA)>
<!ELEMENT mode-point (#PCDATA)>
<!ELEMENT strength-point (#PCDATA)>
(...)
<!ELEMENT conx (partic,discrel,settings,channel)>
  <!ELEMENT partic (roles)>
```

```
  <!ELEMENT roles (speakersubord,hearersubord)>
   <!ELEMENT speakersubord (#PCDATA)>
   <!ELEMENT hearersubord (#PCDATA)>
 <!ELEMENT discrel (theme,rheme)>
   <!ELEMENT theme (#PCDATA)>
   <!ELEMENT rheme (#PCDATA)>
 <!ELEMENT settings (time?,place)>
   <!ELEMENT time (#PCDATA)>
   <!ATTLIST time occ ID #REQUIRED>
(...)
```

Note that with the enhancement some modifications were necessary to maintain a correct syntax: The *time* element of the simple DTD has been integrated in the substructures of the *settings* element, so that it does not appear any more in the content model of the *transcript* element. Furthermore, some of the elements in the DTD expand to just one other element, e.g. f to fsem. The option to enrich the content models by adding more elements is reserved for future integration. This might prove useful for the integration of an SDRT-style structuring of discourse. Here is a fragment of the transcript with enhanced markup:

```
<?xml version="1.0" standalone="no"?>
<!DOCTYPE transcript SYSTEM "transcript.dtd">
<transcript>
  <title>Birgen Air B757 Accident 6 Feb, 1996
  </title>
  <speaker>HCP</speaker>
  <turn-id>094</turn-id>
   <turn>
    <token surf="d" sem="a" syn="c">
 <f>
  <fsem occ="a">
   <force>i Pi-3^command P</force>
   <success>
    <i-o> noise </i-o>
    <point>A(a-i) E(b-i,P)=1</point>
    <mode-point> mode(||command||)(i,P)=1</mode-point>
    <strength-point> k=command   </strength-point>
    (...)
   </success>
   <conx>
    (...)
    <channel>air-waves</channel>
    (...)
   </conx>
  </fsem>
 </f>
<p>
 <psurf occ="d">
   <phon>/diskonekt/, /Di/, /Ot@UpaIl@t/</phon>
```

```
      (...)
    </psurf>
    <psem occ="a">
      <content>
        <ref>levers</ref>
        <pred>thrust</pred>
      </content>
      <tempref occ="b"> delta-tfut prec t-denot</tempref>
    </psem>
    <psyn occ="c">
     <head>
      <maj>verb </maj>
      <verb-mood> imperative </verb-mood>
     </head>
      <subcat> empty </subcat>
    </psyn>
  </p>
</token>
    </turn>
    <speaker>HCO</speaker>
    <turn-id>095</turn-id>
    <time>0346:54</time>
    <turn>
     <token><...>...</...>retard
     </token>
    </turn>
</transcript>
```

The DTDs have been operationally validated with a parser. For the complete
DTD and document instantiation see http://pbns.claudia-sassen.net/.

5.5 Conclusion

Using an extensive crisis talk corpus, a principled and flexible strategy has
been introduced for developing a new set of annotation categories by mapping HPSG-based attribute value matrices into an XML semantics. It has been
shown that this strategy has the power and flexibility to handle crisis talk.
Both approaches are attribute-value formalisms that serve different purposes
and have evolved from complementary motives. While XML is used to model
textual structures (here the verbatim record of dialogue that was supplied by
transcribers), HPSG gives a detailed account of linguistic principles and rules
that determine the well-formedness of linguistic expressions. The mapping of
HPSG-based attribute value matrices onto XML is shown to be a principled way
of extending and enhancing dialogue annotation with a set of categories that is

more adequate for *real life* situations. Future work in this area will be directed towards extending and testing the markup categories with related scenarios.

The investigation presented here seeks to propose a methodology for the speech act-based analysis of data from communication in aviation disasters. It is based on a fine-grained analysis of speech data by means of HPSG-based formalisms. The methodology is intended to be extendable to other sets of crisis talk data. Hence, regularities of speech act sequences have been established, developing at the same time a modified HPSG-formalism for the integration of illocutionary logic and the disambiguation of speech acts. An accompanying goal was to extend HPSG not only to modelling utterances but also to representing dialogue threads in one HPSG-sign. This allows for an *a posteriori* analysis of possible reasons for an aviation disaster. The clock cannot be turned back and a disaster cannot be undone. However, knowledge of possible defects is an invaluable and indispensible means of minimising the number of potential disasters. Elaboration and application of the methodology were employed to detect leaky and thus dangerous points in communication. Ideally, this analysis can be used to minimise escalations during flights and to make aviation safer.

The study has examined communicative patterns of controller-pilot and pilot-pilot interaction. Future research might also consider aspects of transmissions between controllers and ground vehicles as well as other ATC-environment communication apart from tower-ground control: air route traffic control centers, tower-local control and terminal radar control. Since aviation communication is a controlled language, it was convenient to use it as a starting point for the analysis: The grammar that defines the controlled language feeds naturally into an algorithm that recognises the discourse structure.

A clear advantage of the model that has been proposed lies in its applicability to other sorts of crisis talk data, because these types of dialogues share the same basic features (see the definition of crisis talk in Chapter 1.2). In other high-risk environments, however, it is not common to have a restricted subset of natural language in the way a controlled language works. Crisis talk can for instance also be observed in medical scenarios (Grommes & Grote 2001). Unfortunately, surgeons cannot fall back on a language similar to that in aviation communication. Hence, general modelling of crisis talk has to be freed from the strong assumption of a controlled language.

To this end, a theory of discourse structure has to be used that meets two requirements with regard to the data employed: first, the theory must be as unrestricted as possible concerning the domain; second, it must be as surface oriented as possible (ideally, requiring no additional assumptions that go beyond the purely linguistic domain). To clarify these two requirements, some remarks are in order with respect to theories of discourse structure.

One of the earliest theories of this sort is outlined in Grosz & Sidner (1986). A discourse is conceived of as being structured according to three types of criteria: linguistic markers, speakers' intentions, and publicly accessible states that correspond to the focus of attention of the participants involved. It is unclear, however, how the mental states of the speakers should be recognised by the participants involved in order to derive a partial specification of the discourse structure from those mental states.[7] The problem is that the relevant intentions and beliefs that are responsible for some action can be reconstructed in arbitrary ways.

The problem with the recognition of the mental states of other persons (the *other mind problem*) can be explained in various ways. The strongest version is perhaps given by Dennett (1991). He argues that one might be mistaken in the interpretation of linguistic or other behaviour even if there is only a single plausible explanation for it.

> The fact that there *is* a single, coherent interpretation of a sequence of behavior doesn't establish that the interpretation is *true*; it might be only *as if* the "subject" were conscious; we risk being taken in by a zombie with no inner life at all.
> (Dennett 1991:78)

This version of the argument is only a strengthening of the corresponding arguments of Bennett (1973) and Bennett (1976).

Moeschler argues for an extension of speech act theory by a *radical pragmatic* theory to arrive at a speech act-based description of discourse structure, having in mind the theory of relevance set up by Sperber & Wilson (1986). He states in accord with the present analysis that "the main purpose of discourse analysis is the definition of necessary and sufficient conditions for sequencing and [interpreting] utterances in discourse" (Moeschler 2001:239).
He claims that these two aspects are intrinsically related and could not be accounted for independently of each other. He continues:

> I claim furthermore that speech act theory cannot give any insight into the sequencing and interpretation problems, because speech act theory is neither a theory of interpretation (it is a theory of meaning) nor a global theory of action. Finally I show how a radical pragmatic theory (in the Gricean sense) accounts for the sequencing and interpretation problem.
> (Moeschler 2001:239)

But the latter, of course, though attributed by Moeschler to Sperber & Wilson (1986), is arguably just what Grosz & Sidner (1986) intended, and what is not easily achieved in a computationally tractable way. Another theory is that of Allen & Litman (1987). Their theory is certainly more surface oriented than that of Grosz & Sidner (1986). The problem, however, is that, while Grosz and Sidner aim at generality and domain independence, Allen's and Litman's theory is highly domain specific, i.e. restricted. This drawback is not really compensated by the fact that the theory is speech act-driven (or at least compatible with it), and hence would provide a good interface for the account discussed in this paper.

The work might be done by employing *rhetorical structure* theory (RST) as an additional apparatus. RST in its origin was designed as a descriptive tool for the identification of discourse relations according to the *functions* by which spans of text are related. The leading heuristic principle was to assume those relations that established the highest possible coherence in discourse. As the founders of RST remarked, however, it can serve as a basis for text generation, in particular for planning large texts of various kinds (Mann & Thompson 1987).

Meanwhile, RST has undergone a number of transformations and has produced a variety of offsprings. One of the most recent is SDRT as developed by Lascarides & Asher (1993) and Asher (1998). A natural way of extending the proposed account would be to adopt some version of SDRT. The idea of a dynamic semantics that was outlined in Section 5.2 in fact is the core idea of SDRT as far as truth-functional semantics is concerned.[8]

Building on RST, Marcu (2000) formulates two compositionality criteria of valid text structures; in an attempt to implement a discourse parser, they explain the relationship between discourse relations that hold between large spans of text and discourse relations that hold between elementary discourse units. Marcu's research program, however suffers from the failure to take into account the most recent developments in the field of research, e.g. the newer versions of SDRT. Thus, an implementation of a follow-up of the present account could expand on Marcu's work by involving more recent linguistic theories.

There are already proposals for annotating RST (see e.g. Stent (2000)). An extension of the present account, if implemented, could utilise this work and take an adequately annotated corpus as a testbed, in just the same manner as the ATC/CVR transcripts have been used here.

In conclusion, it can be said that the method employed here promises to lead to extensions for a comprehensive modelling of discourse that is both theoretically well founded and empirically testable. The analysis at hand is thus intended to remedy a drawback that was expressed by Sag (1991), who stated that computer scientists "loudly and pointedly derided the linguistic community for its lack of concern with computational issues and its failure to concern itself with a sufficiently broad range of phenomena relevant to the interpretation of naturally occurring texts" (Sag 1991:69–70).

Crisis talk is one of the phenomena that needs to be treated if this inadequacy is to be rectified.

Notes

1. For a definition of *thread* see 5.1.

2. If Sperber & Wilson (1986) are right it is possible to make the notion of a thread dependent on that of Relevance. This idea, however, is not pursued here. My notion of a thread conforms to the notion that is used by Poesio & Traum (1997).

3. This definition accords to some extent with what Grimes (1975:101) calls *thematic partitioning* of a discourse.

4. Foley & Van Valin (1984:321) observe that

> the monitoring of coreference of core arguments across [peripheral junctures] is a central function of the grammar of any language. The use of the full noun phrase to refer to all participants in each junct is a potential solution to this problem, but not an actual one, given the pervasive tendency in language to omit or pronominalize given and topical information. Therefore, the problem of participant identification in an ongoing discourse is a very real one.

5. This expression is shorthand for an utterance with the illocutionary force *directive* and the force *command*.

6. The speech act label *elaborate* has been borrowed from rhetorical structure theory (see e.g. Mann & Thompson 1987) and refers to utterances that explain and extend preceding utterances.

7. The theory as laid down in Grosz & Sidner (1986) is even more complicated and questionable; discussion of this, however, would exceed the scope of the present analysis.

8. It has long been disputed whether DRT is compositional; but see Muskens (1996) for an undoubtedly compositional version.

Select glossary of relevant aviation terms

The terms presented here are of prominent use in the current study. The source of the definition has been appended to each entry. This glossary does not claim to be exhaustive.

AIM – Airman's Information Manual, which forms part of the *Aeronautical Information Manual*, as well as the *Pilot/Controller Glossary* (Federal Aviation Administration 2000a).

aircraft call sign – the complete aircraft identification. For Part 121 carriers this consists of an airline name and flight number (Cardosi, Falzarano, & Han 1999: 25).

air traffic – all aircraft in flight or operating on the maneuvering area of an aerodrome (Federal Aviation Administration 2000e).

air traffic clearance – an authorization by air traffic control for the purpose of preventing collision between known aircraft, for an aircraft to proceed under specified traffic conditions within controlled airspace (Federal Aviation Administration 2000e).

air traffic control service – a service provided for the purpose of preventing collisions between aircraft and on the maneuvering area between aircraft and obstructions. Further, the service expedites and maintains an orderly flow of air traffic (Federal Aviation Administration 2000e).

altitude deviation – a departure from, or failure to attain, an altitude assigned by ATC (Cardosi, Falzarano, & Han 1999).

approach control service – air traffic control service for arriving or departing controlled flights (Federal Aviation Administration 2000e).

ASRS – Aviation Safety and Reporting System (Cardosi, Falzarano, & Han 1999)

ATC – Air Traffic Control, see also

ATCT – Air Traffic Control Tower

ATIS – Automated Terminal Information Service

azimuth – a magnetic bearing extending from an microwave landing system navigation facility. Note: Azimuth bearings are described as magnetic and are referred to as "azimuth" in radio telephone communications (Federal Aviation Administration 2000e).

callout – special type of verbal feedback to PIC's instruction, but may also be the instruction itself.

CAM – cockpit area microphone Aviation Safety Network (2000a)

complete readback – a pilot's acknowledgement of a controller's transmission, which repeats all of the key information the controller conveyed. (Note that the information does not have to be repeated verbatim, or in the same order, in this use of complete readback.) Also, see partial readback.

FAA – Federal Aviation Administration

FARS – Federal Aviation Regulations

FDR – Flight Data Recorder (Federal Aviation Administration 2002)

flameout – an emergency condition caused by a loss of engine power (Federal Aviation Administration 2000e).

flight level – a level of constant atmospheric pressure related to a reference datum of 29.92 inches of mercury. Each is stated in three digits that represent hundreds of feet. For example, flight level (FL) 250 represents a barometric altimeter indication of 25,000 feet; FL 255, an indication of 25,500 feet (Federal Aviation Administration 2000e).

go-around – instructions for a pilot to abandon his approach to landing. Additional instructions may follow (Federal Aviation Administration 2000e).

hearback error Type I – the failure on the controller's part to notice or correct a pilot's readback error (Cardosi, Falzarano, & Han 1999).

hearback error Type II – the failure on the controller's part to notice his own error in the pilot's correct readback. For example, if the controller instructed an aircraft to descend to 11,000, but meant to descend the aircraft to 10,000 and did not notice his own error when the pilot read back the descent to 11,000, this would be a hearback error type II (Cardosi, Falzarano, & Han 1999).

IAS – Indicated Air Speed (Federal Aviation Administration 2002)

less than standard separation – less than the legal separation between two airborne aircraft (as defined by the airspace involved) (Cardosi, Falzarano, & Han 1999).

ICAO – International Civil Aviation Organization (Federal Aviation Administration 2002)

NMAC (Near-Midair Collision) – a conflict situation in which the flight crew reports (either directly, or as quoted by the controller) that the reported miss distance is less than 500 feet (Cardosi, Falzarano, & Han 1999).

NTSB (National Transportation Safety Board) – an independent federal agency that investigates every civil aviation accident in the United States and significant accidents in the other modes of transportation, conducts special investigations and safety studies, and issues safety recommendations to prevent future accidents. Safety Board investigators are on call 24 hours a day, 365 days a year (National Transportation Safety Board 2001).

operational error – less than standard separation (between two or more aircraft, or between aircraft and terrain, obstacles or obstructions, including vehicles/equipment/personnel on the runway) that occurred as a result of ATC actions, inactions, or ATC equipment malfunction (Cardosi, Falzarano, & Han 1999).

PA – public address microphone (Federal Aviation Administration 2002)

PIC – pilot in command, the pilot responsible for the operation and safety of an aircraft during flight time (Federal Aviation Administration 2000e).

pilot's discretion – when used in conjunction with altitude assignments, means that ATC has offered the pilot the option of starting climb or descent whenever he wishes and conducting the climb or descent at any rate he wishes. He may temporarily level off at any intermediate altitude. However, once he has vacated an altitude, he may not return to that altitude (Federal Aviation Administration 2000e).

radar – a radio detection device that provides information on range, azimuth and/or elevation of objects (Federal Aviation Administration 2000e).

RDO – radio microphone (Federal Aviation Administration 2002)

readback – a pilot's acknowledgement of a controller's transmission that repeats the information that the controller conveyed (Cardosi, Falzarano, & Han 1999).

readback error – an incorrect repeat of the controller's transmission by the pilot. For example, if the controller said, "AirCarrier 123, descend and maintain one one thousand" and the pilot responded with "Roger, one zero thousand for AirCarrier 123", this would be a readback error, since the pilot should have read back the altitude of 11,000 (Cardosi, Falzarano, & Han 1999).

reporter – a pilot or controller who files an ASRS report (Cardosi, Falzarano, & Han 1999).

partial readback – a pilot's acknowledgement of a controller's transmission that repeats some, but not all, of the key information that the controller conveyed. For example, if the controller issued both an altitude and heading, but only the altitude was read back, this would constitute a partial readback. Also see complete readback (Cardosi, Falzarano, & Han 1999).

readback behaviour full readback, partial readback, one-word acknowledgement; Morrow et al. (1994:236): an explicit acknowledgement procedure where pilots repeat the ATC message so that the controller can check its interpretation. Cushing (1994:40): full readback: an entire instruction or a fully synonymous equivalent is repeated in full. They play a crucial role in air traffic control through both their presence and their absence. These are required for any instruction a controller issues to a pilot, as a way of confirming that instructions are correctly received and understood (Cardosi, Falzarano, & Han 1999).

runway transgression – the erroneous or improper occupation of a runway or its immediate vicinity by an aircraft, which poses a potential collision hazard to other aircraft using the runway, even if no other aircraft is actually present (Cardosi, Falzarano, & Han 1999).

SPD SEL – speed selector (Hoesch 2000)

STAR – Standard Terminal Arrival Route (Federal Aviation Administration 2002)

taxi into position and hold – used by ATC to inform a pilot to taxi onto the departure runway in take-off position and hold. It is not authorization for takeoff. It is used when take-off clearance cannot immediately be issued because of traffic or for other reasons (Federal Aviation Administration 2000e).

tower – a terminal facility that uses air/ground communications, visual signalling, and other devices to provide ATC services to aircraft operating in the vicinity of an airport or on the movement area. It authorises aircraft to land or take off at the airport controlled by the tower or to transit the Class D airspace area (that airspace from the surface to 2,500 feet above the airport elevation) regardless of flight plan or weather conditions. A tower may also provide approach control services (radar or nonradar) (Federal Aviation Administration 2000e).

TRACON – Terminal Radar Approach Control (Federal Aviation Administration 2002)

VHF – Very High Frequency Federal Aviation Administration (2002). The frequency band between 30 and 300 MHz. Portions of this band, 108 to 118 MHz, are used for certain NAVAIDs (navigational aids); 118 to 136 MHz are used for civil air/ground voice communications (Federal Aviation Administration 2000e).

VOR – Very High Frequency Omni-directional Range Federal Aviation Administration (2002). A ground-based electronic navigation aid transmitting very high frequency navigation signals, 360 degrees in azimuth, oriented from magnetic north. Used as the basis for navigation in the National Airspace System. The VOR periodically identifies itself by Morse Code and may have an additional voice identification feature (Federal Aviation Administration 2000e).

Abbreviations

This list refers to the abbreviations used for the attribute-value matrix of the HPSG-based sign (see, for example Section 5.3). The items are listed in their order of appearance.

SURF – surface interpretation
SEM – semantics
SYN – syntax
DTRS – daughters
HEAD-DTR – head-daughter
COMP-DTRS – complement-daughters
F – illocutionary force
SUCCESS – conditions of success
I/O – input-output condition
POINT – illocutionary point condition
A – action
a_i – speaker
b_i – hearer
i – context
P – proposition
E – elicitation
MODE$_{POINT}$ – mode of achievement of the illocutionary point
STRENGTH$_{POINT}$ – degree of strength of the illocutionary point
K – degree of strength, with k $in\ \mathbb{Z}$
PREPI–III – preparatory condition
Aut – authority
Cap – capability
C – common knowledge
SINC – sincerity condition
W – want
STRENGTH$_{SINCERITY}$ – degree of strength of the sincerity condition
$\sqcup$ – semantic unification-operator
PUNC – punctuation
ORTH – orthography
CONX – context
PARTIC – participants
DISCREL – discourse relation
TEMPREF – temporal reference
VF$_U$ – verb of the utterance in first position

A key to the atomic representation of speech act types

ad – advise
as – ask
cl – clarify
co – command
con – confirm
cu – curse
dis – disconfirm
el – elaborate
gr – greet
pr – presume
pre – predict
pro – prod
prom – promise
re – request
rfc – request for clarification
st – state
su – suggest
th – thank
wa – warn

Examples: Minimal sequences and their modifications

seq ↦ st+∅
seq ↦ st+con

(110) CCP148: 2119:30 Mode selector approach land checklist. (st/co)

CFE149: 2119:32 Landing check. (con)

CFE150: 2119:41 Speed brake lever. (st/co)

CCP151: 2119:42 Full forward. (con)

CFE152: 2119:43 Spoiler switches. (st/co)

CFO153: 2119:45 On. (con)

The alternative reading of a(n indirect) command has been given after the preferred reading.

seq ↦ st(+st)+con

(111) CFE390: 2132:39 Flame out! Flame out on engine number four. (st+st)

CAM391: 2132:41 [Sound of momentary power interruption to the CVR]

CCP392: 2132:42 Flame out on it. (co)

seq ↦ st(+st)+con+con

(112) CCP235: 2124:00 I don't know what happened with the runway. (st) I didn't see it. (st)

CFE236: 2124:00 I didn't see it. (con)

CFO237: 2124:00 I didn't see it. (con)

seq ↦ st+rfc+∅+∅

(113) CFO133: 23:42:05 We did something to the altitude (st)

CCP134: What? (rfc)

CFO135: 23:42:07 We're still at two thousand right?

CCP136: 23:42:09 Hey, what's happening here?

CAM137: [Sound of click]

```
CAM138: 23:42:10 [Sound of six beeps similar to radio altime-
ter increasing in rate]
CAM139: 23:42:12 [Sound of impact]
```

seq ↦ st+rfc+cl+con

(114) CSO112: I don't see it down there (st)

CCP113: Huh? (rfc)

CSO114: I don't see it (cl)

CCP115: You can't see that indis ... for the nosewheel ah,
there's a place in there you can look and see if they're
lined up (con)

(115) RCP042: 23:34:21 Okay, going up to two thousand, one
twenty-eight six (st)

CCP045: What frequency did he want us on, Bert? (rfc)

CFO046: One twenty-eight six (cl)

CCP047: I'll talk to 'em (con?)

seq ↦ st+rfc+cl(+el)+∅

(116) CFE006: 2103:56 Then the go-around procedure is stating that
the power be applied slowly and to avoid rapid accelerations
and to have a minimum of nose up attitude. (st)

CCP007: 2104:09 To maintain what? (rfc)

CFO008: 2104:10 Minimum, minimum nose up attitude, that means
the less nose up attitude that one can hold. (cl(+el))

seq ↦ st+st+rfc+cl+cl/el+dis/con

(117) CFE059: 2109:11 They got us, they already vectoring us. (st)

CFO060: 2109:21 They accomodate us ahead of an ... (st)

CCP061: 2109:27 What? (rfc)

CFO062: 2109:27 They accomodate us. (cl)

CFE063: 2109:29 They already know that we are in bad
condition. (cl/el)

CCP064: 2109:30 No, they are descending us. (dis/con)

CFO065: 2109:35 One thousand feet.

CCP066: 2109:36 Ah yes.

CFO067: 2109:38 They are giving us priority.

seq ↦ co+∅

(118) CCP138: 2117:55 Tell me things louder, because I'm not
       hearing it. (co)
       CCP266: 2125:08 Advise him we don't have fuel.

seq ↦ co+con

(119) CCP088: 2111:32 Give me flaps fourteen. (co)
       CFO090: 2111:33 Flaps fourteen. (con)

seq ↦ co+dis

(120) APP355: 2130:32 Avianca fifty two, climb and maintain three
       thousand.(co)
       CAM356: 2130:33 [Sound of landing gear warning horn.]
       RFO357: 2130:36 Ah, negative sir. (dis)
       We just running out of fuel. We okay three thousand. Now okay.

seq ↦ co+rfc+cl+∅

(121) TWR159: 2119:58 Avianca zero five two, two two left, wind one
       niner zero at two zero, cleared to land. (co)
       CCP173: 2120:21 Are we cleared to land, no? (rfc)
       CFO174: 2120:23 Yes sir, we are cleared to land. (cl)

seq ↦ co+rfc+cl+con This is an example from a different transcript, i.e. ATC-
transcript US Air Flight 1493 collision – 01 FEB 1991 (32)

(122) XXX042: 6:01:50 Lights on (?taxiway) uniform (co)
       LCB043: 6:01:53 Calling ground say a eh tower, say again (rfc)
       XXX044: 6:01:56 Landing lights on uniform? (cl)
       LCB045: 6:02:02 Affirmative (con)

seq ↦ co(+co)+rfc+cl?/∅+rfc+∅

(123) TWR128: 2117:42 Increase, increase! (co(+co))
       CCP129: 2117:42 What? (rfc)
       RXX130: 2117:44 Increasing (cl?)
       CCP131: 2117:45 What? (rfc)
       TWR132: 2117:46 Okay

seq ↦ co+co+con+con

(124) TWR128: 2117:42 Increase, increase! (co+co)
       CCP129: 2117:42 What?

```
RXX130: 2117:44 Increasing (cl?) (con)
CCP131: 2117:45 What?
TWR132: 2117:46 Okay (con)
```

seq ↦ as+∅

(125)   CCP136: 23:42:09 Hey, what's happening here? (as)
CAM137: [Sound of click]
CAM138: 23:42:10 [Sound of six beeps similar to radio altimeter increasing in rate]
CAM139: 23:42:12 [Sound of impact]

seq ↦ as+con

(126)   CCP246: 2124:22 Advise him we are emergency!
CCP247: 2124:26 Did you tell him? (as)
CFO249: 2124:28 Yes sir. (con)
CFO250: 2124:29 I already advised him.
CCP251: 2124:31 Flaps four ... fifteen.

The confirm is indirect/inexplicit in that CCP goes on giving commands. If he had not understood CFO's clarification he would probably request for clarification again and enter the loop again.

seq ↦ as+con+con

(127)   TWR187: 2121:07 Avianca zero five two heavy, can you increase your airspeed one zero knots at all? (as)
RXX188: 2121:09 Yes, we're doing it. (con)
TWR189: 2121:12 Okay, thank you. (con)

seq ↦ as+st(+st)

(128)   CCP222: 2123:23 The runway! Where is it? (as)
GPW223: 2123:25 Glideslope [repeated 2 times]
CFO224: 2123:27 I don't see it! I don't see it! (st+(st))
CCP225: 2123:28 Give me the landing gear up. Landing gear up.
GPW226: 2123:29 Glideslope [repeated 2 times]
CXX227: 2123:32 [Sound of landing gear warning horn.]
CCP228: 2123:33 Request another traffic pattern.

seq ↦ as+dis

(129)   CCP119: Itt's not lined up? (as)
CSO120: I can't see it, (dis)
it's pitch dark and I throw the little light I get ah nothing

seq ↦ as+rfc+cl+con/dis

(130) CCP086: 23:39:37 Did you ever take it out of there? (as)
       CFO087: Huh? (rfc)
       CCP088: Have you ever taken it out of there? (cl)
       CFO089: Hadn't till now (con/dis)

seq ↦ as+rfc+cl+con/dis

(131) CAX121: 23:41:31 Wheel-well lights on? (as)
       CSO122: Pardon? (rfc)
       CAX123: Wheel-well lights on? (cl)
       CSO124: Yeah wheel well lights always on if the gear's down
               (con/dis)

Two sample transcripts

The two transcripts that were employed to exemplify an analysis of sequences in aviation communication are included below. They were taken from the corpus without undergoing any modifications.

```
# CVR transcript Eastern Air Lines Flight 401 - 29 DEC 1972 (10)
#
# CVR transcript of the December 29, 1972 accident of Eastern Flight
# 401, a
# Lockheed L-1011 TriStar in the Everglades near Miami, FL, USA.
#
# Original legend missing! According to ASN database
# CAM-1 voice identified as Captain -- CCP
# CAM-2 voice identified as First Officer == CFO
# CAM-3 voice identified as Second Officer == CSO
# TWR   Miami Tower == TWR
# RDO-1 radio transmission of captain? == RCP?
# CAM   cockpit area microphone == CAM
# APP   Miami Approach? == APP
# CAM-? unidentified voice == CXX
# CAM-4 not explained in database == CAX
#
# Transcript: first column: source of turn, turn number,
# time line, second column: transcribed recording
# The codes "#", "...", "* * *" are unexplained, # is interpreted as
# an expletive deleted, * * * is interpreted as unintelligible text
# and changed into ***
#
RCP000: 23:32:35 Miami Tower, Eastern 401 just turned on final
TWR001: 23:32:45 Who else called?
CCP002: 23:32:48 Go ahead and throw 'em out
RCP003: 23:32:52 Miami Tower, do you read, Eastern 401? Just turned
                 on final
TWR004: 23:32:56 Eastern 401 Heavy, continue approach to 9 left
RCP005: 23:33:00 Coninue approach, roger
CSO006: 23:33:00 Continuous ignition.. No smoke
CCP007:          Coming on
CSO008:          Brake system
CCP009:          Okay
CSO010:          Radar
CCP011:          Up, off
```

```
CSO012:            Hydraulic panels checked
CFO013:            Thirty-five, thirty three
CCP014:            Bert, is that handle in?
CXX015:            ***
CSO016:            Engine crossbleeds are open
CXX017: 23:33:22   Gear down
CXX018:            ***
CCP019:            I gotta
CXX020:            ...
CCP021: 23:33:25   I gotta raise it back up
CCP022: 23:33:47   Now I'm gonna try it down one   more time
CFO023:            All right
CAM024: 23:33:58   [sound of altitude alert horn]
CFO025:            (?Right) gear.
CFO026:            Well, want to tell 'em we'll take  it around and
                   circle around and # around?
RCP027: 23:34:05   Well ah, tower, this is Eastern,  ah, 401. It looks
                   like we're gonna have to circle, we don't have  a
                   light on our nose gear yet
TWR028: 23:34:14   Eastern 401 heavy, roger, pull up, climb straight
                   ahead to two thousand, go back to approach control,
                   one twenty eight six
CFO029: 23:34:19   Twenty-two degrees.
CFO030:            Twenty-two degrees, gear up
CCP031:            Put power on it first, Bert. Thata boy.
CCP032:            Leave the # # gear down till we fid out what we got
CFO033:            Allright
CSO034:            You want me to test the lights or not?
CCP035:            Yeah.
CXX036:            *** seat back
CCP037:            Check it
CFO038:            Uh, Bob, it might be the light. Could you jiggle
                   tha, the light?
CSO039:            It's gotta, gotta come out a little bit and then
                   snap in
CXX040:            ***
CXX041:            I'll put 'em on
RCP042: 23:34:21   Okay, going up to two thousand, one twenty-eight six
CFO043: 23:34:58   We're up to two thousand
CFO044:            You want me to fly it, Bob?
CCP045:            What frequency did he want us on, Bert?
CFO046:            One twenty-eight six
CCP047:            I'll talk to 'em
CSO048:            It's right ...
CCP049:            Yeah, ...
CSO050:            I can't make it pull out, either
CCP051:            We got pressure
CSO052:            Yes sir, all systems
CCP053:            # #
RCP054: 23:35:09   All right ahh, Approach Control, Eastern 401, we're
                   right over the airport here and climbing to two
                   thousand feet. in fact, we've just
```

```
APP055: 23:35:20 Eastern 401, roger. Turn left heading three six zero
                 and maintain two thousand, vectors to 9 Left final
RCP056: 23:35:28 Left three six zero
CCP057: 23.36:04 Put the ... on autopilot here
CFO058:          Allright
CCP059:          See if you can get that light out
CFO060:          Allright
CCP061:          Now push the switches just a ... forward.
CCP062:          Okay.
CCP063:          You got it sideways, then.
CXX064:          Naw, I don't think it'll fit.
CCP065:          You gotta turn it one quarter turn to the left.
APP066: 23.36:27 Eastern 401, turn left heading three zero zero
RCP067:          Okay.
RCP068: 23:36:37 Three zero zero, Eastern 401
CCP069: 23:37:08 Hey, hey, get down there and see if that damn nose
                 wheel's down. You better do that.
CFO070:          You got a handkerchief or something so I can get a
                 little better grip on this? Anything I can do with
                 it?
CCP071:          Get down there and see if that, see if that # thing
                 ...
CFO072:          This won't come out, Bob. If I had a pair of pliers,
         I could cushion it with that Kleenex
CSO073:          I can give you pliers but if you force it, you'll
                 break it, just believe me
CFO074:          Yeah, I'll cushion it with Kleenex
CSO075:          Oh, we can give you pliers
APP076: 23:37:48 Eastern, uh, 401 turn left heading two seven zero
RCP077: 23:37:53 Left two seven zero, roger
CCP078: 23:38:34 To # with it, to # with this. Go down ans see if
                 it's lined up with the red line. That's all we care.
                 # around with that twenty-cent piece
CAM079:          ***
RCP080: 23:38:46 Eastern 401 'll go ah, out west just a little
                 further if we can here and, ah, see if we can get
                 this light to come on here
APP081: 23:38:54 Allright, ah, we got you headed westbound there now,
                 Eastern 401
RCP082: 23:38:56 Allright
CCP083:          How much fuel we got left on this # # # #
CXX084:          Fifty two five
CFO085:          (?It won't come out) no way
CCP086: 23:39:37 Did you ever take it out of there?
CFO087:          Huh?
CCP088:          Have you ever taken it out of there?
CFO089:          Hadn't till now
CCP090:          Put it in the wrong way, huh?
CFO091:          In there looks * square to me
CXX092:          Can't you get the hole lined up?
CXX093:          ***
CXX094:          Whatever's wrong?
```

```
CCP095:              (?What's that?)
CFO096: 23:40:05 I think that's over the training field
CXX097:              West heading you wanna go left or *
CFO098:              Naw that's right, we're about to cross Krome Avenue
                     right now
CAM099: 23:40:17 [Sound of click]
CFO100:              I don't know what the # holding that # # # # in
CFO101:              Always something, we coulda make schedule
CAM102: 23:40:38 [Sound of altitude alert]
CCP103:              We can tell if that # # # # is down by looking down
                     at our indices
CCP104:              I'm sure it's down, there's no way it couldnt help
                     but be
CFO105:              I'm sure it is
CCP106:              It freefalls down
CFO107:              The tests didn't show that the lights worked anyway
CCP108:              That 's right
CFO109:              It's a faulty light
CFO110: 23:41:05 Bob, this # # # # just won't come out
CCP111:              Allright leave it there
CSO112:              I don't see it down there
CCP113:              Huh?
CSO114:              I don't see it
CCP115:              You can't see that indis ... for the nosewheel ah,
                     there's a place in there you can look and see if
                     they're lined up
CSO116:              I know, a little like a telescope
CCP117:              Yeah
CSO118:              Well...
CCP119:              It's not lined up?
CSO120:              I can't see it, it's pitch dark and I throw the
                     little light I get ah nothing
CAX121: 23:41:31 Wheel-well lights on?
CSO122:              Pardon?
CAX123:              Wheel-well lights on?
CSO124               Yeah wheel well lights always on if the gear's down
CCP125:              Now try it
APP126: 23:41:40 Eastern, ah 401 how are things comin' along out
                     there?
RCP127: 23:41:44 Okay, we'd like to turn around and come, come back
CCP128:              in Clear on left?
CFO129:              Okay
APP130: 23:41:47 Eastern 401 turn left heading one eight zero
CCP131: 23:41:50 Huh?
RCP132: 23:41:51 One eighty
CFO133: 23:42:05 We did something to the altitude
CCP134:              What?
CFO135: 23:42:07 We're still at two thousand right?
CCP136: 23:42:09 Hey, what's happening here?
CAM137:              [Sound of click]
CAM138: 23:42:10 [Sound of six beeps similar to radio altimeter
                     increasing in rate]
```

```
CAM139: 23:42:12 [Sound of impact]
#
# Copyright    © 1996-1999 Harro Ranter / Fabian Lujan
#              Aviation Safety Network; updated 12 August, 1999
-----------------------------------------------------------------


#     CVR transcript Avianca Flight 052 - 25 JAN 1990 (31)
#
#Cockpit voice recorder transcript of the January 25, 1990
#crash of an Avianca Boeing 707 (Flight 052) at Cove Neck,
#NY
#Accident details: 1990 database
#Source: NTSB Aircraft accident report; Avianca, the
#Airline of Columbia Boeing 707-321B, HK-2016 Fuel
#Exhaustion Cove Neck, New York January 25, 1990
#(NTSB/AAR-91/04)
#
# Legend
# RDO = Radio transmission from accident aircraft == R..
# CAM = Cockpit Area Microphone sound or source == C..
# -1 = Voice identified as Captain == .CP
# -2 = Voice identified as First Officer == .FO
# -3 = Voice identified as Flight Engineer == .FE
# TWR = New York-JFK Tower == TWR
# APPR = New York Approach Controller == APP
# * = Unintelligible word changed into ***
# # = Expletive deleted
# () = Questionable text changed into (? )
# (()) = Editorial insertion changed into [ ]
# - = Pause changed into - - -
# (-?  unidentified speaker        == .XX
# AA 40 == AAX
# AA 692 == AAB
# EVG 102 == EVG
# PA 11 == PAA
# PA 1812 == PAB
# TWA 542 == TWB
# GPWS = Ground Proximity Warning System == GPW
# Avianca APPR = Avianca Approach == APA
# TWA801 == TWA
# CAM = cockpit area microphone == CAM)
# [pre-annotation == ANN]
# <text deleted>
# Transcript: first column: source of turn + turn number,
# time line, second column: transcribed recording
# "..." unexplained
# This transcript does not indicate that some of the utterance were
#                                              in Spanish.
#
RXX000: 2103:07 New York approach Avianca zero five ah two leveling
               five thousand.
```

APA001: 2103:11 zero five two heavy, New York approach good evening, fly heading zero six zero.

RXX002: 2103:15 Heading zero six zero, Avianca zero five two heavy.

CFO003: 2103:18 Zero six zero on the heading.

CFE004: 2103:46 When we have...with thousand pounds or less in any tank, it is necessary to do.

CFO005: 2103:53 Yes sir.

CFE006: 2103:56 Then the go-around procedure is stating that the power be applied slowly and to avoid rapid accelerations and to have a minimum of nose up attitude.

CCP007: 2104:09 To maintain what?

CFO008: 2104:10 Minimum, minimum nose up attitude, that means the less nose up attitude that one can hold.

CFE009: 2104:10 This thing is going okay.

CFE010: 2104:27 Then flaps to twenty five position and maintain vee ref plus twenty...The highest go around procedure is starting.

CFE011: 2104:34 The flaps, sorry, retract the landing gear with positive rate of climb...if any low pressure light comes on do not select the switch in the off position... the low pressure lights of the pumps comes on, reduce the nose up altitude, the nose up attitude.

CFE012: 2104:57 The forward pumps...

CCP013: 2104:59 What heading do you have over there?

CCP014: 2105:04 Select Kennedy on my side.

CFO015: 2105:04 Kennedy is on the number two, but if want Commander, I can perform the radio setup right now that we are now being vectored, we are like on down wind position now.

CCP016: 2105:11 We passed already, no?

CFO017: 2105:12 Yes sir.

APP018: 2105:13 Avianca zero five two heavy turn left, heading three six zero.

RXX019: 2105:17 Left, heading three six zero, Avianca zero five two heavy.

CFE020: 2105:22 Three six zero.

CFO021: 2105:24 Yes Commander, thats what he say.

CCP022: 2105:26 Perform the radio setup, but leave to me the VOR, the in Kennedy, then select here, tell me what.

CCP023: 2105:34 Two what?.

CFO024: 2105:34 Two twenty three.

CXX025: 2105:35 ***sound of altitude alert tone***

CCP026: 2105:38 Two twenty three.

CCP027: 2105:39 What heading he provide us?

CFO028: 2105:42 New, he give us three six zero.

CCP029: 2105:42 Okay.

CFO030: 2105:42 I am going to perform the radio setup on number two.

CCP031: 2105:42 Perform the radio setup.

CXX032: 2105:49 *** [sound of landing gear warning horn] ***

CCP033: 2105:52 Hey, understand that the nose must be maintained as low as possible, yes?

CFE034: 2105:52 That's correct, it says that the forward pumps...
APP035: 2106:02 Avianca zero five two heavy, turn left heading of three zero zero.
RXX036: 2106:04 Left heading three zero zero, Avianca zero five two heavy.
CFO037: 2106:09 Three zero zero on the heading.
CFE038: 2106:10 The forward boost pumps could be uncovered on fuel during the go around.
CFE039: 2106:15 What it means it doesn't contain fuel for feeding itself and a flameout can occur... and it is necessary to lower the nose again.
CCP040: 2106:44 Heading three hundred.
CFO041: 2106:45 Three hundred.
CFO042: 2106:51 Right now we are proceeding to the airport inbound and we have twentyseven, seventeen miles.
CFE043: 2106:58 Roger.
CFO044: 2107:04 This means that we'll have hamburger tonight.
APP045: 2107:17 Avianca zero five two heavy, turn left heading two niner.
RXX046: 2107:20 Left heading two niner zero, Avianca zero five two heavy.
CFO047: 2107:24 Two niner zero on the heading please.
CCP048: 2107:29 Two twenty three course counter standby the frequency number.
CFO049: 2107:32 Standby for the frequency.
CCP050: 2107:34 Leave the ILS frequency in Kennedy until I advise you select your own there.
CFO051: 2107:36 It is ready.
CCP052: 2107:37 Well ...
CFO053: 2107:42 Markers are set.
APP054: 2108:34 Avianca zero five two heavy, descend and maintain, ahh, descend and maintain three thousand.
RXX055: 2108:40 Descend and maintain three thousand, Avianca zero five two heavy.
CFO056: 2108:40 Three thousand feet.
CCP057: 2109:01 The localizer, are we going to intercept it with two thousand?
CFO058: 2109:06 Yes, the initial approach altitude is two thousand or according to the ATC.
CFE059: 2109:11 They got us, they already vectoring us.
CFO060: 2109:21 They accomodate us ahead of an ...
CCP061: 2109:27 What?
CFO062: 2109:27 They accomodate us.
CFE063: 2109:29 They already know that we are in bad condition.
CCP064: 2109:30 No, they are descending us.
CFO065: 2109:35 One thousand feet.
CCP066: 2109:36 Ah yes.
CFO067: 2109:38 They are giving us priority.
APP068: 2109:44 Avianca zero five two heavy, turn left heading two seven zero.
RXX069: 2109:47 Left heading two seven zero.
CFO070: 2109:50 Two seven zero on the heading.

```
CCP071: 2109:54 Two seventy.
CFO072: 2110:03 It is ahead of us.
CFE073: 2110:05 Yes.
CCP074: 2110:16 Standby for the localizer there.
CFO075: 2110:18 Yes Sir.
CFO076: 2110:21 Outer marker is seven miles.
APP077: 2110:21 Avianca zero five two heavy, turn left heading two
                five zero, intercept the localizer.
RXX078: 2110:31 Heading two five zero, intercept the localizer,
                Avianca zero five two heavy.
CFO079: 2110:37 Two fifty is the heading to intercept the localizer.
CFO080: 2111:04 This is final vector, do you want the ILS Commander?
APP081: 2111:07 Avianca zero five two heavy, you are one five miles
                from the outer marker, maintain two thousand until
                established on the localizer, cleared ILS two two
                left.
RXX082: 2111:14 Cleared ILS two two left, maintain two thousand until
                established, Avianca zero five two heavy.
CFE083: 2111:14 Two thousand.
CCP084: 2111:16 Select the ILS on my side.
CFO085: 2111:20 The ILS in number one, one hundred ten point nine is
                set.
CFO086: 2111:29 For two thousand feet.
CFE087: 2111:29 Localizer alive.
CCP088: 2111:32 Give me flaps fourteen.
CFO089: 2111:33 We are thirteen miles from the outer marker.
CFO090: 2111:33 Flaps fourteen.
CCP091: 2111:47 Navigation number one.
CCP092: 2111:49 Did you already select flaps fourteen, no?
CFO093: 2111:51 Yes sir, are set.
CFO094: 2111:53 Navigation number one.
APP095: 2111:55 Avianca zero five two heavy, speed one six zero, if
                practical.
CFE096: 2111:57 Fourteen.
RXX097: 2111:59 One six, Avianca zero five two heavy.
CCP098: 2112:05 Give me flaps twenty five.
CFO099: 2112:06 Flaps twenty five.
CFO100: 2112:09 Reduce to a minimum.
CFO101: 2112:15 We have traffic ahead of us.
CCP102: 2112:28 We can maintain one hundred and forty with this flap
                setting.
CCP103: 2112:52 How many miles is that thing located?
CFO104: 2112:53 It is at seven miles commander, and we are at ten
                miles at the moment from the outer marker.
CCP105: 2113:25 Reset frequency, the ILS please.
CFO106: 2113:29 Okay.
CCP107: 2113:36 Do it.
CCP108: 2113:34 Thankyou.
CFO109: 2113:47 Now the course is going to be intercepted at the
                outer marker. This means there is not a problem,
                Commander.
CFO110: 2114:00 Localizer to the left.
```

```
APP111:  2115:08  Avianca zero five two heavy, contact Kennedy Tower,
                  one one niner point one, good day.
RXX112:  2115:12  One one niner point one, so long.
RXX113:  2115:19  Kennedy Tower, Avianca zero five two established two
                  two left.
TWR114:  2115:23  Avianca zero five two heavy, Kennedy Tower, two two
                  left, you're number three following seven two seven
                  traffic on a, ah, niner mile final.
RXX115:  2115:32  Avianca zero five two, roger.
CCP116:  2116:19  Can I lower the landing gear yet?
CFO117:  2116:21  No, I think its too early now.
CFO118:  2116:53  If we lower the landing gear, we have to hold very
                  high nose attitude.
CFE119:  2116:53  And its not very...
TWR120:  2116:56  American six ninety two, runway two two left, wind
                  one niner zero at two one, cleared to land.
AAB121:  2117:01  Cleared to land, American six ninety two.
TWR122:  2117:17  Avianca zero five two, what's your airspeed?
RXX123:  2117:20  Avianca zero five two, one four zero knots.
CCP124:  2117:25  they was asking for the American.
TWR125:  2117:30  Avianca zero five two, can you increase your airspeed
                  one zero knots?
CCP126:  2117:40  One zero.
RXX127:  2117:41  Okay, one zero knots, increasing
TWR128:  2117:42  Increase, increase!
CCP129:  2117:42  What?
RXX130:  2117:44  Increasing
CCP131:  2117:45  What?
TWR132:  2117:46  Okay
CFE133:  2117:46  Ten knots more.
CFO134:  2117:48  Ten little knots more.
CFE135:  2117:48  Ten little knots more.
CCP136:  2117:48  One hundred and fifty.
CCP137:  2117:52  Here we go.
CCP138:  2117:55  Tell me things louder, because I'm not hearing it.
CFO139:  2118:11  We are three miles to the outer marker now.
CCP140:  2118:13  Right.
CCP141:  2118:15  Resetting the ILS.
CFO142:  2118:17  Here it is already intercepted.
CFO143:  2118:32  Glide slope alive.
CCP144:  2118:38  I'm going to approach at one hundred and forty, it is
                  what he wants or what is the value he wants?
CFO145:  2118:41  One hundred and fifty; We had one hundred and forty,
                  and he required ten little knots more.
CCP146:  2119:09  Lower the gear.
CFO147:  2119:10  Gear down.
CCP148:  2119:30  Mode selector approach land checklist.
CFE149:  2119:32  Landing check.
CFE150:  2119:41  Speed brake lever.
CCP151:  2119:42  Full forward.
CFE152:  2119:43  Spoiler switches.
CFO153:  2119:45  On.
```

```
CFE154: 2119.45 On.
CFE155: 2119:46 Engine start selectors on.
CXX156: 2119:50 [Engine igniter sound starts and continues until end
                of tape.]
CFE157: 2119:56 No smoking switch on,
CFO158: 2119:57 On.
TWR159: 2119:58 Avianca zero five two, two two left, wind one niner
                zero at two zero, cleared to land.
CFE160: 2120:00 Gear.
RXX161: 2120:01 Cleared to land, Avianca zero five two heavy.
RXX162: 2120:03 Wind check please?
TWR163: 2120:05 One niner zero at two zero.
RXX164: 2120:07 Thankyou.
CFO165: 2120:08 One hundred and ninety with twenty is in the wind.
CCP166: 2120:10 With what?
TWR167: 2120:10 Avianca zero five two, say airspeed
CFO168: 2120:10 With twenty,
RXX169: 2120:12 Vero five two is, ah, one four five knots.
TWR170: 2120:15 TWA eight oh one heavy, if feasible reduce airspeed
                one four live.
CCP171: 2120:17 Give me fifty.
TWA172: 2120:19 Okay, we'll do our best.
CCP173: 2120:21 Are we cleared to land, no?
CFO174: 2120:23 Yes sir, we are cleared to land.
CFE175: 2120:25 Hydraulic pressure quantities, normal.
CFO176: 2120:28 Localizer to the left, slightly below glide slope.
CFE177: 2120:33 Standby flaps fifty, landing checklist complete.
CFO178: 2120:36 Stand by flaps fifty.
CCP179: 2120:39 give me fifty.
CFO180: 2120:40 Flaps fifty now.
CFE181: 2120:41 Fifty, fifty, green light, final set.
CFE182: 2120:45 All set for landing.
CFO183: 2120:48 Below glide slope.
TWR184: 2120:53 TWA eight oh one heavy, if feasible reduce to final
                approach airspeed at this time.
TWA185: 2120:56 Yes sir, we're indicating one five zero now, thats
                about the best we can do.
CCP186: 2121:06 Confirm the wind.
TWR187: 2121:07 Avianca zero five two heavy, can you increase your
                airspeed one zero knots at all?
RXX188: 2121:09 Yes, we're doing it.
TWR189: 2121:12 Okay, thankyou.
CCP190: 2121:15 Confirm the wind.
CFO191: 2121:16 The wind is one hundred ninety with twenty knots.
CCP192: 2121:20 I got it.
TWR193: 2121:30 TWA eight oh one, you're gaining on the heavy seven
                oh seven, turn left, heading of, ah, one five zero,
                and, ah, maintain two thousand.
CCP194: 2121:35 I'm going to leave the runway to the right, okay?
CFO195: 2121:36 To the right, yes sir.
TWA196: 2121:38 Okay TWA eight oh one heavy, left to one five zero,
                maintain two thousand.
```

```
CCP197: 2121:41 Localizer, glide slope one thousand feet, standby
                for lights.
CFO198: 2121:46 Standing by for lights.
CFO199: 2121:59 Slightly below glide slope.
CFO200: 2122:07 One thousand feet above field.
CFO201: 2122:10 Instruments cross checked, slightly below.
CFO202: 2122:17 All set for landing.
CFE203: 2122:19 Stand by for lights.
CCP204: 2122:21 Stand by.
CFO205: 2122:26 The wind is slightly from the left, one hundred
                ninety with twenty.
AAX206: 2122:33 Tower, American Forty heavy's with ya outside LORRS.
TWR207: 2122:36 American forty heavy, Kennedy Tower, roger, runway
                two two left, you're number two following heavy seven
                oh seven traffic on a two mile final. Wind two zero
                zero at one eight. RVR five thousand, five hundred,
                Cleared to land.
CFO208: 2122:44 Below glide slope.
AAX209: 2122:50 Cleared to land, American forty heavy.
CFO210: 2122:52 Glide slope.
TWR211: 2122:56 American forty heavy, whats your airspeed?
CFO212: 2122:57 This is the wind shear.
CFE213: 2138:08 Glide slope.
GPW214: 2123:08 Whoop whoop, pull up!
CFO215: 2123:09 Sink rate.
CFO216: 2123:10 Five hundred feet.
GPW217: 2123:11 Whoop whoop, pull up! [repeated 3 times]
CCP218: 2123:13 Lights.
GPW219: 2123:14 Whoop whoop, pull up! [repeated 4 times]
CCP220: 2123:20 Where is the runway?
GPW221: 2123:21 Whoop whoop, pull up! [repeated 3 times]
CCP222: 2123:23 The runway! Where is it?
GPW223: 2123:25 Glideslope [repeated 2 times]
CFO224: 2123:27 I don't see it! I don't see it!
CCP225: 2123:28 Give me the landing gear up. Landing gear up.
GPW226: 2123:29 Glideslope [repeated 2 times]
CXX227: 2123:32 [Sound of landing gear warning horn.]
CCP228: 2123:33 Request another traffic pattern.
RFO229: 2123:34 Executing a missed approach, Avianca zero five two
                heavy.
CFE230: 2123:37 Smooth with the nose, smooth with the nose, smooth
                with the nose.
TWR231: 2123:39 Avianca zero five two heavy, roger, ah, climb and
                maintain two thousand, turn left, heading one eight
                zero.
CCP232: 2123:43 We don't have the flae...
CFO233: 2123:45 Maintain two thousand feet, one eight zero on the
                heading.
CCP234: 2123:54 Flaps twenty five.
CCP235: 2124:00 I don't know what happened with the runway. I didn't
                see it.
CFE236: 2124:00 I didn't see it.
```

```
CFO237: 2124:00 I didn't see it.
TWR238: 2124:04 Avianca zero five two, you are making a left turn,
                correct sir?
CCP239: 2124:06 Tell them we are in emergency.
CFE240: 2124:06 Two thousand feet.
RFO241: 2124:08 Thats right to one eight zero on the heading, and,
                ah, we'll try once again. We're running out of fuel.
TWR242: 2124:15 Okay.
CCP243: 2124:17 What did he say?
CFO244: 2124:18 Maintain two thousand feet, one eight on the heading.
                I already advise him that we are going to attempt
                again, because we now can't.
TWR245: 2124:21 American forty heavy, two two left, wind two zero
                zero at one niner, cleared to land. Wind shear
                reported, gain and loss of ten knots, seven hundred
                feet to the surface by a DC-9.
CCP246: 2124:22 Advise him we are emergency!
CCP247: 2124:26 Did you tell him?
AAX248: 2124:27 American forty.
CFO249: 2124:28 Yes sir.
CFO250: 2124:29 I already advised him.
CCP251: 2124:31 Flaps four ... fifteen.
TWR252: 2124:32 Avianca zero five two heavy, continue the left turn,
                heading one five zero, maintain two thousand.
RXX253: 2124:36 One five zero, maintaining two thousand, Avianca zero
                five two heavy.
TWR254: 2124:39 Avianca zero five two heavy, contact approach on one
                one eight point four.
CFO255: 2124:40 One hundred and fifty on the heading.
RXX256: 2124:42 One one eight point four.
CCP257: 2124:45 They put us to reduce airspeed, that's the thing man,
                hundred and fifty.
CFO258: 2124:50 One hundred and fifty on the heading.
APP259: 2124:51 Five forty two heavy, thank you for your help,
                contact Kennedy Tower, one one niner point one.
TWB260: 2124:51 Good day, thank you.
CCP261: 2124:55 Flaps fifteen.
RFO262: 2124:55 Approach, Avianca zero five, ah, two heavy, we just
                missed a missed approach, and ah, we're maintaining
                two thousand and five on the...
CFE263: 2124:58 Flaps fourteen.
CCP264: 2125:00 Flaps fourteen.
APP265: 2125:07 Avianca zero five two heavy, New York, good evening,
                climb and maintain three thousand.
CCP266: 2125:08 Advise him we don't have fuel.
RFO267: 2125:10 Climb and maintain three thousand, and ah, we're
                running out of fuel, sir.
APP268: 2125:12 Okay, fly heading zero eight zero.
RFO269: 2125:15 Flying heading zero eight zero, climb to three
                thousand.
CFO270: 2125:19 Three thousand feet please.
APP271: 2125:19 TWA eight zero one heavy, turn left, heading zero
```

```
                    four zero.
CCP272: 2125:20 What, zero eighty?
CFO273: 2125:20 Hundred and eighty.
CCP274: 2125:22 Ah ...
TWA275: 2125:22 Zero four zero, TWA eight oh one heavy.
CFO276: 2125:22 Hundred and eighty.
CCP277: 2125:28 Did you already advise that we don't have fuel?
CFO278: 2125:29 Yes sir, I already advise him, hundred and eighty on
                    the heading. We are going to maintain three thousand
                    feet, and he's going to get us back.
CCP279: 2125:29 Okay.
APP280: 2125:41 Evergreen one zero two heavy, fly two seven zero.
EVG281: 2125:44 Two seven zero, one oh two heavy.
CFO282: 2125:47 One hundred and eighty.
CCP283: 2125:50 Give me bugs.
CFO284: 2125:52 One eighty on the heading.
APP285: 2125:53 American four zero heavy, present heading. I'll give
                    you a turn here in a minute.
AAX286: 2125:56 American four zero heavy, wilco.
CFO287: 2126:00 Three thousand feet.
APP288: 2126:07 American four zero heavy, turn left, heading one
                    eight zero. You're nine miles from the outer marker,
                    maintain  two thousand until established on the
                    localizer. Cleared for ILS two two left.
CFO289: 2126:11 ***
AAX290: 2126:15 Okay, one eight zero, two thousand, maintain two
                    until established, cleared ILS two two left,
                    American four zero heavy.
CCP291: 2126:21 Okay.
APP292: 2126:21 Evergreen one zero two heavy, descend and maintain
                    three thousand.
EVG293: 2126:24 Okay, leveling four for three, Evergreen one oh two
                    heavy.
APP294: 2126:27 Avianca zero five two heavy, turn left, heading zero
                    seven zero.
RXX295: 2126:31 Heading zero seven zero, Avianca zero five two heavy.
CFO296: 2126:34 Zero seven zero.
APP297: 2126:35 And Avianca zero five two heavy, ah, I'm going to
                    bring you about fifteen miles northeast, and then
                    turn you back onto the approach, is that fine with
                    you and your fuel?
RFO298: 2126:43 I guess so, that you very much.
CCP299: 2126:46 What did he say?
CFE300: 2126:46 The guy is angry.
CFO301: 2126:47 Fifteen miles in order to get back to the localizer.
APP302: 2126:50 Mvergreen one zero two heavy, turn left, heading two
                    five zero, you're one five miles from the outer
                    marker,  maintain three thousand until established
                    on the localizer. Cleared for ILS two two left.
CCP303: 2126:50 zero seventy.
APP304: 2126:50 Evergreen one zero two heavy, turn left, heading two
                    five zero. You're one five miles from the outer marker,
```

```
                    maintain three thousand until established on the
                    localizer. Cleared for ILS two two left.
CCP305: 2126:50     Zero seventy.
CFO306: 2126:52     Zero seven zero on the heading, maintaining three
                    thousand feet.
EVG307: 2126:59     Cleared for the approach, Evergreen one zero two
                    heavy.
APP308: 2127:02     TWA eight zero one heavy, turn left, heading two
                    nine zero.
CCP309: 2127:03     Give me the Kennedy LLS in number one.
TWA310: 2127:04     Two nine zero, TWA eight oh one.
CFO311: 2127:08     The LLS or the VOR?
CCP312: 2127:09     I like say the VOR.
CFO313: 2127:11     Fifteen point nine is on number one.
CCP314: 2127:13     Zero ninety.
CFO315: 2127:14     Zero seven zero on the heading.
CFE316: 2127:20     Zero seventy.
CFE317: 2127:20     We must follow that LLS.
APP318: 2127:28     Arnerican four zero heavy, contact Kennedy Tower,
                    one one niner point one, good evening.
CFO319: 2127:29     It is not centered, the localizer of the radial, no.
CCP320: 2127:31     I'm going to follow this...
CFO321: 2127:32     We must follow the identified ILS.
AAX322: 2127:32     Nineteen one for American four heavy. You have a good
                    evening sir.
APP323: 2127:35     Thankyou.
CCP324: 2127:36     To die.
PAB325: 2127:38     Kennedy Approach, Clipper eighteen twelve heavy with
                    alpha's descending to five thousand, heading zero six
                    zero.
APP326: 2127:43     Clipper eighteen twelve New York, good evening.
APP327: 2127:52     TWA eight zero one heavy, turn left, heading two
                    seven zero.
TWA328: 2127:54     Two seven zero, TWA eight zero one heavy.
APP329: 2128:11     Tlipper eighteen twelve heavy, descend and maintain
                    four thousand.
PAB330: 2128:15     Eighteen twelve heavy to four thousand.
CCP331: 2128:16     Take it easy, take it easy.
EVG332: 2128:42     Ah, approach for Evergreen one oh two heavy, is one
                    seven zero a good speed on final?
APP333: 2128:47     Ah, what's it gonna be in knots? Ah, I don't know the
                    mach, ah.
EVG334: 2128:54     Ah, yes sir, a hundred and seventy knots on final for
                    Evergreen, is that okay?
APP335: 2128:58     Yeah, that's fine, ah, I have a heavy jet seven
                    ahead, and he's about twenty knots slower, that's
                    due to the winds. I'm gonna need you to slow twenty
                    knots in three or four miles.
EVG336: 2129:09     Okay sir.
RFO337: 2129:11     Ah, can you give us a final now? Avianca zero five
                    two heavy.
APP338: 2129:20     Avianca zero five two, affirmative sir, turn left,
```

```
                    heading zero four zero.
CCP339: 2129:30 Give me a bug.
CFO340: 2129:33 Zero four zero, okay, that's fine.
CFO341: 2129:36 I'm giving you bugs for...
APP342: 2129:42 Evergreen one zero two heavy, contact Kennedy Tower,
                    one one niner point one. Good day.
EVG343: 2129:46 Ah, good day.
PAA344: 2129:58 New York Approach control, it's Clipper one one heavy,
                    maintaining four thousand feet, turning right to zero
                    three zero, what speed would you like?
APP345: 2130:05 Clipper eleven heavy, New York, good evening. Speed
                    one eight zero please
PAA346: 2130:09 Back to one eight zero for eleven heavy.
CFE347: 2130:11 I have the lights on.
APP348: 2130:14 TWA eight zero one heavy, turn left, heading two five
                    zero, you're one five miles from the outer marker.
                    Maintain  two thousand until established on the
                    localizer. Cleared for ILS two two left.
RXX349: 2130:21 Avianca zero five two heavy, left turn two five zero,
                    and ah, we're cleared for ILS.
CCP350: 2130:25 What heading? Tell me.
APP351: 2130:26 Okay, two called Trans World eight oh one, you were
                    cleared for the approach.
CFO352: 2130:27 Two five zero.
TWA353: 2130:30 Affirmative, TWA eight oh one, we got it. We're out
                    of three for two.
CFO354: 2130:32 Two five zero in the heading.
APP355: 2130:32 Avianca fifty two, climb and maintain three thousand.
CAM356: 2130:33 [Sound of landing gear warning horn.]
RFO357: 2130:36 Ah, negative sir. We just running out of fuel. We
                    okay three thousand. Now okay.
CCP358: 2130:39 No, no, three ... three thousand, three thousand.
APP359: 2130:44 Okay, turn left, heading three one zero sir.
RXX360: 2130:47 Three one zero, Avianca zero five two.
CCP361: 2130:50 Tell me...
APP362: 2130:50 Clipper eighteen twelve heavy, turn left, heading
                    three one zero.
PAB363: 2130:52 Eighteen twelve heavy, left three one zero.
CFO364: 2130:52 Three one zero in the...
CCP365: 2130:53 Flaps fourteen.
CFO366: 2130:54 Three one zero.
CFE367: 2130:54 No sir, are in...
CCP368: 2130:55 Set flaps fourteen.
APP369: 2130:55 Avianca fifty two, fly heading of three six zero
                    please.
CFO370: 2130:56 Fourteen degrees.
CCP371: 2130:56 Tell me heading, what?
RXX372: 2130:58 Okay, we'll maintain three six zero now.
CFE373: 2130:59 Three six zero now.
APP374: 2131:01 Okay, and you're number two for the approach. I just
                    have to give you enough room so you can make it
                    without, ah, having to come out again.
```

```
RXX375: 2131:07 Okay, we're number two and flying three six zero now.
APP376: 2131:10 thankyou sir.
CCP377: 2131:22 Three sixty, no?
CFO378: 2131:23 Three sixty.
CCP379: 2131:26 Flaps fourteen.
APP380: 2131:27 TWA eight zero one heavy, you're eight miles behind
                a heavy jet. Contact Kennedy Tower, one one niner
                point one. Thanks for the help.
TWA381: 2131:33 Okay, eight oh one roger and what's his ground...
                what's his airspeed, do you know?
APP382: 2131:36 Ah, he's indicating ten knots slower, eight miles.
TWA383: 2131:39 Okay, thank you.
APP384: 2131:45 Clipper eighteen twelve heavy, speed one six zero,
                if practical.
PAB385: 2131:47 eighteen twelve heavy slowing to one fifty.
APP386: 2132:08 Avianca zero five two heavy, turn left, heading
                three three zero.
RXX387: 2132:11 Three three zero on the heading, Avianca zero five
                two.
CFO388: 2132:14 Three three zero, the heading.
ANN389: 2132:38 [Sound of momentary power interruption to the CVR.]
CFE390: 2132:39 Flame out! Flame out on engine number four.
CAM391: 2132:41 [Sound of momentary power interruption to the CVR]
CCP392: 2132:42 Flame out on it.
CFE393: 2132:43 Flame out on engine number three, essential on number
                two, one number one.
CCP394: 2132:49 Show me the runway.
RFO395: 2132:49 Avianca zero five two, we just, ah, lost two engines
                and, ah, we need priority, please.
APP396: 2132:54 Avianca zero five two, turn left, heading two five
                zero, intercept the localizer.
CAM397: 2132:56 [Sound of engine spooling down.]
CFO398: 2132:57 Two five zero.
RXX399: 2132:59 Roger.
CCP400: 2133:00 Select the ILS.
CFO401: 2133:01 ILS.
CFO402: 2133:03 It is on the number two.
CCP403: 2133:04 Select the ILS, let's see.
APP404: 2133:04 Avianca zero five two heavy, you're one five miles
                from the outer marker, maintain two thousand until
                established on the localizer. Cleared for ILS two
                two left.
RXX405: 2133:12 Roger, Avianca.
APP406: 2133:14 Clipper eighteen twelve, turn left, heading two two
                zero.
CCP407: 2133:22 Did you select the ILS?
CFO408: 2133:22 It is ready on two.
CAM409: 2133:24 [End of recording]
#
#
#   Copyright © 1996-1999 Harro Ranter / Fabian Lujan
#    Aviation Safety Network; updated 12 August, 1999
```

Background information to samples

The information in the current section has been taken from the database of the Aviation Safety Network (2000b) and Aviation Safety Network (2000c).

```
Date:                29.12.1972
Time:                23.42 EST
Type:                Lockheed L-1011 TriStar 1
Operator:            Eastern Air Lines
Registration:        N310EA
C/n:1011
Year built:          1972
Total airframe hrs:  986 hours
Cycles:              502 cycles
Crew:                5 fatalities / 13 on board
Passengers:          94 fatalities / 163 on board
Total:               99 fatalities / 176 on board
Location:            Everglades, FL (USA)
Phase:               Final Approach
Nature:              Scheduled Passenger

Flight:              New York-John F. Kennedy IAP, NY - Miami
IAP, FL (Flightnumber 401)
```

Remarks:
Flight EA401 departed New York-JFK at 21.20h EST for a flight to Miami. The flight was uneventful until the approach to Miami. After selecting gear down, the nosegear light didn't indicate 'down and locked'. Even after recycling the gear, the light still didn't illuminate. At 23.34h the crew called Miami Tower and were advised to climb to 2000ft and hold. At 23.37h the captain instructed the second officer to enter the forward electronics bay, below the flight deck, to check visually the alignment of the nose gear indices. Meanwhile, the flightcrew continued their attempts to free the nosegear position light lens from its retainer, without success. The second officer was directed to descend into the electronics bay agin at 23.38h and the captain and first officer continued discussing the gear position light lens assembly and how it might have been reinserted incorrectly. At 23.40:38 a half-second C-chord sounded in the cockpit, indicating a +/- 250ft deviation from the selected altitude. None of the crewmembers commented on the warning and no action was taken. A little later the Eastern

Airlines maintenance specialist, occupying the forward observer seat went into the electronics bay to assist the second officer with the operation of the nose wheelwell light. At 23.41:40 Miami approach contacted the flight and granted the crew's request to turn around by clearing him for a left turn heading 180 deg. At 23.42:05 the first officer suddenly realised that the altitude had dropped. Just seven seconds afterwards, while in a left bank of 28deg, the TriStar's no.1 engine struck the ground, followed by the left maingear. The aircraft disintegrated, scattering wreckage over an area of flat marshland, covering a 1600ft x 300ft area. PROBABLE CAUSE: "The failure of the fightcrew to monitor the flight instruments during the finall 4 minutes of flight, and to detect an unexpected descent soon enough to prevent impact with the ground. Preoccupation with a malfunction of the nose landing gear position indicating system distracted the crew's attention from the instruments and allowed the descent to go unnoticed." (NTSB-AAR-73-14)

Source: (also check out sources used for every accident) NTSB-AAR-73-14

Date:	25.01.1990
Time:	21.34 EST
Type:	Boeing 707-321B
Operator:	Avianca
Registration:	HK-2016
C/n:	19276/592
Year built:	1967
Crew:	8 fatalities / 9 on board
Passengers:	65 fatalities / 149 on board
Total:	73 fatalities / 158 on board
Location:	Cove Neck, NY (USA)
Phase:	Initial Approach
Nature:	Scheduled Passenger
Flight:	Medellin-Olaya Herrera APT - New York-John F. Kennedy IAP, NY (Flightnumber 052)

Remarks:
Avianca Flight AV052 (Bogota - Medellin - New York-JFK) took off from Medellin shortly after 15.00h with approx. 81000lb of fuel on board When arriving near New York, the aircraft had to enter 3 holding patterns. The first for 12-16 mins over Norfolk, the second for 27mins over new Jersey, and the third pattern over CAMRN for 46mins. At that moment the Avianca crew advised ATC that they could only hold for 5 more minutes and that their alternate Boston couldn't be reached anymore due to the low state of fuel. New York TRACON (Terminal Radar Approach Control) guided AV052 to Runway 22L ILS. Due to the bad weather

(300ft ceiling, 400m visibility, RVR - Runway Visual Range of
2400ft and wind shear of ca. 10kt) the crew had to carry out a
missed approach. During the go-around, at 12mls SE of JFK
Airport, 2 of the 4 Pratt & Whitney JT3D-3B engines ran down.
Shortly afterwards followed by the remaining two. At 21.34h,
heading 250 and flaps at 14 and gear up, the aircraft crashed
into some trees.

Source: (also check out sources used for every accident)
AW&ST 2.4.1990 (52-53); NTSB/AAR-91/04

References

Aczel, A. (1996). *Fermat's last theorem*. Harmondsworth: Penguin.

Alexandersson, J., Buschbeck-Wolf, B., Fujinami, T., Maier, E. et al. (1997). *Dialogue Acts in VERBMOBIL-2* (Tech. Rep.). Verbmobil Verbundvorhaben. (Report 204)

Allan, K. (1986). *Linguistic Meaning* (Vol. 2). London: Routledge and Kegan Paul.

Allan, K. (1998). Speech act Theory – An overview. In J. Mey (Ed.), *Concise encyclopedia of pragmatics* (927–939). Amsterdam, etc.: Elsevier.

Allan, K. & Core, M. (1997). *Draft of DAMSL: Dialogue Act Markup in Several Layers.*

Allen, J. & Litman, D. (1987). A plan recognition model for subdialogues in conversation. *Cognitive Science*, *11*(2), 163–200.

Allwood, J. (1977). A critical look at speech act theory. In *Logic, pragmatics and grammar* (53–69). Lund.

Allwood, J. (1997). *Dialog on Dialog – An Appetizer to the Study of Dialog*. Contribution to a festschrift for Ivan Havel.

Allwood, J., Nivre, J., & Ahlsen, E. (1992). On the Semantics and Pragmatics of Linguistic Feedback. *Journal of Semantics*, 9.

Anderson, S. (1971). *On the lingistic status of the performative–constative distinction*. Bloomington: Indiana University Linguistics Club.

Aristoteles (1975). *Lehre vom Schluß oder Erste Analytik. Organon III.* Hamburg: Felix Meiner Verlag. (Philosophische Bibliothek Band 10. Nachdruck der Übersetzung von Eugen Rolfes, 1921)

Asher, N. (1998). Varieties of discourse structure in dialogue. *Twendial (Proceedings of the Second International Workshop on Dialogue)*. Twente, the Netherlands.

Asher, N., Busquets, J., & Le Draoulec, A. (2001). Cooperativity in Dialogue. In M. Bras & L. Vieu (Eds.), *Semantic and pragmatic issues in discourse and dialogue* (217–45). Elsevier.

Asher, N., & Lascarides, A. (2003). *Logics of discourse*. Cambridge UP.

Austin, J. (1962). *How to do things with words*. London: Oxford University Press.

Bach, K. (2001). *Routledge Encyclopedia of Philosophy Entry: Ambiguity.* online.sfsu.edu/~kbach/ambguity.html.

Bange, P. (1983). Points de vue sur l'analyse conversationnelle. In *Drlav* (Vol. 29, pp. 1–28).

Bäuerle, R., Schwarze, C., & Stechow, A. v. (Eds.). (1983). *Meaning, use, and interpretation of language*. de Gruyter.

Bennett, J. (1973). The meaning-nominalist strategy. *Foundations of Language*, *10*, 141–68.

Bennett, J. (1976). *Linguistic Behaviour*. Cambridge UP.

Benthem, J. v. (1996). *Exploring logical dynamics*. CSLI & FoLLI.

Bergmann, J. (1981). Ethnomethodologische Konversationsanalyse. In P. Schröder & H. Steger (Eds.), *Dialogforschung. Jahrbuch 1980 des Instituts für Deutsche Sprache* (9–51). Düsseldorf.

Beveren, T. van (1995). *Runter kommen sie immer. Die verschwiegenen Risiken des Flugverkehrs*. Frankfurt/Main, etc.: Campus.

Bird, S., & Liberman, M. (1999a). Annotation graphs as a framework for multidimensional linguistic data analysis. *Towards Standards and Tools for Discourse Tagging, Proceedings of the Workshop*, 1–10.

Bird, S., & Liberman, M. (1999b). *A formal framework for linguistic annotation* (Tech. Rep.). Department of Computer and Information Science, University of Pennsylvania. (ms-cis-99-01)

Bochenski, J. (1970). *Formale Logik*. Freiburg i. Br., etc.: Alber, 1970. (3. Aufl., unveränd. Neudr. d. 2., erw. Aufl.)

Bodenheimer, A. (1992). *Verstehen heißt antworten*. Stuttgart: Philipp Reclam jun.

Buerki-Cohen, J. (1995). *Say again? How complexity and format of air traffic control instructions affect pilot recall* (Tech. Rep.). USDOT-Volpe National Transportation Systems Center, Cambridge, Massachusetts. www.volpe.dot.gov/opsad/pubs.html

Bürki-Cohen, J. (1995). *An analysis of tower (ground) controller-pilot voice communications* (Tech. Rep.). United States. Federal Aviation Administration. Office of Research and Development John A. Volpe National Transportation Systems Center (U.S.). www.volpe.dot.gov/opsad/grd-view.html

Burnard, L. (1991). What is TEI? In D. Greenstein (Ed.). *Modelling historical data* (130–145). St. Katharinen: Scripta Mercaturae Verlag.

Bußmann, H. (1990). *Lexikon der Sprachwissenschaft* (No. 452). Alfred Kröner Verlag.

Cardosi, K. (1994). *An analysis of tower (local) controller-pilot voice communications* (Tech. Rep.). United States. Federal Aviation Administration. Research and Development Service John A. Volpe National Transportation Systems Center (U.S.). (Washington D.C.: Office of Research and Development, U.S. Dept. of Transportation, Federal Aviation Administration; Springfield, VA: Available through the National Technical Information Service).

Cardosi, K., Falzarano, P., & Han, S. (1999). *Pilot-Controller Communication Errors: An Analysis of Aviation Safety Reporting System (ASRS) Reports* (Tech. Rep.). Volpe Center. DOT/FAA/AR-98/17, www.volpe.dot.gov/opsad/pubs.html

Cassidy, S., & Harrington, J. (2001). *The Emu speech database system*. www.shlrc.mq.edu.au/emu/.

Chierchia, G. (1995). *Dynamics of meaning–anaphora, presupposition, and the theory of grammar*. Chicago UP.

Chomsky, N. (1957). *Syntactic structures*. The Hague: Mouton.

Chomsky, N. (1970). Remarks on nominalization. In *Readings in English transformational grammar* (184–221). Waltham, Massachusetts: Ginn and Company.

Chomsky, N., & Halle, M. (1968). *The sound pattern of English*. New York: Harper and Row.

Clark, H. (1996). *Using language*. Cambridge: Cambridge University Press.

Clark, H., & Schaefer, E. (1987). Contributing to discourse. *Cognitive Science, 13,* 259–294.

Cohen, P. R., Morgan, & Pollack, M. E. (1990). *Intentions in communication*. Cambridge: MIT Press.

Coulon, A. (1987). *L'ethnométhodologie*. Paris. ("Que sais-je?", no. 2393)

Cushing, S. (1994). *Fatal words. Communication clashes and aircraft crashes*. Chicago, London: University of Chicago Press.

Dennett, D. C. (1991). *Consciousness explained*. Penguin Books.

Devlin, K. (2001). *Infosense*. Freeman.

Duncan Jr., S. (1973). Toward a grammar for dyadic conversation. *Semiotica*, *9*, 29–46.

Duncan, S. J. (1974). On the structure of speaker-auditor interaction during speaking turns. *Language in Society*, *2*, 161–180.

Duncan, S., & Niederehe, G. (1974). On signalling that it's your turn to speak. *Journal of Experimental Social Psychology*, *10*, 234–247.

Duncan, S., & Fiske, D. W. (1985). *Interaction structure and strategy* (Editions de la Maison des Sciences de l'Homme ed.). Cambridge University Press.

Eckstein, R. (2000). *XML – kurz & gut*. Köln, etc.: O-Reilly Verlag.

Edmondson, W. (1981). *Spoken discourse: A model for analysis*. Longman.

Edmondson, W., & House, J. (1981). *Let's talk and talk about it*. Munich: Urban and Schwarzenberg.

Ehlich, K., & Rehbein, J. (1977). Wissen, kommunikatives Handeln und die Schule. In H. C. Goeppert (Ed.), *Sprachverhalten im Unterricht*. Fink.

Essler, W. (1970). *Induktive Logik: Grundlagen und Voraussetzungen*. Freiburg: Alber.

Foley, W., & Van Valin, R. (1984). *Functional syntax and universal grammar*. Cambridge: Cambridge University Press.

Fraser, B. (1974). An examination of the performative analysis. *Papers in Linguistics*, *7*, 1–40.

Frege, G. (1969). *Funktion, Begriff, Bedeutung: fünf logische Studien*. Göttingen: Vanden-hoeck & Ruprecht. (Herausgegeben und eingeleitet von Günther Patzig.)

Frege, G. (1971). *Schriften zur Logik und Sprachphilosophie: aus dem Nachlaß*. Hamburg: Meiner. (Hrsg. von Gottfried Gabriel)

Fuchs, W., Klima, R., Lautmann, R., Rammstedt, O., & Wienold, H. (Eds.). (1978). *Lexikon zur Soziologie*. Opladen: Westdeutscher Verlag.

Gamut, L. (1991). *Logic, language, and meaning. Introduction to logic* (Vol. 1). Chicago and London: The University of Chicago Press.

Garofalo, J. S., L. F. Lamel, W. M. Fisher, J. G. Fiscus, D. S. Pallett, & N. L. Dahlgren (1986). *The DARPA TIMIT acoustic-phonetic continuous speech corpus cdrom*. CD-ROM. (printed documentation; available on request from the LDC)

Gibbon, D. (1976). Performatory categories in contrastive intonation analysis. In D. Chitoran (Ed.), *2nd International Conference of English contrastive projects* (145–156). Bukarest: University Press.

Gibbon, D. (1981). Idiomaticity and functional variation. A case study of international amateur radio talk. *Language in Society*, *10*, 21–42.

Gibbon, D. (1985). Context and variation in two–way radio–discourse. *Discourse Processes*, *8*, 395–419.

Gibbon, D., Mertins, I., & Moore, R. (2000). *Handbook of audiovisual, multimodal and spoken dialogue and systems resources and terminology for development and product evaluation.* Doordrecht, New York: Kluwer. (Final Report of LE EAGLES Phase II project (LE3-4244 10484/0) for the European Commission)

Gibbon, D., Moore, R., & Winski, R. (Eds.). (1997). *Handbook of standards and resources for spoken language systems.* Mouton de Gruyter.

Gibbon, D., & Sassen, C. (1997). *Prosody-Particle Pairs as Discourse Control Signs* (Report– Situierte Künstliche Kommunikatoren No. 97/11). SFB 360.

Ginzburg, J., Sag, I., & Purver, M. (2001). Integrating conversational move types in the grammar of conversation. In P. Kühnlein, H. Rieser, & H. Zeevat (Eds.), *Bi-dialog 2001 proceedings of the 5th workshop on formal semantics and pragmatics of dialogue, June, 14th–16th at ZIF, Bielefeld, 2001.*

Gülich, E. (1990). Pour une éthnométhodologie linguistique. Description de séquences conversationnelles explicatives. In M. Charolles, S. Fisher, & J. Jayez (Eds.), *Le discours. représentations et interprétations* (71–109). Nancy: Presses Universitaires. (Coll. Processus Discursifs)

Goffman, E. (1963). *Behaviour in public places.* Free Press of Glencoe, New York.

Grice, H. P. (1957). Meaning. *Phil. Rev.*, 66, 377–88.

Grice, H. P. (1969). Utterer's Meaning and Intentions. *Phil. Rev.*, 78, 147–77.

Grice, H. P. (1975). Logic and conversation. In P. Cole & L. Morgan (Eds.), *Syntax and semantics* (Vol. 3: Speech Acts). Academic Press, New York.

Grimes, J. E. (1975). *The thread of discourse.* Mouton.

Groenendijk, J., & Stokhof, M. (1991). Dynamic Predicate Logic. *Linguistics and Philosophy*, 14, 39–100.

Grommes, P., & Grote, G. (2001). Coordination in action. Comparing two work situations with high vs. low degrees of formalization. In P. Kühnlein, A. Newlands, & H. Rieser (Eds.), *Proceedings of the workshop on coordination and action* (27–29).

Grosz, B., & Sidner, C. (1986). Attention, intentions, and the structure of discourse. *Computational Linguistics*, 12(3), 175–204.

Gut, U., & Milde, J.-T. (2001). The TASX-environment: an XML-based corpus database for time aligned language data. In *Proceedings of the ircs workshop on linguistic databases, Philadelphia.*

Halliday, M. (1973). *Explorations in the Functions of Language.* London: Edward Arnold.

Harnish, R. (1975). The argument from *lurk. Linguistic Inquirer*, 6, 145–154.

Heim, I. (1983). *File change semantics and the familiarity theory of definiteness.* (in Bäuerle, Schwarze, & Stechow 1983)

Hempel, C. G. (1974). *Grundzüge der Begriffsbildung in der empirischen Wissenschaft.* Düsseldorf: Bertelsmann-Universitätsverlag.

Heydrich, W., Kühnlein, P., & Rieser, H. (1998). *A DRT-Style Modelling of Agents' Mental States in Construction Dialogue–Revised and Extended Version* (Tech. Rep.). Collaborative Research Center SFB 360 'Situated Artificial Agents', Report 98/5. ftp://ftp.uni-bielefeld.de/.mnt2/papers/sfb360/report-98-05.ps.gz

Hjelmslev, L. (1969). *Prolegomena to a theory of language.* Madison, Wisconsin: University of Wisconsin Press.

Hoesch, D. (2000, 1 December). *DC-9 sample oral questions.* www.nauticom.net/www/leoni/MD80Mainfiles/DC9SG.htm. (This is part of the unofficial MD-80/DC9 study site)

House, J. (1982). Opening and closing phases in German and English dialogues. *Grazer Linguistische Studien, 16,* 52–82.

Hymes, D., & Gumperz, J. (1972). *Directions in sociolinguistics. The ethnography of communication.* New York: Holt, Rinehart and Winston.

Jackendoff, R. (1972). *Semantic interpretation in generative grammar.* Cambridge, Mass.: MIT Press.

Jakobson, R. (1960). Closing statement: Linguistics and poetics. In *Style in language* (350–377). Cambridge, Mass., MIT Press.

Jekat, S., Klein, A., Maier, E., Maleck, I., Mast, M., & Quantz, J. (1995). *Dialogue Acts in VERBMOBIL* (Tech. Rep.). Verbmobil Verbundvorhaben. (VM-Report 65)

Kadmon, N. (2001). *Formal pragmatics.* Blackwell.

Kamp, H., & U.Reyle (1993). *From discourse to logic: An introduction to modeltheoretic semantics, formal logic and discourse representation theory.* Kluwer Academic Publishers, Dordrecht, Germany.

Kautz, H. A. (1987). *A Formal Theory of Plan Recognition* (Tech. Rep. No. 215). University of Rochester, Computer Science Dept. (PhD Thesis)

Kempen, G. (Ed.). (1987). *Natural language generation* (No. 135). Martinus Nijhoff Publishers.

Kendon, A., & Ferber, A. (1973). A description of some human greetings. In R. Michael & J. Crook (Eds.), *Comparative ecology and behaviour of primates* (591–668). London: Academic Press.

Kienle, R. (1982). *Fremdwörterlexikon.* Hamburg. Xenos.

Kilroy, C. (2001). *Voice recorders.* www.airdisaster.com/cvr/.

Kindt, W. (2001). *Koordinations-, Konstruktions- und Regulierungsprozesse bei der Bedeutungskonstitution: Neue Ergebnisse der Dynamischen Semantik* (Tech. Rep. No. 01/4). SFB 360.

Kindt, W., & Rieser, H. (1999). Syntax- und Semantikkoordination im Diskurs. *Kognitionswissenschaft.* (Eds.: G. Rickheit and I. Wachsmuth)

Kiss, T. (1995). *Merkmale und Repräsentationen. Eine Einführung in die deklarative Grammatikanalyse.* Westdeutscher Verlag.

Klein, E., & Veltman, F.(Eds.). (1991). *Natural language and speech.* Springer.

Kohler, K. (1994). *Handbuch zur Datenaufnahme und Transliteration in tp14 von Verbmobil–3.0. Technisches Dokument Nr. 11.*

Kowtko, J. C., Isard, S. D., & Doherty, G. M. (1993). *Conversational games within dialogue* (Research Paper No. RP-31). HCRC, Edinburgh & Glasgow. http://www.hcrc.ed.ac.uk/Site/KOWTJ922.html

Kripke, S. (1977). Speaker's reference and semantic reference. *Midwest Studies in Philosophy, 2,* 255–76.

Kripke, S. (1980). *Naming and necessity.* Oxford: Blackwell.

Kühnlein, P., Rieser, H., & Zeevat, H. (2003). *Perspectives on dialogue in the new millenium.* Amsterdam: John Benjamins.

Kutschera, F. von. (1982). *Grundfragen der Erkenntnistheorie.* Berlin, etc.: de Gruyter.

Labov, W., & Fanshel, D. (1977). *Therapeutic Discourse: Psychotherapy as Conversation*. New York: Academic Press.

Ladkin, P. (1999, February). *Computer-related incidents with commercial aircraft*. www.rvs.uni-bielefeld.de/publications/Incidents. (last visit: 18 December, 1999)

Lambert, K., & Brittan, G. (1991). *Eine Einführung in die Wissenschaftsphilosophie*. Berlin, New York: Walter de Gruyter.

Landsberg, B. (1995–2000). *Landmark Accidents: Deadly Surprise. Thunderstorms require a wide berth*. www.aopa.org/asf/asfarticles/sp9808.html. (Aircraft Owners and Pilots Association)

Lascarides, A. (2001). Imperatives in dialogue. *BIDIALOG-Proceedings*.

Lascarides, A., & Asher, N. (1993). Temporal interpretation, discourse relations and common sense entailment. *Linguistics and Philosophy*, *16*(5), 473–493.

Lascarides, A., Asher, N., & Oberlander, J. (1992). Inferring discourse relations in context. In *Proceedings of the 30th annual meeting of the Association of Computational Linguistics*.

Laver, J. (1974). Communicative functions of phatic communion. In A. Kemp, E. Uldall, & R. Sommerville (Eds.), *Work in progress* (Vol. 7). Edinburgh University.

Levinson, S. (1983). *Pragmatics*. Cambridge University Press.

Lewandowski, T. (1990). *Linguistisches Wörterbuch*. UTB: Quelle und Meyer.

Lewis, D. (1998). *Papers in philosophical logic*. Cambridge, etc.: Cambridge Univ. Press.

Linter, T., & Buckles, J. (1993). Why can't we talk to each other? *Journal of Air Traffic Control*.

Llisterri, J. (1996). Eagles *preliminary recommendations on spoken texts* (Eagles document No. EAG-TCWG-SPT/P). Eagles.

Lobin, H. (2000). *Informationsmodellierung in xml und sgml*. Berlin, Heidelberg, etc.: Springer.

Lyons, J. (1977). *Semantics, Vol. II*. Cambridge: Cambridge University Press.

MacWhinney, B., & Gillis, S. (1998). *CHILDES Child Language Data Exchange System*. childes.psy.cmu.edu/.

Malinowski, B. (1923, repr. 1969). The problem of meaning in primitive languages. In *The meaning of meaning*. London: Routledge and Kegan Paul.

Mann, W., & Thompson, S. (1988). Rhetorical structure theory: Toward a functional theory of text organization. *Text*, *8*(3), 243–281.

Mann, W. C., & Thompson, S. A. (1987). *Rhetorical Structure Theory: Description and construction of text structures*. in: (Kempen 1987:). (85–95)

Marcu, D. (2000). *Theory and practice of discourse parsing and summarization*. MIT Press.

Matthiessen, C., & Thompson, S. (1987). The structure of discourse and "subordination". In J. Haiman & S. Thompson (Eds.), *Clause combining in discourse and grammar*. Amsterdam: John Benjamins.

Aviation Safety Network. (2000a). *CVR and ATC transcripts*. aviation-safety.net/investigation/cvr/transcripts/

Aviation Safety Network. (2000b). *Recordings*. aviation-safety. net/cvr/cvrwav.htm.

Aviation Safety Network. (2002a). *Accident Coverage: Tenerife Collision*. aviation-safety.net/database/record.php?id=19770327-???.

Aviation Safety Network. (2002b). *Accident Description: Boeing 707-321B.* aviation-safety.net/database/1990/900125-0.htm.

Aviation Safety Network. (2002c). *Accident Description: Lockheed L-1101, TriStar-1.* aviation-safety.net/database/1972/721229-0.htm.

Aviation Safety Network. (2002d). *Accident Description: Tenerife, 1977.* aviation-safety.net/database/1977/770327-1.htm.

Commonwealth Department of Transport and Regional Services. (1999). *Flight Data and Cockpit Voice Recorders.*

DSTO Commonwealth of Australia. (1999). *The Black Box: An Australian Contribution to Air Safety.* www.dsto.defence.gov.au/corporate/history/jubilee/ blackbox.html.

DSTO Commonwealth of Australia. (2000). *World's first flight memory recorder (Black Box).* www.dsto.defence.gov.au/corporate/history/jubilee/sixtyyears5.html.

Dublin Core Metadata Initiative. (2002). *About the Dublin Core Metadata Initiative.* dublincore.org/about/.

EU Kommission. (2001). *Die europäische Verkehrspolitik bis 2010: Weichenstellung für die Zukunft* (Tech. Rep.). Kommission der europäischen Gemeinschaften. www.uic.asso.fr/sdocumentation/~documentation/legislation/com2001370de.pdf

Federal Aviation Administration. (1995). *Air traffic control procedures.* (aviation-charts.com/atc01.htm)

Federal Aviation Administration. (1998). *Flight Operations Manual PNNL-MA-530.* www.pnl.gov/atmossciences/pnnlma530.html

Federal Aviation Administration. (2000a). *Aeronautical Information Manual. Official Guide to Basic Flight Information and ATC Procedures.* www.faa.gov/ATPubs/AIM/

Federal Aviation Administration. (2000b). *Aeronautical Information Manual. Phonetic Alphabet.* www.faa.gov/atpubs/aim/Chap4/TBL422.GIF

Federal Aviation Administration. (2000c). Chapter 4. Air Traffic Control, Section 2. Radio Communications Phraseology and Techniques. In *Aeronautical Information Manual. Official Guide to Basic Flight Information and ATC Procedures.* www.faa.gov/ATPubs/AIM/Chap4/aim0402.html

Federal Aviation Administration. (2000d). *International Flight Information Manual.* www.faa.gov/atpubs/IFIM/INDEX.htm

Federal Aviation Administration. (2000e). *Pilot/Controller Glossary.* www.faa.gov/atpubs/PCG/PCGTOC.htm

Federal Aviation Administration. (2000f). Preface: Federal Aviation Administration (FAA). In *Aeronautical Information Manual. Official Guide to Basic Flight Information and ATC Procedures.* www.faa.gov/ATPubs/AIM/Preface/aim-bscflight.html

Federal Aviation Administration. (2001a). *Federal Aviation Administration Order, 7110.65M Air Traffic Control.* www.faa.gov/atpubs/ATC/index.htm

Federal Aviation Administration. (2001b). *Federal Aviation Administration Order, 7110M Air Traffic Control: Foreword.* www.faa.gov/ atpubs/ATC/65m-fwd.html

Federal Aviation Administration. (2002). *Aeronautical Information Manual. Appendix 3. Abbreviations/Acronyms.* www.faa.gov/atpubs/aim/Appendices/aimapd3.html #Appendix3

National Safety Board. (2000). *Cockpit Voice Recorders (CVR) and Flight Data Recorders (FDR).* www.ntsb.gov/Aviation/_FDR.htm.

National Transportation Safety Board. (2001). *About the NTSB.* www.ntsb.gov/Abt-NTSB/ guide.htm.

ServiceTasmania Online. (2000). *Metadata guidelines.* www.tased.edu.au/tasonline/ metadata/.

Mc Kevitt, P., Partridge, D., & Wilks, Y. (1992). *Approaches to natural language discourse processing* (Tech. Rep.). 3CRL, Box 30001, New Mexico State University, Las Cruces: Computing Research Laboratory Dept.

McLaughlin, M. (1984). *Conversation: How talk is organized.* Beverly Hills, Calif.: Sage Publications.

Mengel, A., Dybkjaer, L., Juanma, G., Heid, U., Klein, M., Vito, P. et al., (1999). *MATE Dialogue Annotation Guidelines.* Le Telematics Project LE4-8370 1 March 1998–31 October 1999.

Menne, A. (1986). *Einführung in die Logik* (Vol. 34). Francke.

Miller, P. (1999). *Metadata: Definition.* www.ukoln.ac.uk/interop-focus/presentations/ cimi/taiwan/rdf/iap-html/.

Moeschler, J. (2001). *Speech act theory and the analysis of conversations.* (in Vanderveken & Kubo 2001)

Montague, R. (1974). *Formal philosophy: Selected papers of Richard Montague.* New Haven: Yale University Press.

Morrow, D., Lee, A., & Rodvold, M. (1993). Analysis of problems in routine controller-pilot communication. *International Journal of Aviation Psychology*, *3*(4), 285–302.

Morrow, D., & Rodvold, M. (1993). The influence of ATC message length and timing on pilot communication. *NASA Contractor Report 177621.* (see also: United States. National Aeronautics and Space Administration Ames Research Center Decision Systems, Los Altos, CA : Decision Systems, [1993])

Morrow, D., & Rodvold, M. (1998). Communication issues in air traffic control. In S. M. & E. Stein (Eds.), *Human factors in air traffic control* (421–456). New York: Academic Press.

Morrow, D., Rodvold, M., & Lee, A. (1994). Nonroutine transactions in controller-pilot communication. *Discourse Processes*, *17*, 235–258.

Mortimer, H. (1988). *The logic of induction.* Ellis Horwood.

Murray, D. (1989). Turn-taking in computer conversations. In C. Hywel (Ed.), *A multi-disciplinary consideration of language use in work contexts* (323–337). New York.

Muskens, R. (1994). A compositional discourse representation theory. In P. Dekker & M. Stokhof (Eds.), *Proceedings of the 9th Amsterdam colloquium* (467–86).

Muskens, R. (1996). Combining Montague semantics and discourse Representation. *Linguistics and Philosophy*, *19*, 143–86.

Newton-Smith, W. H. (2000). *A companion to the philosophy of science* (No. 18). Blackwell.

Percival, P. (2000). *Theoretical Terms: Meaning and Reference.* (in Newton-Smith (2000))

Peregrin, J. (2000). The 'Natural' and the 'Formal'. *Journal of Philosophical Logic*, *29*, 75–101.

Poesio, M., & Traum, D. (1997). *Conversational actions and discourse situations* (Tech. Rep. No. HCRC/RP-92). HCRC.

Pollard, C., & Sag, I. A. (1987). *Information-based syntax and semantics. Volume 1: Fundamentals.* Stanford: CSLI Publications.

Pollard, C., & Sag, I. A. (1994). *Head-driven phrase structure grammar.* Chicago & London: The University of Chicago Press, CSLI.

Popper, K. (1971). Conjectural knowledge. My solution of the problem of induction. *Rev. Int. Philos.*

Rickheit, G., & Strohner, H. (1985). *Grundlagen der kognitiven Sprachverarbeitung. Modelle, Methoden, Ergebnisse.* Tübingen, Basel: Francke.

Rickheit, G., & Strohner, H. (1997). *Textverarbeitung–von der Proposition zur Situation* (Tech. Rep. No. 97/3). Univ. Bielefeld, SFB 360.

Rieser, H., & Skuplik, K. (2000). Multi-speaker utterances and coordination in task-oriented dialogue. In *Gothenburg papers in computational linguistics 00-5.* www.ling. gu.se/gotalog/FinalP/rieser2.ps

Rife, B. (2000, 15 August). *ATC Communications* (Tech. Rep.). Fort Worth Air Route Traffic Control Center.

Ringle, M., & Bruce, B. (1982). Conversation failure. In W. Lehnert & M. Ringle (Eds.), *Strategies for natural language processing.* Hillsdale, NJ: Erlbaum.

Rintel, E., & Pittam, J. (1997). Strangers in a strange land: interaction management on Internet Relay Chat. *Human Communication Research, 23,* 507–534.

Rosencrantz, R. D. (1977). *Inference, method and decision: towards a bayesian philosophy of science.* Reidel.

Ross, J. (1970). On declarative sentences. In R. Jacobs & P. Rosenbaum (Eds.), *Readings in English transformational grammar* (222–272). Waltham, Massachusetts, etc.: Ginn and Company.

Sacks, H. (1971). *Lecture notes.* (School of social Science, University of California at Irvine)

Sacks, H. (1984). Notes on methodology. In J. Atkinson & J. Heritage (Eds.), *Structures of Social Action, Studies in Conversation Analysis* (21–27). Cambridge.

Sacks, H., Schegloff, E. A., & Jefferson, G. (1974). A simplest systematics for the organization of turn-taking for conversation. *Language, 50*(4), 696–735.

Sag, I. (1991). *Linguistic theory and natural language processing.* (in Klein & Veltman 1991)

Sag, I. (2001). *Head-driven phrase structure grammar: some leading ideas.* hpsg.stanford. edu/hpsg/leading-ideas.html.

Sag, I., & Wasow, T. (1999). *Syntactic theory – A formal introduction.* CSLI.

Sassen, C. (2003). An HPSG-based representation model for illocutionary acts in crisis talk. In *Perspectives on dialogue in the new millenium.* Amsterdam: Benjamins. (in Kühnlein, Rieser, & Zeevat 2003)

Sassen, C., & Gibbon, D. (2002). Enhanced dialogue markup for crisis talk scenario resources. In *Lrec 2002. third international conference on language resources and evaluation. las palmas.*

Schegloff, E. (1972). Notes on a conversational practice: formulating place. In D. Sudnow (Ed.), *Studies in social interaction.* New York: Free Press.

Schegloff, E. (1992). *The last site for intersubjectivity.* American Sociological Review.

Schegloff, E., & Sacks, H. (1973). Opening up closings. *Semiotica, 8,* 289–327.

Schegloff, E., & Sacks, H. (1977). The preference for self-correction in the organization of repair in conversation. *Language, 53*(2), 361–382.

Schiel, F., Burger, S., Greumann, A., & Weilhammer, K. (1998). The Partitur format at BAS. *Proceedings of the First International Conference on Language Resources and Evaluation.*

Schiffrin, D.(1994). *Approaches to discourse*. Cambridge, Massachusetts: Blackwell.

Searle, J.(1969). *Speech acts*. Cambridge University Press.

Searle, J.(1979a). *Expression and Meaning*. Cambridge: Cambridge University Press.

Searle, J. (1979b). Metaphor. In A. Ortony (Ed.), *Metaphor and thought* (92–123). Cambridge: Cambridge University Press.

Searle, J., & Vanderveken, D. (1985). *Foundations of illocutionary logic*. Cambridge: Cambridge University Press.

Seeboerger-Weichselbaum, M. (2000). *Das Einsteigerseminar XML*. Kaarst: Bürohandels- und Verlagsgesellschaft mbH.

Sells, P.(1985). *Lectures on Contemporary Syntactic Theories*. CSLI.

Sinclair, J.(Ed.). (1987). *Collins COBUILD English language dictionary*. London, Glasgow: Collina; Stuttgart: Klett.

Sinclair, J., & Coulthard, R. (1975). *Towards an analysis of discourse: the english used by teachers and pupils*. Oxford University Press.

Sperber, D., & Wilson, D.(1986). *Relevance*. Blackwell.

Sperberg-McQueen, C., & Burnard, L.(Eds.). (1994). *Guidelines for electronic text encoding and interchange (TEI P3)*. Chicago and Oxford: Association for Computers and the Humanities/Association for Computational Linguistics/Association for Literary and Linguistic Computing.

Spohn, W. (2003). Die Logik und das Induktionsproblem. In P. Schröder-Heister & W. Spohn (Eds.), *Logik in der Philosophie*. Synchron-Verlag.

Stegmüller, W. (1975). *Das Problem der Induktion: Humes Herausforderung u. moderne Anforderungen. Der sogenannte Zirkel des Verstehens*. Darmstadt: Wiss. Buchges.

Stenström, A.(1994). *An introduction to spoken interaction*. Longman.

Stent, A. (2000). *Rhetorical structure in dialog*.

Stubbs, M.(1983). *Discourse analysis*. Chicago UP.

Taylor, A. (1995). *Dysfluency annotation stylebook for the switchboard corpus*. University of Pennsylvania, Department of Computer and Information Science. ftp.cis.upenn.edu/pub/treebank/swbd/doc/DFL-book.ps, original version by Marie Meteer et al.

Traum, D. R., & Hinkelman, E. A. (1992). Conversation acts in task-oriented spoken dialogue. *Computational Intelligence*, 8(8). (Special Issue on Non-Literal Language)

Trippel, T., & Gibbon, D. (2001). PAX – an annotation based concordancing toolkit. In *Proceedings of the IRCS workshop on linguistic databases, Philadelphia* (238–244). (see also coral.lili.uni-bielefeld.de/ ttrippel/papers/ircspaper.pdf)

Vanderveken, D., & Kubo, S. (Eds.). (2001). *Essays in speech act theory* (No. 77). John Benjamins.

Van Dijk, T. (1972). *Some aspects of text grammars*. The Hague: Mouton.

Webopedia (2002). *Multiplexing*. www.pcwebopedia.com/TERM/M/ multiplexing.html.

Willkopp, E.-M. (1988). *Gliederungspartikeln im Dialog. Studien Deutsch, Band 5*. Iudicium Verlag, München.

Wittgenstein, L. (1961). *Philosophical investigations*. Oxford: Blackwell.

Wunderlich, D. (Ed.). (1976). *Wissenschaftstheorie der Linguistik*. Kronberg: Athenaeum.

Yngve, V. (1970). On getting a word in edgewise. In *Papers from the Sixth Regional Meeting Chicago Linguistic Society* (567–577).

Subject index

In the *Pragmatics & Beyond New Series* the following titles have been published thus far or are scheduled for publication:

113 **PANTHER, Klaus-Uwe and Linda L. THORNBURG (eds.):** Metonymy and Pragmatic Inferencing. 2003. xii, 285 pp.

112 **LENZ, Friedrich (ed.):** Deictic Conceptualisation of Space, Time and Person. 2003. xiv, 279 pp.

111 **ENSINK, Titus and Christoph SAUER (eds.):** Framing and Perspectivising in Discourse. 2003. viii, 227 pp.

110 **ANDROUTSOPOULOS, Jannis K. and Alexandra GEORGAKOPOULOU (eds.):** Discourse Constructions of Youth Identities. 2003. viii, 343 pp.

109 **MAYES, Patricia:** Language, Social Structure, and Culture. A genre analysis of cooking classes in Japan and America. 2003. xiv, 228 pp.

108 **BARRON, Anne:** Acquisition in Interlanguage Pragmatics. Learning how to do things with words in a study abroad context. 2003. xviii, 403 pp.

107 **TAAVITSAINEN, Irma and Andreas H. JUCKER (eds.):** Diachronic Perspectives on Address Term Systems. 2003. viii, 446 pp.

106 **BUSSE, Ulrich:** Linguistic Variation in the Shakespeare Corpus. Morpho-syntactic variability of second person pronouns. 2002. xiv, 344 pp.

105 **BLACKWELL, Sarah E.:** Implicatures in Discourse. The case of Spanish NP anaphora. 2003. xvi, 303 pp.

104 **BEECHING, Kate:** Gender, Politeness and Pragmatic Particles in French. 2002. x, 251 pp.

103 **FETZER, Anita and Christiane MEIERKORD (eds.):** Rethinking Sequentiality. Linguistics meets conversational interaction. 2002. vi, 300 pp.

102 **LEAFGREN, John:** Degrees of Explicitness. Information structure and the packaging of Bulgarian subjects and objects. 2002. xii, 252 pp.

101 **LUKE, Kang Kwong and Theodossia-Soula PAVLIDOU (eds.):** Telephone Calls. Unity and diversity in conversational structure across languages and cultures. 2002. x, 295 pp.

100 **JASZCZOLT, Katarzyna M. and Ken TURNER (eds.):** Meaning Through Language Contrast. Volume 2. 2003. viii, 496 pp.

99 **JASZCZOLT, Katarzyna M. and Ken TURNER (eds.):** Meaning Through Language Contrast. Volume 1. 2003. xii, 388 pp.

98 **DUSZAK, Anna (ed.):** Us and Others. Social identities across languages, discourses and cultures. 2002. viii, 522 pp.

97 **MAYNARD, Senko K.:** Linguistic Emotivity. Centrality of place, the topic-comment dynamic, and an ideology of *pathos* in Japanese discourse. 2002. xiv, 481 pp.

96 **HAVERKATE, Henk:** The Syntax, Semantics and Pragmatics of Spanish Mood. 2002. vi, 241 pp.

95 **FITZMAURICE, Susan M.:** The Familiar Letter in Early Modern English. A pragmatic approach. 2002. viii, 263 pp.

94 **McILVENNY, Paul (ed.):** Talking Gender and Sexuality. 2002. x, 332 pp.

93 **BARON, Bettina and Helga KOTTHOFF (eds.):** Gender in Interaction. Perspectives on femininity and masculinity in ethnography and discourse. 2002. xxiv, 357 pp.

92 **GARDNER, Rod:** When Listeners Talk. Response tokens and listener stance. 2001. xxii, 281 pp.

91 **GROSS, Joan:** Speaking in Other Voices. An ethnography of Walloon puppet theaters. 2001. xxviii, 341 pp.

90 **KENESEI, István and Robert M. HARNISH (eds.):** Perspectives on Semantics, Pragmatics, and Discourse. A Festschrift for Ferenc Kiefer. 2001. xxii, 352 pp.

89 **ITAKURA, Hiroko:** Conversational Dominance and Gender. A study of Japanese speakers in first and second language contexts. 2001. xviii, 231 pp.

88 **BAYRAKTAROĞLU, Arın and Maria SIFIANOU (eds.):** Linguistic Politeness Across Boundaries. The case of Greek and Turkish. 2001. xiv, 439 pp.

87 **MUSHIN, Ilana:** Evidentiality and Epistemological Stance. Narrative Retelling. 2001. xviii, 244 pp.

86 **IFANTIDOU, Elly:** Evidentials and Relevance. 2001. xii, 225 pp.

85 **COLLINS, Daniel E.:** Reanimated Voices. Speech reporting in a historical-pragmatic perspective. 2001. xx, 384 pp.

84 **ANDERSEN, Gisle:** Pragmatic Markers and Sociolinguistic Variation. A relevance-theoretic approach to the language of adolescents. 2001. ix, 352 pp.

83 **MÁRQUEZ REITER, Rosina:** Linguistic Politeness in Britain and Uruguay. A contrastive study of requests and apologies. 2000. xviii, 225 pp.

82 **KHALIL, Esam N.:** Grounding in English and Arabic News Discourse. 2000. x, 274 pp.

81 **DI LUZIO, Aldo, Susanne GÜNTHNER and Franca ORLETTI (eds.):** Culture in Communication. Analyses of intercultural situations. 2001. xvi, 341 pp.

80 **UNGERER, Friedrich (ed.):** English Media Texts – Past and Present. Language and textual structure. 2000. xiv, 286 pp.

A complete list of titles in this series can be found on the publishers' website, *www.benjamins.com*